Praise for *Izzy's Fire*

"Having known Izzy Ipson as a congregant, this book conveys the very essence of his character. *Izzy's Fire* demonstrates the hidden miracles that are in our lives and the ability of individuals to persevere and maintain their integrity through very trying circumstances. This book conveys a very positive, moral message with good ethical teaching. It will allow students to learn about the Holocaust through the experience of the Ipsons' personal story. "

Rabbi Zvi Ron, Keneseth Beth Israel (Orthodox)

~

"The author has done a masterful job of portraying a gripping saga of one family's courageous fight for survival in the midst of the most horrendous event in human history. The story plumbs the depths of horror and despair of the Holocaust, yet, through it all, speaks strongly of hope and faith.

"Though fully recognizing the pattern of treachery, deceit, and betrayal that characterizes too much of human life, *Izzy's Fire* depicts an example of human caring that bridges the deep chasm that often separates Jewish and Christian communities. As a staunch Catholic acts to protect a Jewish family, the Ipson story tells us that human solidarity is still possible even in the darkest moments of human history."

Tom Graves, President, Baptist Theological Seminary of Richmond
Member, Board of Directors, Virginia Holocaust Museum

Izzy's Fire

Nancy Wright Beasley

Izzy's Fire

Finding Humanity in the Holocaust

NANCY WRIGHT BEASLEY

PALARI PUBLISHING
Richmond, Virginia

This is a true story. The characters are authentic, the events real. Quotations have
been recreated as accurately as long-term memory allows and, where possible,
have been documented by two or more witnesses.

World War II Chronology reproduced from the Hidden History of the Kovno
Ghetto by the United States Holocaust Memorial Museum. ©1997 by Walter
Reich. By permission of Little, Brown and Company, Inc.

Maps courtesy of the United States Holocaust Memorial Museum and
The Routledge Atlas of the Holocaust, 3rd edition by Martin Gilbert.

Library of Congress Cataloging-in-Publication Data

Beasley, Nancy Wright, 1945-
Izzy's fire : finding humanity in the Holocaust / Nancy Wright Beasley.
p. cm.
Includes bibliographical references (p.) and index.
ISBN-13: 978-1-928662-94-5 (pbk.)
1. Ipson family. 2. Jews—Lithuania—Kaunas—Biography. 3. Ipson, Izzy—
Family. 4. Holocaust, Jewish (1939-1945)—Lithuania—Kaunas—Personal
narratives. 5. Holocaust survivors—Virginia—Richmond—Biography.
6. Kaunas (Lithuania)—Biography. 7. Richmond (Va.)—Biography.
I. Title: Finding humanity in the Holocaust. II. Title.
DS135.L53I67 2008
940.53'1809224793—dc22
2008020657

Manufactured in the United States of America on acid-free paper

Book design by Steve Hedberg

10 9 8 7 6 5 4 3 2 1

For Beulah Mae Wright,
my precious mother, of blessed memory,
who inspired me three years into
this project by saying,
"Don't give up so easy."

Acknowledgments

Edna Ipson and my precious mother, Beulah Mae Wright, were the abiding inspiration for *Izzy's Fire*.

Emmanuel Shlom — "Mannie" to family and friends — opened his heart from Israel, mailing his and his mother's memoirs before I even met him. Jacob Kalamitskas, of Israel, offered valuable insight into his father's deep faith. Dr. Sara Pliamm, daughter of the late Moshe Gillman and Sheina Gillman, and Neil Bienstock, grandson of Israel and Sheina Gillman, all of Canada, provided invaluable assistance.

In addition to Izzy's memoirs, as well as memoirs written by others, this book is based on interviews, telephone conversations, letters, and e-mails and some previously published works. Although I tried to adhere to the information presented, I haven't met several of the individuals about whom I've written. It's reasonable to note that, over sixty years, some memories have faded or differ from those of others. I've tried to bridge the gap, adhering to Izzy's memoirs when there was a difference. Any errors, although unintentional, are mine.

Many friends and family have walked beside me during this arduous seven-year journey, holding the tides at bay until I finally made it to shore. Chief among them would be Gay Neale, an exceptional friend and mentor.

Neil November helped me in every imaginable way. Neil introduced me to Carole Weinstein, a perfect stranger, whose aid and personal vigilance brought this work to fruition. I owe her a debt I can never repay. I experienced similar encouragement the first time three years earlier when Nina Imajo, also a stranger, wrote a check, in 1999, to help support my research.

Also, Inge Horowitz, Patty O'Connor, and Diane Dillard could be the perfect pattern for unrelenting support of a friend. I consider them special gifts from God.

I hope *Izzy's Fire* conveys my honest belief – that it is only by seeing each other through love and understanding that we recognize how truly similar we all are.

Table of Contents

Introduction

Izzy's Fire was seven years in the making. It's fair to say that the book "chose" me, rather than the other way around. It all began in the fall of 1997 when Gwen Woolf, an editor at the Fredericksburg, Virginia, *Free Lance-Star*, offered me an assignment to cover the newly opened Virginia Holocaust Museum in Richmond. Although I was trying to sustain myself as a freelance writer, I declined the assignment because I have always found the Holocaust so disturbing.

Gwen, a long-time friend, persisted. Out of respect for her, I decided to attend a *Kristallnacht* ceremony, an annual event held in Richmond at the Emek Sholom Holocaust Memorial Cemetery in November to commemorate Holocaust martyrs and honor survivors.

I was able to remain composed until the end of the ceremony when Alan Zimm, a slender man of just over five feet, stepped to the microphone and began reciting the names of his family members who died during the Holocaust. For some odd reason, I began counting the names on my fingers.

When I ran out of fingers and he was still reciting names, I began to cry.

I introduced myself to Mr. Zimm, a native of Poland who had been an inmate in Buchenwald and three other camps in Europe. He and one brother were the only members of their family to survive the Holocaust. I told him I was so sorry for his loss and that hearing him had made me realize the importance of telling stories like his.

As I left the cemetery amid a drizzling rain, I looked up at a gray sky and said, "OK, God, what do you want?" I didn't know the answer then, but I did know I had been profoundly changed and that the change would somehow be reflected in my work.

During the following year, I wrote numerous stories about the Virginia Holocaust Museum and Holocaust survivors, which appeared in the *Free Lance-Star, Richmond* magazine and other publications, and I met Edna Ipson and realized the "calling" of the book. Since then, I have interviewed the surviving members of the Ipson family and most of the others who lived underground with them during that harrowing time.

Izzy's Fire has not been without a price. There have been countless tears and many sleepless nights, but there has also been unbridled joy and profound memories.

While my newfound friends' abiding closeness and wonderful conviviality have sustained me, a Christian, during immeasurable hours of work and editing, Izzy Ipson's poignant memoirs have given a singular voice to the suffering his family endured, as well as their bravery. He held a mirror that reflects the untold stories of so many others.

Izzy's words, and especially those of Edna Ipson, to whom I owe so much, have made such an impression on my heart that I will never be the same.

— *Nancy Wright Beasley*

But they that wait upon the Lord shall renew their strength;
they shall mount up with wings as eagles; they shall run, and
not be weary; and they shall walk, and not faint.
Isaiah 40:31

1

My name is Edna Ipson. Many years ago, before I came to America, it was Eta Ipp. My son, Jay, was known as Jacob. This is our family's story.

T he sound of the guard's boots on the hard street ripped the silence of the night. It was a familiar sound to all of us. I was having trouble trying to discern whether the sound was coming toward us or going away. The thump of my heartbeat kept drowning it out.

Jay, now a scrawny, wasp-waisted eight-year-old, was standing close beside Izzy and me. Over the past two years, our son had learned to keep quiet when he heard that noise. He knew it could mean death. Although silence was what we listened for now, it was rare in the ghetto. There always seemed to be a fight over food or some squabble going on. We were all so crowded. No one had enough to eat, space to live in, or decent clothes to wear.

Izzy, Jay, and I stood beside the fence for what seemed like an eternity. When we were sure of the return of complete silence, Izzy deftly began to unhook the strands of barbed

~ 5 ~

wire from the fence post. He took turns with his cousin, Leibel Gillman, who was more adept, more practiced at cutting and swiftly unfurling, then repairing the thorny maze.

The two men worked feverishly, standing just inside the ugly fence on Paneriu Street that surrounded the ghetto. I paused for a moment, thinking of how Jay and his little friends used to chase each other back and forth across the bridge that once connected the two camps of Kovno Ghetto. The children had entertained themselves by playing tag on the bridge while their parents were at work.

Izzy had given Jay instructions before we left the house. They had been carefully reviewed and rehearsed many times before. No reminders were needed now. With a swift, almost rough, movement, Izzy leaned against the fence, as much to protect Jay from the piercing barbs as to help guide his frail body through the gaping hole. Whispering *"Gay,"* he pushed Jay with his hands. No embrace. No other sound. Just movement.

Jay hurried through the fence without even looking back. He probably wondered if he would ever see Izzy or me again. Or his grandparents. He must have been halfway across the road before I suddenly remembered that dogs sometimes ran loose in the yard at the abandoned house where he was to rejoin us. I wondered what would happen if they started to bark.

We had tried to think of something he could tell anyone who might discover him. He decided he would simply say he had lost his way trying to find the entrance to the ghetto. I'm sure it never occurred to him that his explanation made no logical sense. Anyone in Lithuania would know, as he did, that no Jewish boy would be outside the ghetto confines at midnight. Still, his planned reply probably gave him comfort.

I could hear the heels striking the cobblestone a long time

before the guard got near me again. Each click sounded like a crack of thunder. I could feel every footstep, as if it were traveling across the surface of the road, through the dirt and up my legs to my belly. I had to swallow to keep from being sick. I kept wondering how long I had been standing there and tried to remember exactly what Izzy had said. I went over the instructions again and again. My head hurt from trying to remember the sound of Izzy's voice. It seemed so very far away.

"Get across the road as fast as you can," Izzy had told Jay. "Find the place. Lie down. Don't move. Don't make a sound. Wait — no matter how long it is." As time dragged, Jay had no way of knowing how long he had been huddled on the ground. The night was starless, so it was impossible to see anything in the inky sky. All he could possibly do was wrestle with his inner thoughts, as I was now doing, listen for the footsteps to come back and hug the comforter he had taken with him.

I was second through the hole in the fence. A few yards beyond the road, I dropped to my knees and used my hands to sweep the area in front and to the side of my body, even though I knew it was too soon to find Jay. The thought haunted me: had I sent him to his death?

Not finding him immediately paralyzed me with fear. I could only imagine how much more frightened Jay must be. I moved a few feet and stopped where I thought he should be. I sat motionless for a few minutes, using the respite to massage my hands and knees, which had started bleeding from crawling over the gravel. There had been plenty of time. It didn't make sense that Jay hadn't reached the appointed meeting place.

I tried to convince myself that Jay was safe. I knew he was out there. I just had to find him. He wouldn't make a sound, even if a guard seized him or threatened to kill him. Jay understood the seriousness of the escape. One sound and we would all be dead and probably the remainder of our family as well. No, Jay would never cry out. The war had hardened him. He could be trusted.

A little rested, I started searching again. My hand suddenly touched Jay's elbow and then his shoulder. Even though he was too old to be cuddled, I pulled him close to my breasts and rocked him like a baby once again. I held him to my heart and dared to hope for his life, Jay — my grandfather's namesake, the family's only lifeline. As he clung to me, Jay took deep breaths and buried his head in the familiar softness of my sweater. I held him so tightly the buttons probably began cutting into his face, but I don't think he paid any attention to that. Having him in my arms again almost caused me to cry out with relief.

While I comforted Jay, I wondered if Izzy was on his way back to us. He had returned to the house one more time. He wanted a final goodbye with his mother. Although he didn't dare say it, I think Izzy sensed it would be the last time he would ever see his family.

Izzy's mother never cried, but last night she couldn't keep the tears from running down her cheeks. I could envision her grabbing Izzy again, hugging and kissing him. She had already kissed Jay and me the night before. Izzy hoped he would see Dvoira or Golde, his younger sisters. It must have been so terrible for him trying to keep his composure.

When Izzy reunited with us, he moved like a man made of stone, as if all the feeling had been drained from him. He took my hand and Jay's and walked stiffly down the road where Marchuk, my Uncle Itzhak's friend, was waiting for us beside a wagon on Paneriu Street. While Izzy and Marchuk lifted Jay quickly into the wagon bed, I hoisted myself onto the seat and put on a scarf, a big one that made me look like a countrywoman. Jay quickly scooted under the straw as

Marchuk gave Izzy a heavy coat and a farmer's hat to put on. Marchuk placed sheep pelts over Jay and rearranged the straw to better protect him while Izzy went to the front and stood beside the horse.

Marchuk picked up the reins and slightly flicked his wrist, causing the reins to move across the horse's withers, a signal to leave. Without a sound, Izzy led the horse into the darkness. Later, as a few pink streaks shot through the sky, I finally dared to look back at the mound of straw where Jay was buried. Would he remember to remain quiet? Would the straw send him into fits of sneezing? Would he know to move to one side of the cart if the Germans stopped us and stuck pitchforks through the straw? Why didn't I prepare him better?

Unable to answer my own questions, I concentrated on watching Marchuk's hands and how he deftly guided the raw-boned horse through the pocked road. He held the reins loosely in his right hand between two fingers and his thumb, while his left hand rested on his knee. It was a comforting sight. When I was a little girl, I had seen my Uncle Itzhak ride like that, on days when I went to the market with him to sell apples. Now I rode silently beside Marchuk, as Izzy tried to keep time with the horse's plodding steps. Izzy and I were so close; I could almost read his mind. I knew his thoughts, like mine, matched the gray of the morning. I wondered if his heart was racing and if the same questions were crowding inside his head.

Had he made the right decision? Would our escape ensure Jay's life or guarantee our deaths? What would his mother be doing now? Praying, no doubt, as she always did. Izzy took comfort in the knowledge of her prayers. I'm sure it buoyed his courage to meet the dawning day.

The lurch of the wagon's motion reminded me of the ghetto. Reporting to work in the pre-dawn hours was like stepping into a harness. No free will existed. The reins of forced labor were used to turn human beings into animals.

I thought of the other nine women who worked in the coal detail with me. What would they say as they gathered at dawn? I felt a pang of guilt thinking how the guards would beat them and try to extract information when it was discovered that I was missing. I vividly recalled an incident when we had dared to stop shoveling coal on a rainy day. Our thin coats were plastered against us and rain had run down our legs into our ragged boots. When the guards moved away, as they often did to warm themselves beside barrels of fire, we women decided to huddle for a moment trying to stave off being frozen. Sometimes a slight respite gave us an opportunity to encourage each other. We always talked of home and what it might be like after the war. Our bodies were so deprived of food, we didn't even have the strength to shiver. By standing close to each other, we could benefit from the group's body heat and try to shore up the weaker ones. Engaged in our memories, we didn't hear the footsteps of the approaching guard. He went unnoticed until he split open my skull with his rifle butt, sending me to my knees and the others running back to their shovels.

As the guard cursed and beat the other women, I found some rags to wrap my bleeding, throbbing head. I had to run to escape another bludgeoning before beginning the three-mile walk back to the ghetto hospital, where a doctor sutured and bandaged my wounds. The next morning, the same doctor took my temperature. When it was normal, I was declared fit to work and had to return to the coal detail.

My head began throbbing now, as Marchuk's wagon rocked, and I remembered again how much my head had hurt that day. I wondered if the woman who took my place had been strong enough to survive.

I put the questions aside and replaced them in my mind with hope that the women wouldn't be angry with me for not saying goodbye. They would understand why I dared not confide in anyone. Maybe my disappearance would inspire them to also escape from the work camp. Work camp. What a ridiculous description for a slave labor camp. But, for a moment, I almost missed the safety of the monotonous work routine. At least it was predictable.

I thought of Sarah, even smaller than I, but able to shovel coal for ten hours a day. Because we were both less than five feet tall, we had to work harder than the others to keep up. Our impetus was the meager rations we'd get at the end of the day to share with our children. Or we might find an opportunity to slip away from the work detail long enough to trade a piece of clothing for food from the locals that we could share once we were back inside the confines of the ghetto. I knew one guard who was particularly fond of eggs, so I always tried to bring at least two back with me on the days that he worked, to ensure passage through the gate where we were always stopped and searched.

As the daylight began to show just above the horse's ears, my thoughts shifted to memories of Rachel, a co-worker who described her home and dining room while the women toiled endlessly. Rachel was excellent at describing *Shabbat*. She made it come alive through her words.

"Oh, it was something fine, I tell you," Rachel always started. "The china, the finest bone china with a little rose pattern at the edge, was always set for my mother's family. I used my grandmother's silverware, four pieces for each plate with a scroll pattern in each handle, and her special lace tablecloth. My grandmother, my special *bubbe*, had always let me set the table for her when I was a little girl. She promised that she would save the table dressings for me, and she kept her promise.

"The last time I saw her, she drew me to her bedside, pulled my head close to hers and whispered, 'Your pretties are in a special box with your name on them, child. Don't ever forget to keep *Shabbat*. Remember that you are a Jew. Never deny who you are.'

"That's what she said, all right. I memorized every word so that I could repeat it when my time came to pass on the treasure," Rachel carefully explained every time she had the chance. Her descriptions of *Shabbat* were always preceded with her grandmother's admonitions.

"That tablecloth, I tell you, the stitches were so fine and so close that the eye could barely see them. It was a masterpiece. We were always careful not to spill food on it. And the candlesticks — why, they were the same ones that my *elderbubbe* had prayed over. Tall, branched candlesticks of the finest silver, polished, always polished before *Shabbat*, until you could see your face in them. Gone. All gone now. Our so-called neighbors grabbed the candlesticks right off the table the night we were forced into the ghetto. I saw them with my very own eyes. When I looked back to see my home one last time, the Lithuanians were coming through the door with my *bubbe's* candlesticks and her silverware in their arms. The sight made me sick, I tell you."

Sarah would listen for a few minutes but inevitably would lash out at Rachel. "Why do you talk so foolishly, stupid woman?" Sarah hissed. "Look at us. We are walking skeletons. You describe *challah* bread rich with eggs when we only have scraps of bread made gritty with sand and shriveled potato peelings. I'm sick of your stories." Sarah twisted her body toward Rachel in a menacing stance and spat at her. "That is what I think of your memories."

Rachel took a step sideways but went on, ignoring Sarah as if she were a vapor. No matter how much Sarah protested, Rachel told the same story, slowly choosing each word carefully as if she were placing bricks one upon the other to construct a wall of memory.

I kept shoveling coal, the cadence of the words helping the monotony of the repetitious work. I often thought of my grandmother, *Frumme* Leah. She was known as "Righteous Leah" because she always kept the Sabbath and was so devoted to her faith. She died in the ghetto as much from heartbreak as from lack of medical attention.

~

Swaying with the wagon, I could almost hear Rachel again describing how her family used to make matzo ball soup. Her descriptions were so vivid that sometimes I could actually smell the chicken broth bubbling on the stove, making my mouth water from the hunger. Thoughts of the delicious soup brought back memories of *Pesach* – Passover – a time of deliverance. Just thinking of it gave me hope.

Was it Rachel who said a few weeks back, "If only I had enough chicken to fill my stomach one more time before they kill me, then I would be satisfied to die"?

Sometimes, when time permitted between the guard's rounds, I would describe how I prepared the lemon cookies that Jay loved so much. I could no longer bake the cookies, but I smiled to myself, remembering how he always enjoyed them. That was one time I didn't have to coax him to eat.

With the sun now fully up, I realized that I didn't recognize anything. I tried to get my bearing by thinking of the date, November 26, 1943. Somehow, knowing the date gave me an accomplished feeling. I decided I would remember it always. November 26, 1943. November 26, 1943. I said it over and over to myself, hoping that it would help me concentrate on the escape rather than my hunger. I wondered if we would eat this day or the next.

While we were waiting for the escape hour the night before, Izzy and I had refused to eat the loaf of bread his mother offered. Instead, Izzy carefully pulled open the end of it, hollowed out the middle and stuffed what few valuables we had inside the opening. Izzy carefully replaced the end before wrapping the loaf in a brown bag and handing it to me for safekeeping. As a woman, it made sense that I should take care of the food.

While Izzy's mother offered Jay a slice from another loaf, Izzy and I ate the bread scraps he had piled on the table and pondered once again our decision to escape. We refused more food, knowing it would just be wasted if we were caught. Thinking of the bread now brought the ever-present hunger to the forefront again, a part of the uncertainty that I had lived with for the last two years. I could hardly remember the time before we were forced into the ghetto. Somehow, our former life seemed like a daydream.

I had prayed for a windy day so I could huddle beside Marchuk on the wagon. A cold wind would justify hiding my face. God had honored my prayers. A drizzling rain began falling as well. Wet and chilled, I comforted myself with the knowledge that at least Jay was with us. At least he was alive, for the moment.

Clutching the sweater around my body, I suddenly thought of its buttons. I instinctively reached to count them with my fingers, fearing that I might have torn one off against the wheel as I had climbed onto the wagon. Five in all. Good. All accounted for. I would have to remember to be more careful of them in the future. I drew my damp, thin dress and apron around my knees, tucking them under my legs to prevent the frigid draft of air from wrapping around my almost numb body. I was so thin, my bones rubbed against the seat, making me even more uncomfortable.

I wondered how Jay could possibly be warm, but I didn't allow myself to turn around and check on him. I hoped the comforter would be enough, along with the straw and the pelts, to keep him from freezing. Trying to ignore our distress, I strained to see ahead, as if I could discern the end of the path we were taking.

2

Life in Lithuania – 1938

In the late 1930s in Lithuania, we led a simple, but meaning-ful, life. I liked standing at the kitchen window and watching the sun stream through the curtains. Sometimes I watched it dancing in jagged patterns on the newly scrubbed kitchen floor. I always looked out that window so I could see Izzy on his way to and from work. On sunny days, like today, he would leave a little early and walk to the office. It gave him a few minutes to stop along the way and talk to the neighbors about their gardens and flowers. We lived on a short street in Slobodka, Lithuania, not too far from Poland's border. It was a gentle, well-kept neighborhood, where everyone looked out for each other. The children could play outside for hours, and the mothers knew the children were being watched from several kitchen windows.

Before I knew it, it was midday. As I unwrapped a scarf from around my hair, I saw a cobweb in the corner that had evaded me yesterday. Grabbing a cloth, I removed the culprit and began thinking about what I'd offer Jay for lunch. My

Leibel Gillman (1939).

little son, now three years old, was such an easy child except for his very picky appetite. Some days I resorted to bribery.

Through trial and error, I had found ways to trick him into eating. It was a sure thing if I promised him a ride on Leibel's motorcycle. Leibel Gillman, my husband's first cousin, was so young, just a teenager, and sometimes reckless in his speed. I tried not to listen to the stories told about his daring. I often wondered if his daredevil antics were just a way of proving his manliness or living up to "Little Lion," the meaning of his name.

No matter how fearless Leibel might have been, he was always very careful with Jay. I would watch him sometimes as he rode Jay slowly on his motorcycle and I could see the tenderness in his face when Jay would squeal with delight. I think Leibel actually regarded Jay much the same as he would a little brother. He was such a thoughtful young man and besieged by girls because of his handsome looks and debonair ways, but he would always find time to stop by every day or two to check with me. He was always willing to offer Jay a ride as a bribe for a meal if I needed him to help.

Today I was letting Jay ride his tricycle around the kitchen table, but only if he stopped for a bite of something to eat each time he passed me. He was really excited by the game, giggling and making loud noises and going as fast as he could, trying not to fall over as he rounded the end of the table on two wheels. He thoroughly enjoyed playing with me, and it was a relief for me to get food inside him without a struggle.

I laughed each time he came by me pretending to be a big truck. He was such a happy child and perfectly content to play by himself. My sweet son, named Jacob to honor my maternal grandfather, Jacob Kalamitsky, was the joy of my life. I often marveled at my good fortune. I loved being Izzy's wife and relished doing the little things that made him happy, like cooking special meals or rubbing his back when he was tired. Who could believe that I would be so happy, especially when I never dreamed I would end up married to Izzy. My father was a cobbler and I didn't have a big dowry, so I knew Izzy's parents didn't think I was suitable. And Izzy, so handsome, so well educated and hard working, was sought out by many parents for their daughters. One matchmaker even brought Izzy's parents an offer of a bride with 100,000 litas, an absolute fortune. Imagine. Izzy told me about it and laughed when I suggested he take the offer, even though I loved him deeply.

"Are you *meshuggah*?" he asked. "You are worth more than that to me. In fact, you're priceless to me. But, don't you even think about me leaving you for someone else. You're the woman I love and the one I want to marry."

Our courtship started after we met briefly in a neighborhood yard. We spoke only a few words, but I felt something turn over inside me when I first saw him — maybe it was my heart. He wasn't terribly tall, probably not more than five feet nine inches, but I was barely five feet. I felt small and protected standing beside him. His brown hair was neatly swept back from his forehead, framing a very handsome and clean-shaven face. He had a strong jaw, even white teeth, and blue eyes that seemed to know my very soul.

I wasn't sure Izzy felt the same way, but after he saw me he asked Benjamin, my friend, to arrange a meeting so we could talk with each other privately. Izzy and I went to the movies and for a long walk on our first date. That's what most of the young people did at that time. We would see each other very often after that, sometimes squeezing in a visit between Izzy's law classes at Vytautas University in Kaunas.

It took Izzy a long while to tell me that his parents, especially his mother, objected to our plans to marry. They wanted him to rise in society by becoming a doctor and marrying a wealthy woman. Izzy had asked me whether he should become a doctor or a lawyer. I suggested he study law. I thought that as a doctor he might be gone all the time, and we'd never have a family life, which was very important to both of us.

Even as a lawyer, Izzy would be rising in status, something his parents wanted very badly. Both of them had humble jobs: his father was a brewer; his mother, a seamstress. But Izzy, handsome and smart, was a man with a future. He could pick and choose a bride. I can't say that I blamed his parents too much, but their objections did nothing to dissuade Izzy from courting me. We always managed to see each other every week, even if it was only for a few minutes to go for a walk and hold hands. Izzy usually found an out-of-the-way place for a quick kiss, never anything more.

He wasn't the first boyfriend I'd had, but he was the only one I ever took home. My mother talked to me a long time about Izzy, saying that I should bring him to meet her and father. I held back until I was very sure that Izzy was serious. I didn't want to take a chance on embarrassing my parents.

I was very devoted to my mother. She had such a hard life, but she knew what real love was and had been fortunate enough to have two men who loved her in a very special way. My father, of blessed memory, died when I was quite young, and my mother was left with five children to care for alone. I don't know how my father, Moshe Butrimowitz, died. Maybe it was cancer, maybe a series of small strokes. He had a thriving butcher business and then one day he got really sick. There was supposed to be something wrong with his head. I don't remember much, except that he got sicker and sicker. It was very quick. People didn't speak about illnesses much in those times, and my mother wouldn't talk about it. I think she was trying to protect us children.

After he died, my mother struggled to feed us and finally sent my brother and sister, Abraham and Sadie, to America to live with her sister, my Aunt Bessie. Mother asked if I wanted to go, but I couldn't bear to leave her. It was several years before she remarried. I remember when she asked my grandmother, Leah, if she should remarry. My grandmother replied, "Marry. Your children will grow up and leave you; then you'll be alone. Better to have a husband of straw than a child of gold. Better to marry." My mother ended up marrying a man with the same last name, although I don't think the men were related to each other.

Chananya Butrimowitz was the only father I ever really remember. He was so good to me; no one ever thought of him as a stepfather, especially me. I remember how he made boots for me, touching the pieces of leather just so, smoothing them between his palms, to make sure my feet were cushioned properly. He was a master at fashioning footwear and always had standing orders from faithful customers. His work was so fine that people had to place their orders two months in advance. He worked very hard, but he was never too busy to spend a few minutes with me, even when he was dog-tired. His skin always carried that wonderful musky leather smell, even after a bath. And although he tried, he just couldn't shed the brown dye that stained his fingers. It seemed so natural, as if he had been born that way. We used to have such special times singing together. He had a beautiful baritone voice and could stay on tune, no matter who was singing off-key beside him.

He was very attentive to me. People used to be surprised when I said he was my stepfather. I remember when I became sick with yellow fever. My older sister, Yentaleh, had already come down with it and died in the hospital after my mother agreed for her to be treated there. When I got sick, I remember the doctor recommending that I also go to the hospital and hearing my mother say, "No. Isn't it enough that I've already lost one daughter? Eta stays with us." I was delirious with fever, but I can clearly remember my father sitting beside my bed all night long, night after night until the fever broke. The first thing I wanted to do when I got better was sing with him.

My father always treated my mother with such reverence, never raising his voice, always complimenting her cooking. He would push away from the table at night, pat his full stomach and say, "Well, Chai Esther, that was the best meal I've had since the last one you cooked for me. Now come and sit with me for a while before I go to bed. Tell me about your day and what the children learned in Hebrew school."

Mother always insisted on washing the dishes before

sitting down. She did it very meticulously, adding one plate to the water at a time, carefully washing and drying each one and putting it away before starting the next. Father would always try to hurry her. Sometimes he'd sneak up behind her, slip his arms around her waist, and take a chance at a quick hug and say, "These children of ours. They are such smart children, you know, because we are their parents."

Mother and Daddy had two children of their own, Fievel and Chaim, rambunctious boys born a few years apart. Some days I would see Mother looking at them as they ran and played in the yard. She would have such pride on her face. I think she must have been thinking how good it was that God gave her two more children, the exact number she felt she had to send away to America.

Seeing the love my parents had for each other made me long for someone special to share my life with. Not until I met Israel Ipp did I understand their singular devotion to each other, the real joy they felt when they were together. That's why I had to be very sure before I took Izzy home to meet them. They would be able to see right away that Izzy had eyes only for me and that he would offer me and our children a good life.

We were hoping that Izzy's parents would come to accept me. We reasoned that if we waited a long time, they would have to see that we were serious and weren't going to change our minds.

Izzy's sisters pleaded with their mother not to force Izzy to give me up. One day I heard Dvoira say, "Please, Mother, don't break up Izzy and Eta. She's Izzy's fire." I was always exuberant and outgoing. When I was very young, someone started calling me "*Simchah* Fire." I don't remember who gave me the nickname, but it stuck. Some people say it means everlasting flame. Others say it means unquenchable fire or a celebration that goes on and on. Either way, it always made me smile and feel special when someone called me that.

After Izzy and I had dated for three years, my mother said, "Enough. It's time to marry." We were still afraid that Izzy's parents would object, so we went to a rabbi in secret. He agreed to perform the ceremony. I didn't even have time for a *mikvah*, the ritual bath Jewish women take before marriage. There were only a few witnesses, my parents and several friends. We had to have at least ten men, the necessary number to make a *minyan*, which constitutes the synagogue as a congregation.

Izzy and I wanted a large family. After all, family is what matters the most. What do you have without a family, without roots, without history? That's why I took my job as a wife so seriously. I worked at it every day, just like when I was a saleslady after my high school years.

I used to be called the best saleslady in the store because I was always cheerful and tried to engage the customers in conversation. The manager would often say, "Eta, I don't know what it is about you. No matter what's going on in your life, you're always cheerful. The customers really like that. When I see someone coming into the store and heading toward you, I say to myself, 'Now that man doesn't know it, but he's going to leave some of his money here.'"

After I got married, I felt my husband was my job. I determined very early that I should smile for Izzy and have a pleasant look when he leaves for work in the morning. Who likes a sourpuss anyway? What did I have to be unhappy about? I was very close to my mother and I could talk with her every day if I wanted. Jay was healthy, and Izzy and I were discussing having another baby before too long. Should that happen, I would be making new little dresses for her; I really wanted a little girl. Izzy's mother would help me, I was sure. She was such a good woman, but so very serious, especially about her work. She was a wonderful dressmaker.

Eta and Israel Ipp (1934).

Little by little she came to accept me, especially after she saw how devoted I was to Izzy. After she accepted me, she showed me how to make a hem and do other sewing. The times we sewed together were very special. We actually became quite close, especially after Jay was born. She had been thrilled recently when Izzy told her that we were thinking of adding to our family.

When I wasn't busy with Jay, I tried especially hard to keep the house clean and ready for company at any time.

I made sure that I always had a fresh dress on and dinner waiting when Izzy got home from work. Izzy traveled some then, and he'd come home and describe a really delicious meal that he had eaten. Right away I would learn to make that dish, and sometimes I served it during the weekend visits when his friends dropped by. I eventually became a very good cook from all that practice.

Most weekends we had his friends over for a card game. The card games were always very casual and a lot of fun. We never knew exactly how many there would be, but several of Izzy's friends always dropped by. The ones who were married would bring their wives, of course, and we would enjoy talking about our homes and our children and comparing new recipes while the men played cards.

I would set up the card table and have the drinks ready to be served when they got there. After the first game or two, I always served special cakes or cookies and little sandwiches, tiny little things cut into triangles and stuffed with egg salad or chicken salad. Some even had jam in them. The men always looked at Izzy with a little jealousy in their eyes.

David, who wasn't married, teased Izzy that he planned to come and steal me away while Izzy was at work. When the games were over and I would be getting their coats, David always said, "I tell you one thing, Izzy. I've been coming here every weekend for a long time. You'd better keep your eye on that beautiful wife of yours. If I catch you not looking, I'm stealing her for sure."

But this particular evening — the same day Jay and I had played with each other around the table — I remember especially well. The sandwiches were already arranged on the serving tray. I had made my special lemon cookies that day, the kind Jay loved so much. He had hopped from foot to foot, waiting for the first pan to come out of the oven. Something strange happened while I was stirring the

Jacob Ipp (1939).

dough and baking them though. I had this gray feeling, like something was amiss. I shrugged it off. After all, I had done quite a bit of extra housework that day and I was a little more tired than usual.

Our friends arrived on time. I hung up their coats, while Izzy led the way into the dining room and began to prepare the drinks.

"I've been waiting for tonight all week," Izzy said as he retrieved the glasses from the cabinet. "I want to tell you something funny that happened at work."

"Wait, Izzy," David interrupted. "I think you'll want to save that story for another time. The card game will have to wait, too. All of us need to talk tonight about a very serious matter. They've started killing Jews in Poland."

3

Ominous Signs

I zzy and I had both lived our whole lives in Lithuania. For the most part, we had been very happy. Even though most Lithuanian Jews could not attend public high schools or secure positions within government departments, we had made ourselves reasonably content by sharing religious holidays and primarily enjoying life among our families and neighbors. That changed when the influence of the Nazis became prevalent in Germany. Every time I heard one of Hitler's hysterical anti-Semitic speeches, I felt exhausted, as if I'd had the life beaten out of me. His voice was so oppressive that I had a hard time even breathing when I heard him on the radio. It was apparent that Hitler's power was beginning to seep across all strata of European Jewish life like a blinding snowstorm, covering everything in its path.

Systematically, with precise planning, every which way we turned, our lives and those of other Jews in bordering countries were being squeezed relentlessly through restrictions. We couldn't help but notice how these limitations were designed to alienate us from everyday life.

Anti-Semitism, always obvious in the past but somewhat restrained, was now given full leash. Lithuania was once considered a somewhat safer place for Jews to live, but recently many Lithuanian Jews, including several of our friends, abandoned their homes and livelihood, took a few possessions, and went to other countries to avoid the ever-increasing restrictions. It was so unfair. The local *yeshiva*, a seminary for Orthodox Jews, was world-renowned for turning out the most learned rabbis, and we had the best of artistic events. Napolean even referred to Vilna (Vilnius), the capital of Lithuania, as "Little Jerusalem," because of its large Jewish population and cultural ties.

It became especially hard on the Jewish shop owners. They were forced to give up establishments they had spent their whole lives developing. Businessmen with links to the Nazis began moving to Lithuania and opening businesses, competing with long-established Jewish enterprises. When the new stores opened, I hoped things might be different, that somehow they could live in peace with the Jewish merchants. That was very naive thinking on my part. Within days, the new owners started plastering their doors and windows with advertisements calling on Lithuanians to avoid shopping at Jewish stores and urging everyone to attend public lectures that denigrated Jews.

Boiling hatred awaited us wherever we turned. Mammoth billboards and signs were posted depicting huge-nosed, vicious-looking vile creatures, meant to represent Jews. The signs featured horrible messages equating Jews with vermin. Editorials either openly presented derogatory and slanderous lies about Jews or demanded that Lithuanians boycott Jewish businesses. Art shows were even held for the express purpose of presenting derogatory art about Jewish life and religious practices. It was indescribable. All the while, our everyday life was becoming ever more cloistered through restrictive legislation.

How could we help but be constantly nervous? It was like waiting for a guillotine to drop. We weren't sure what was ahead, but we knew something terrible wasn't far off. For example, Izzy had already lost his right to work as an attorney. A law had been passed that forbade Jews to practice law unless they had ten years of experience. That left only about 100 Jewish attorneys in all of Lithuania who weren't affected. After a couple of months, Izzy was desperate to find work to support our family. We were running out of food. Thank goodness our families were nearby, and we all made out by sharing with each other. My mother's brother, Itzhak Kalamitsky, was my favorite uncle. He helped by bringing us produce raised on his farm. Izzy came home one day with good news though.

"Guess what, Eta," he started. "I saw one of my former classmates from law school today. He told me that the import duty had been reduced for automobiles and motorcycles. While I'm no expert, I do have some experience with motorcycles. What do you think about me starting a business for motorcycles and parts? A lot of people have them, many more than own a car."

"That's a good idea, Izzy," I said, trying to encourage him. I wasn't sure if he could make a go of it, but what did we have to lose? He had to do something. Izzy owned a motorcycle made by Fabrique Nationale, which was referred to as an FN in those days. It was a very sleek machine that he dearly loved. Izzy kept it spotless and showed it off every chance he had. Oh, I tell you, it was a beauty. Jay especially loved it, and Izzy was always letting him stand beside him and hold a bolt or two while he pretended to do a little tinkering on it. Although just a little boy, Jay took special pride in holding his father's tools, and Izzy delighted in pretending to let him use them.

Izzy always said that Jay would grow up to be a wonderful mechanic because he was so interested in machines.

Izzy thought about the business venture for a few days and finally decided to become a distributor for Fabrique Nationale, which was located in Belgium. He got lucky again. He also became the agent for a company in England that made the Ariel, another beautiful motorcycle. He had only one motorcycle as a beginning inventory, but he ended up selling a couple of hundred during the season. I was really proud of him. I always knew he was enterprising, but he never failed to amaze me by finding a way to provide for us.

It took quite a while, but Izzy finally began to make a comfortable living and had a very good business going. I helped, too, by keeping the shop when Izzy had to be away. I was really good at talking with customers. It reminded me of when I used to work as a saleslady. I never met a stranger, and that came in handy in working with the public. I became very proficient in learning about the motorcycle parts as well. One day I had closed the shop a little early and had gone home, just a short distance away, to cook dinner. Suddenly Izzy burst into the kitchen, out of breath from running.

"Eta, do you remember that beautiful FN that I had parked next to the shop? The expensive one? Well, it's gone. It must have been stolen," he said, trying to catch his breath. I started laughing so hard I couldn't speak.

"What's the matter with you?" he demanded angrily. "I just told you that one of my motorcycles has been stolen and all you can do is laugh?"

I was able to finally constrain myself long enough to ask, "Izzy, did you see where anyone broke into the shop?"

"No," he said. "I checked at all the locks and they seemed to be in place."

"Well, did you see where any of the fence was broken down?"

"No," he answered again, looking at me rather quizzically as I started laughing again.

"Don't you know that you had the best saleslady in Lithuania in charge today?" I asked. "I sold that motorcycle while you were gone, and I got a higher price than what you would have."

You should have seen the look on his face when I said that. It took a few minutes for it to sink in, but when it did, he began laughing right along with me. Izzy had a good time the next few weeks retelling that story.

Eventually Izzy branched out and became a distributor for ammunition, streetcars and elevators, among other things. During those times I counted my blessings. Other Jews were having a terrible go of it, but Izzy proved himself time and time again. He was always trying to think of a way to help us survive and worked relentlessly to care for us. We even started a small paperclip enterprise where we manually made the paperclips and packaged them in small boxes. Many times Izzy would help others as well, giving them jobs or repairing their motorcycles for free. He even did free legal work for some of the farmers, neighbors of Uncle Itzhak's. Some of them weren't even Jewish, but Izzy did it as a favor to Uncle Itzhak. Everyone was having a terrible time, and Izzy just couldn't say no to someone in need, no matter who they were. At times, I would accompany him and actually became quite proficient in some of the legal matters.

Everything seemed to be going well until Izzy was walking to work one day and saw paperboys running up and down the street waving papers over their heads. They were yelling, "Extra! Extra! Hitler walked into Austria!"

Izzy told me about it that night.

"Eta, I don't know what will become of us now. When I heard those paperboys, I felt just like someone had stabbed me in the chest. All day long, everywhere I went, people were in turmoil, confused and crying, terribly upset and saying, 'We're going to have a war.' "

Hitler annexed Austria on March 13, 1938 and continued his aggressive campaign across Europe. Within a year, the German army had control of all of Czechoslovakia. The defining blow came on September 1, 1939. With a *blitzkrieg* − a military tactic using surprise, lightning speed, and overwhelming power − Hitler's army invaded Poland. Four weeks later Poland was in German hands. With the invasion of Poland, the artistic and educated world we knew all but ended in Europe. Thousands of Jews from Poland began fleeing to other countries trying to find safety.

After Hitler invaded Poland, which was just across the border from Lithuania, we knew things were really dire. Letters from relatives and friends in other cities told us that the situation was just as terrible elsewhere. We felt a growing uneasiness, an all-encompassing depression because of the Hitler regime. Restrictions had become so pervasive, that we could no longer buy cars, and were forbidden from such simple things as attending the theater or visiting the zoo.

Increasing restrictions on imports made it especially difficult for any business owner to travel out of the country. German Jews started pouring into Lithuania, looking for ways to get Lithuanian passports to escape their country, where Jews endured backbreaking restrictions.

Izzy had already witnessed the crushing German restrictions firsthand. He had gone on a business trip to Belgium and stopped in Berlin to visit his mother's relatives. While he was there, Izzy's male relatives were so scared they decided to seek shelter in various places away from their homes, believing something awful was going to happen, especially after one of Hitler's crazed speeches. Izzy decided to stay overnight in the apartment with his aunts, feeling secure in his Lithuanian passport and not realizing that he was about to witness the first orchestrated, widespread pogrom in Europe.

The destruction, which eventually became known as *Kristallnacht,* or the Night of Broken Glass, was a sadistic government-sponsored riot that took place November 9-10, 1938, for the express purpose of destroying Jewish property and smashing the windows in every synagogue, especially in Austria and Germany. Jews who tried to intervene or object were severely beaten. During the melee, Jewish businesses, homes, synagogues and schools — some say as many as 2,000 — were systematically destroyed, and priceless books and *Torahs* were burned.

All that night Izzy said he could hear screaming, but no one came to his aunt's apartment. He told me about it later.

"I could see through the window," he said. "There were Germans everywhere in their ugly Nazi uniforms with the swastikas on their arms. They were setting books on fire and they also started a fire in my aunt's synagogue across the street. I couldn't believe what I was seeing. There was no reason for the insanity. I could think of nothing the Jews might have done to deserve this tragedy. Right before my eyes, I watched that beautiful place of worship being destroyed and the precious *Torah* being stomped on and burned openly in the street. For what?"

I couldn't answer him. I didn't understand it, either. There had been no Jewish uprising, no open demonstrations against the government. I just didn't know what to say to him.

Izzy continued. "Eta, if there were a reason, I could accept it. But there is no defiance. In fact, the reverse is true. We Jews are staying inside more and more from fear. I don't know what our fate will be."

Later we learned that Hitler's henchmen purposely orches-trated the riots, supposedly as retribution for the murder of a German diplomat killed in Paris. A young Jewish man, Herschel Grynszpan, who was living in Paris at the time, shot the diplomat in a rage after learning how his parents' home, business and all their belongings were confiscated and they were forced to leave Germany because they were Jews. Even so, why did the act of one man result in the arrest of some 30,000 Jews and the murder of 96, not to speak of the millions of dollars in damage? Unknown to us at the time, it was a harbinger of worse things to come.

None of the Jews in Lithuania knew what to do, where to turn, or how to handle our lives anymore. To make matters worse, we kept hearing rumors that the *Schutzstaffel*, the Nazi special police units called the SS, were continuously attacking Jews in countless towns and cities throughout Europe.

Every time Izzy turned on the radio, we would hear Hitler screaming, saying how he was going to occupy the whole world. In the Soviet Union, Josef Stalin had been talking with England and America, but then he stuck a knife in their backs by making a deal with Hitler.

I can still hear Izzy, how he spoke with such pleasure after hearing Churchill stand up to Hitler. Izzy didn't have the words exactly right, I don't think, but he often quoted Churchill by saying, "We'll fight you with all our power. We'll fight you on land, sea and in the air. We're going to put an end to you."

Uneasiness became a way of life for us. We could be certain of nothing but more trouble. One Saturday afternoon Izzy went to visit his sister, Dvoira, and her husband in Kaunas. After hearing some noise, Izzy walked out into the street less than a block from City Hall. He could hardly believe what he was seeing. Russian tanks, cars and trucks of all kinds began pouring into Kaunas. The streets started filling with Russian soldiers. From that time on, everything began disappearing from the stores, and most of our restaurants and gathering places eventually closed. As the weeks passed, the Communists completely took charge of all the small shops and businesses, as well as the factories, and confiscated all bank accounts. Then one day Izzy came home with terrible news.

"Eta," he began. "I don't know how to tell you this, but we have no money, no business, no motorcycles, nothing. It's all gone. I don't even have a job. I don't know what we'll do."

"What do you mean? Everything is gone? Is nothing left for us?" I asked.

"No, nothing. We're penniless. As I understand it, all the factories are going to stay closed a week or so while they are restructured. When they reopen, I think we're going to have less-experienced working-class individuals, whom the Communists have decided are 'worthwhile,' to replace the owners or presidents of corporations. They say they're trying to rid us of capitalism, but I don't know how we'll survive. I even heard the Russian bureaucrats have removed the owner of a chocolate factory in Kaunas and replaced him with a maid who used to wash the windows and floors. What sense does that make?"

It didn't take long to learn that Izzy's fears were well founded. Many members of the Jewish upper echelon were forbidden to work and were subsequently sent to Kulautuva, the summer place where rich people would normally go on vacation, where food was now scarce and work was nonexistent.

The wealthy people were forbidden to work and were told, "You have enough fat and money to live without our help." They had no alternative, especially since everything was turned over to the government and nationalized.

Emptiness fell into our beautiful city; it became like a desert. It was as if the very last of our freedom had been chopped away.

I asked Dvoira to watch the children one day. She didn't have any children of her own then and she really loved Jay.

I think her favorite was Masha, though, our beautiful little baby daughter who was just a few months old. Masha had become the bright spot in our lives, but we worried about her a lot. She didn't eat well and was somewhat sickly, causing us to treasure her even more.

After Dvoira came that day, Izzy and I took a cup of tea and went just outside and sat down on the porch. We were afraid to go for a walk or do anything to draw attention to ourselves. We just needed some quiet time. We were trying to think what to do.

"Eta, I know it's bad now, but even with all the restrictions, it's better in Lithuania than in Poland with the Gestapo," Izzy said. "At least here, our lives are safe. Nobody is going to kill us, or put us in jail, unless we become enemies of the Communists. We just have to get used to a different culture. Ours has been destroyed."

"I know, Izzy, I know," I said, trying to hide my growing fear. "But what will we do? There are no more theaters, no Maccabi sports organization or Zionist organizations, nothing like we used to have. I guess we're lucky to still have our families. Look at the poor Polish Jews. They came here hoping for visas and now you see what's happened. With the location of consular offices being moved to Latvia, permits are even harder to come by."

"Having a visa doesn't guarantee anything," Izzy said in disgust. "Even with visas, nobody is going anywhere. It's hard to believe any Jews have made it to America or any other country. When they do leave, it is through a miracle of some kind."

Since Izzy's motorcycles were confiscated, he started looking for other work. Lucky for us, he was installed rather quickly as a manager for a recently organized horse-and-buggy cartel. Even a man who had a horse or a buggy couldn't work if he didn't belong to the cartel. The Communists allowed the buggy drivers to work because they thought they were poor people. It was almost impossible for those listed as millionaires to get any type of job. Izzy hired two or three of them to work for him. One, who was named Marcus, traded Izzy a car for a job. He was the happiest person. He figured that with a job he wouldn't have to live in Kulautuva and be in danger of being locked up.

The Communists didn't like people walking around without work. For example, Izzy's former boss, Leib-Itzick Fish, formerly a wealthy man, came asking Izzy for a job. He even offered to take care of the horses. Here was Leib-Itzick, the millionaire, shoveling horse manure, and it made Izzy feel terrible. Still, everybody was begging to work, and Izzy and I were so happy that he had a good job. After two months, the cartels had around 200 former business owners. They soon got their own blacksmith, wagon and wheel maker and began making their own wagons and platforms with the steel they were getting from the Russian government. This all happened around 1940.

While Izzy didn't worry about being jailed, he was still very depressed. Our life was only a shadow of the one we used to have. As the family provider, Izzy felt responsible to make it better. Sometimes we would lie awake at night, and he would ask me, "What can we do? There's a war going on, and Hitler has already occupied half of Europe. Here, at least, we can still get a slice of bread and a potato."

I was always glad for the dark, so Izzy couldn't see the panic on my face. I was so afraid, but even so, I tried to think of a way to encourage him. I'd always answer, "Yes, of course, you're right. We can even get a little butter to put on our bread. At least we have all our family together. That's the important thing."

Just as Izzy predicted, trouble started almost immediately in the factories and in the government offices. It was a natural result of the Communists replacing the Lithuanian managers, primarily with Jewish workers. The situation was already strained, but this new development created more tension. Every day there would be a disruption of some kind. Finally the trouble came to a head when a radio bulletin announced that a Russian/German war had started. Hitler had broken his treaty and attacked Stalin's army near the Lithuanian border. That announcement scared me to death, and I wasn't the only one.

Every hour there were more and more Russian soldiers retreating through Kaunas. By mid-summer of 1941, many of our friends had joined the Russians trying to flee the approaching Germans. Since Lithuania was right at the border, we could see the Russians, the Red Army, retreating through Kaunas and Slobodka. Anywhere there was a road, people began running away on foot, going by trucks and cars, horse and wagon, and even by bicycles, trying to escape the inevitable onslaught of the Germans.

Radios amplified a constant blare of noise, which mixed with people shouting at each other. Guns were being fired randomly, and everyone was frightened and so confused they didn't know what to do. People suddenly came running to the carriage cartel, grabbing horses, buggies and wagons from the stable. What could Izzy do to stop them? They were desperate. They loaded the horses and wagons with a few necessities and then tried to get to the Russian border, which was on the highway through Slobodka. Some of our friends survived by running to the railroad station and taking a train to Russia.

Izzy took a horse with a buggy, too. He came for Jay, who was six years old, and our baby daughter, Masha, who was about six months old, and for me. After all of us were loaded in, Izzy drove the buggy up beside his parents' home and handed me the reins. He was only gone a few minutes. He needed to see if his parents wanted to escape with us, but they said they couldn't leave. Izzy's sister, Dvoira, had just given birth to a baby boy.

Izzy jumped into the buggy and said, "I don't know what to do. I feel like I'm being pulled apart."

We talked for a few minutes, trying to decide if we should stay, but when the bombs began dropping closer and closer, Izzy picked up the reins and shouted at the horse to take off. I had no idea where we were going. I don't think Izzy knew, either. We were just so afraid and thought it would be better to follow the mass of people who were running from Slobodka toward the Russian border. We didn't stop to think about how we would make it 150 kilometers.

I was so scared, I was trembling, but I tried to be brave for Jay's sake. I also had my hands full trying to keep Masha from crying. She wasn't a robust baby, and Izzy always got so upset when she cried and he couldn't help with her.

We left so suddenly that we took no provisions. Who could think of food or water when bombs were flying through the air? As the time dragged on, hunger and thirst multiplied our misery. We were just four among thousands fleeing the terrible approaching German army. There were Jews from all over, holding their children by their hands, some running, some walking. Their flight became more perilous as German planes drew closer, flying over their heads dropping bombs and strafing people as they ran down the road and through the fields. Every time a plane approached, adults would grab the children and run to the side of the road and sometimes lie down on top of them trying to avoid the worst. Sometimes the adults were killed and there were little children standing beside their dead parents. Still others were picked off by rifle fire.

I saw one man go completely mad. He began running around in circles shouting orders at people and demanding a Russian flag from everyone he talked to. He said he was going to tie the flag around his head so he would be safe.

Our retreat had a fast ending, only a day and a half later. German paratroopers cut off our escape by dropping down right in front of us. It was terrifying to see so many Germans. They also overran our positions with motorcycles, which were faster than our horses. They were like bees in a swarm all around us, in trucks and cars, with their hateful Nazi uniforms, and the rest of the army already ahead of us. We had no alternative but to turn back.

4

Kovno Ghetto Formed – 1941

As we headed back toward the city of Janova, we could see great clouds of smoke. All the furniture factories had been set afire, and there were horses and people lying dead all along the highway. Lithuanians were forcing the Jews, including the rabbi from Janova, to clean the highway with shovels and picks. They were removing dead horses and humans off the road by pulling them by their arms and legs, trying to move them to a burial site.

When we came upon this, I was terrified that they would take Izzy, too. Hoping the Lithuanians would not bother him if he were carrying a child, I put Masha in his arms. We had decided to walk at that point to rest the horse. Finally, we were able to pass with several others in a group. I held Jay by the hand. He was walking stiff as a board, not looking to either side and not saying a word. I knew he was terrified, but I couldn't do anything to comfort him. We saw all the bodies being cleared off the road. Izzy and I put Jay between us, trying to shield him from seeing the ones who were slaughtered.

Later we learned that the Lithuanians took several other Jews into the woods and shot them. It was a miracle to get past that place without being touched.

Izzy helped us back into the wagon and we headed toward Slobodka. When we came to a fork in the road, one way was the main highway to Kaunas, and the other was a side road to Slobodka, the suburb across the river where we lived. Izzy thought the road to Slobodka would be less traveled since it was only sand and there were many holes in the road. As we separated from them, it looked like thousands of people were returning to Kaunas over the main highway.

By then, we had not eaten for almost two days. The horse was faltering from exhaustion. I felt so sorry for him. I could see blood running from the open sores where the harness had rubbed wounds in his hide. Izzy chanced stopping at a farmhouse so I could ask for milk for Masha. The farmer's wife gave me a pitiful look. My blouse was hanging half off my shoulder. I had torn it getting into the wagon. The woman must have thought I looked indecent. She went back into the house and returned with a glass of milk for Masha and a blouse for me.

While I tried to feed Masha, the woman warned us to stay on the road to Slobodka. She said Lithuanians were arresting Jews on the highway to Kaunas, putting them in jail or killing them. When we returned to Slobodka, there was an eerie quiet. The streets were completely empty. We looked around trying to find someone and then asked each other, "What's happening?"

All of a sudden, my father and my father-in-law both rushed toward us from my father's house. They were so happy we had come back. They embraced us all but then stood on either side of Izzy describing the terrible things that happened while we were gone. They could hardly get the words out.

"Izzy, you won't believe what happened," my father began. "On Jurbarko Street the Lithuanians have killed every single Jew, including Meise, my neighbor, and the blacksmith who lived just around the corner from him."

"What do you mean?" Izzy asked, his mouth hanging open in amazement. "Didn't the soldiers do anything to stop it?"

"The Germans just watched the slaughter," my father replied with disgust. "In fact, they stood watching as people were dying, all of them laughing and pointing."

My father turned to me next and gently put his arm around me.

"Eta, I'm so grateful you are alive. On the day you left, just at dark, I heard screaming. I ran to the attic where I could see into Meise's backyard. I saw Lithuanians stab Meise, his wife, and his grandfather to death. There were other Jews being killed with hammers and axes. The people were trying to run away screaming with pain. The madmen kept chasing the tormented Jews, as if they were playing a game of hide and seek. When they had killed everyone in the yards, they turned to the Jews who lived near Raudondvario and Tilzes streets and killed every person on the right side of the street."

"Every person? That can't be true," I said. "There are so many houses. How could they kill so many?"

"I don't know," my father said, finally breaking down in sobs. "They went from house to house killing everybody on the right side of the street but skipped the left side for some unknown reason."

I stood beside my father trying to take in what he was saying. Then I noticed his hair had turned completely white. It had to be from fear and what he had witnessed.

My father-in-law took up when my father couldn't continue.

"The first house they went in belonged to the general manager of the newspaper *The Jewish Voice*. I don't know why they targeted him, perhaps because he was a Zionist. He was such a nice man, and his wife, the dentist, a beautiful woman. The Lithuanians killed them, as well as their two children, before going into the rabbi's house, where they continued their unspeakable work."

At this point, my father-in-law became so pale I thought he was going to be sick. It took him several minutes to regain his composure. Finally, he said, "They cut off the rabbi's head, placed it on a platter, and then put it on a dresser. They also killed his wife."

I was suddenly overcome with nausea. I had to steady myself and try to keep Jay from hearing so much about the torture.

My father then said that he watched the Lithuanians go into the Friedmans' house. Friedman, a plumber, was over six feet tall, and a very strong man. My father said Friedman put up quite a fight, but they shot and killed him, along with his wife and son.

Izzy's father and mine broke down and cried several times while they were relaying the horrible news of our friends and neighbors. They kept saying the names of those murdered, as if their repetitious naming might either bring their friends back to life or allow them to accept their demise. The hardest part was describing how helpless they felt watching as the brutality continued from house to house. There was dreadful screaming and everyone ran wild trying to escape their relentless tormenters. Anyone intervening was immediately executed.

Next they told us it was the Lithuanian Home Guard, an organization that was part of the ex-Lithuanian Army. The Lithuanians already hated the Jews, and now with the Jewish youngsters becoming the bosses in factories and stores, the Lithuanians felt that killing them was the way to get their revenge. The Home Guard had an empty lot not far from the

Slobodka Cemetery where they brought together the rest of the Jews from Jurbarko Street and from all over Slobodka.

We were so fortunate. They didn't bother my father-in-law's house or ours because of Voitekunas, the headman from the Lithuanian Home Guard. My father-in-law, Preidl Ipp, had a government whiskey store on the first floor of his house, which was run by a Gentile Lithuanian woman. Lucky for us, she was Voitekunas's mistress. My in-laws felt we would be safe there because we had the Lithuanian woman watching out for us. The woman knew what we were thinking. One day she told us not to worry because nothing would happen to us; she would not let it. She said, "You're good people, good Jews."

We were still terribly afraid. Izzy, Jay and I lived in a little house behind my father-in-law's home. Although it was only a few feet away, I still felt unsafe, even with a strong wall around the houses so tall even Izzy couldn't climb over it. We were so afraid that Izzy finally brought my family to stay at our house overnight.

The next morning the Lithuanians grabbed many young Jews and forced them to gather all the bodies and put them into wagons. Next they dug a mass grave in the Slobodka Cemetery where they buried all those who were murdered. When the burial was complete, the gravediggers were also held captive. After keeping them without food for a couple of days, they gathered two or three hundred Jews and took all of them to a nearby fort. Back in the time of the Russian czars, nine forts were built around Kovno to protect it from German invasion. Now they were being used to imprison Jews and dissenters or as places to execute them.

When Izzy spoke of it later, I could see it just like a picture right in front of me. Izzy was standing in the back of our yard looking through a hole in the gate where he could see the street. Izzy remembered seeing so many, including Meir

During the first days of the German occupation of Lithuania, Lithuanian nationalists carried out a series of deadly attacks against the Jewish population, which they believed were responsible for the hardships endured under the Soviet regime. At Lietukis's Garage, sixty Jewish men were herded together and systematically beaten to death with crowbars.

Courtesy U.S. Holocaust Memorial Museum

Abel, a neighbor and father of a school friend of his. Meir Abel was carrying the *Torah* from the New Synagogue. Next to him were his brother and his son. There was also Rabbi Maiskovski, who owned a hardware store.

So many we knew were herded away like cattle. The Germans, along with Lithuanian collaborators, killed them all. Then we learned that those who returned to Kaunas by taking the good highway were also captured by members of the Lithuanian Home Guard who were waiting there to grab them. How ironic that these same ones thought they were taking the "safer" road.

Izzy had chosen to take the road to the right despite its holes and the sand, while his Uncle Herschel, his wife, who was Izzy's mother's sister, their children, and a lot of our friends took the other road and ended up being killed. Not only did the Lithuanians kill them, we heard they tortured them, raped the young girls and kept them confined without any food. A few who escaped told us how the Lithuanians, people with whom we had lived all of our lives, were massacring people. They treated Jews worse than dogs. It was so unbelievable. No matter how hard we tried, we couldn't find an explanation for it or absorb the insanity of it.

At Fort VII the Lithuanians killed about 3,500 Jews from all around Kaunas. Many who didn't run away were brought together and killed there. In Kaunas, there was a gasoline station near the synagogue called Lietukis's Garage. The Lithuanians grabbed sixty elderly Jews and beat them to death with crowbars. They poured gasoline on some of them and burned them alive. This happened during the last few days of June.

We just wanted to crawl into a grave somewhere and hide, but there was no place to hide from the Lithuanians. They gathered groups of Jews from different places. One of those places was the Platz Parade, where the city government was, and from there they took them to Fort VII. Izzy's good friends David Salzburg and Simon Karnovski were brought there, and they didn't understand what was happening. A Lithuanian, one of the few decent ones, recognized the two men and tried to help them by letting them go home for an hour to see their wives, thinking they would not come back. They were so honest, though, that after visiting their wives for a while, they came back and were taken to Fort VII and killed with all the other Jews.

The killings went on for days without any government intervention. It was a partnership with the Germans, who were allowing the Lithuanians to do their dirty work. The Germans finally started organizing, trying to get a little order after everybody was satisfied with the killings and seeing the Jews in misery. The Germans jailed many Jews in the *Gelbe Turm*, the Yellow Jail. They started arresting Jews who were simply walking in the street. From jail they, too, were taken to Fort VII. The daily murders and continuous destruction were so terrible that we kept our window shades pulled, hiding in our homes behind locked doors, giving the appearance that no one was living there. It got so bad that every Jew I knew was afraid to leave his home even to buy food.

Shortly after the killings, the Gestapo came to Kaunas and established an office. Things slacked off a little, but the Germans still didn't stop the Lithuanians; they could do anything they wanted. The Gestapo issued orders to the acting Lithuanian mayor that Jews were no longer allowed to walk on the sidewalks but had to walk in the gutter. Dogs, however, could walk on the sidewalks.

On July 8, 1941, a decree had been issued that all the Jews in the Baltic States had to wear the Star of David. One yellow star had to be placed over our hearts and the other on our

Courtesy U.S. Holocaust Memorial Museum

Jews move their belongings into Kovno Ghetto in Slobodka. Use of motorized vehicles was forbidden. Inhabitants were crowded together with several families sharing lodging in an impoverished area lacking modern plumbing and sanitation systems. Each inhabitant was allotted less than ten square feet of living space.

backs. In case a Jew ran, they would be able to take aim at the star coming or going.

In Kaunas a mass of suicides started. Day after day we would hear of individuals, particularly from the higher classes, killing themselves. For example, the Wolfe brothers — one of them was the director of the Commerce Bank, and the other was the president of the Central Bank — both committed suicide. Many good people died; it was pitiful.

While life as we knew it was being destroyed, we had to deal with yet another inconceivable loss.

Our tiny daughter had become very ill just after our flight from the Germans. A frail child from birth, Masha, now just a few months old, always needed more sustenance than my milk could provide. I did what I could by making rice milk for her, keeping a constant vigil over her. I wanted to believe that she would live if I stayed with her. But one night I was so exhausted I could barely stand up, so I left the baby in Dvoira's care and went to bed very late. When I woke the next morning, Dvoira was standing in the doorway to the bedroom with my sister. I could tell there was terrible news. My baby was gone. I had tried so hard, but to no avail.

I thought my heart would break as I washed Masha's little body a final time and wrapped her in a shroud. I couldn't bear to accompany them, but stood in the doorway and watched as my father and father-in-law gently carried my tiny baby toward the Jewish cemetery. A part of me had died. As I saw Masha being borne away, I wondered if I would ever carry life within my body again.

～

On July 10, 1941, a decree announced the formation of the Kovno Ghetto, to be established across the river from Kaunas in the suburb of Slobodka near where we lived. The Lithuanians sometimes referred to it as Vilijampole, a name given to it around 1918. Jews had until August 15 to move there.

~

Along with our neighbors, we began packing to move. We were allowed only a few personal items, a couple of changes of clothes apiece, and some shoes. My mother and I discussed which pots and pans I should bring, along with the bedding. I couldn't take our extra set of dishes, the special ones we used to *kasher* for *Pesach*. There wasn't enough room. There was precious little to choose from anyway. All the Jewish households had been searched, and so many of our things had already been stolen by either the Lithuanians or the Gestapo. Many houses, ours included, had been ransacked, with the hoodlums breaking what furniture they didn't cart off.

(left to right, standing) Fievel, Chaim and Minnie Butrimowitz and Eta Ipp; *(left to right, seated)* Chai Esther and Chananya Butrimowitz, *Frumme* Leah Kalamitsky (mother of Chai Esther), and Jacob and Israel Ipp (1937).

Courtesy Virginia Holocaust Museum

(left to right) Toni, Dvoira, Israel, Golde and Preidl Ipp (1930).

My father, a cobbler, was known for his craftsmanship with leather. He was determined not to add to the thieves' plunder. Just before we were forced into the ghetto, there had been a particularly harrowing search, when some of my parents' personal belongings were confiscated. My mother told me that after the search was over and the Germans had left our house, my father had instructed her to build a big fire.

My mother said, "Build a big fire. What for? We need to save the firewood for cooking. Are you cold? Here, put on a sweater."

"Build the fire like I told you and stop with the talking," my father had said in an uncharacteristically harsh voice. "And make sure it's very hot."

My mother didn't really understand the cutting tone of his voice or his request, but not wanting to fret him further, she fed the fire until it roared. Just as she turned to tell my father that she had done his bidding, he walked out of their bedroom carrying his best coat, a full-length leather coat with a fur collar, the one he always reserved for special occasions.

"This is one thing they'll not get," he told her with satisfaction. "I didn't work to make the finest of coats to cover the backs of murderers." With that said, he shoved the prized possession into the fire. He followed the coat with shoes and boots, leaving only a pair or two for the rest of the children and my mother. The fur burst into flames first, as if gasoline had been thrown onto the fire. Within minutes the oiled leather on the items was either burned or charred beyond use. Soon thereafter all the Jews started pouring into the ghetto.

There were certain sections of Slobodka designated to be within the ghetto. Izzy's parents' house and ours, situated in the yard nearby, were located one street outside of the ghetto. Because of that, we had to move in with my parents, whose little blue house was located right on the border of the ghetto. After we all moved in, including Izzy's sisters, one of whom was married and had just given birth, there would be sixteen living in a house built for five or six. We had no inside bathroom or running water and were allowed to use electricity only three or four hours a day. It was miserable, but still better than some other places where many more were crowded into even smaller houses.

When we learned the ghetto was going to be established,

all the Jews from Kaunas started running to Slobodka, trying to trade houses with the few Gentiles who were living there in the west end. Since Jews primarily inhabited Slobodka, only a few homes were available for trading.

As the deadline to be inside the ghetto grew near, throngs of families ran with wagons, buggies, bicycles, and handcarts, moving what few pieces of furniture they still owned from Kaunas to Slobodka to settle there in squalid spaces. The roads were dirt, and when it rained they turned to mud, making them all but impassable. It wasn't unusual to be walking ankle-deep in mud. There wasn't enough room in the ghetto for all the Jews, so the Nazis designated an area for a little ghetto as well. It was established on the other side of Paneriu Street. A bridge was constructed between the two ghettos, crossing Paneriu, so the Jews wouldn't have to mingle with the Gentile community. It also left the main thoroughfare open so that Jews could be marched to the forts nearby for torture and execution.

A population of about 5,000 Jews settled in the small ghetto. In the big ghetto, which was called Kovno Ghetto, 25,000 or more Jews also took up residence, squeezed together like sardines, with only a few wells to sustain their needs.

The Gestapo gave an order to Dr. Elkhanan Elkes, a well-known Jewish physician, who had been asked to lead the Jewish community, to organize a Jewish police force, which helped to maintain order, and to manage our own businesses inside the ghetto. Dr. Elkes was also told to organize a labor department from the ghetto community, which would supply all the labor from the ghetto for the Germans. We were instructed to organize a Jewish hospital. We had good doctors, specialists, surgeons and general practitioners. From now on, only a few of them could work in the ghetto hospital.

A barbed-wire fence surrounded the ghettos. Lithuanian and Jewish police were stationed at the gate to guard the entrance and confiscate unauthorized items. Lithuanian police walked the perimeter with rifles on their shoulders like it was an armed camp. On August 15, 1941, the ghetto gates were locked.

Some rooms had as many as ten people in them. As soon as we got locked in, everyone felt trapped, like rats in their holes, scared to death, crowded together miserably. We didn't have adequate sanitary facilities, and food was very restricted. It's impossible to describe how we all suffered.

I felt like I was smothering all the time because I had to breathe someone else's air. We did our best to protect Jay. I think he felt comforted in some strange way. All of his family was surrounding him. He was just six years old and couldn't understand much of what was going on. At least he had his feather comforter to keep him warm.

5

Learning to Survive

We had been imprisoned in Kovno Ghetto for just three days. Late that afternoon, August 18, some of the women were standing outside our homes when we noticed a large group gathering not too far away. Although I was really afraid of what was happening, I eased closer, just to see what the crowd was looking at. I shuddered, hoping no one was being beaten or shot. As I got closer, I could see a crowd trying to read a notice that had been posted. One of the men standing up front started to read it aloud to the others.

It was an order from the governor of Kaunas, transmitted through SA Captain Fritz Jordan, a member of the hated *Sturm Abteilung*, or Storm Troopers, who were being used to incite riots against Jews all over Europe. The order directed the Jewish Council to provide 500 Jews, namely men from among the educated classes, to be brought to the authorities at the ghetto gate.

The Gestapo request was interpreted to mean the men

were needed for clerical work or reorganizing archives the Russians had left in Kaunas. Interested parties were to gather by 7 a.m. the next day. The excitement generated by the opportunity for something other than manual labor and the possibility of a monetary reward or food resulted in 534 men reporting to the Lithuanian police and Gestapo officials for the assignment.

Many of Izzy's childhood friends and schoolmates, all lawyers, clerical bosses, doctors, "the cream of the crop" from Kaunas, began to gather early the next morning. Some of them got thirsty and ran into our house for a drink. One of them asked me to make him a sandwich for lunch, which I gladly did. About the time I was wrapping it up, Gdalia Berkman, a good friend and my Uncle Itzhak's brother-in-law, stepped inside.

"Hey, Eta," Gdalia said, flashing me a mischievous grin, "while you're at it, make one of those for me."

"Of course, Gdalia," I replied. "I want you to keep up your strength." Gdalia was giving me one of his famous hugs when Izzy stepped inside from the back door.

One of the men said, "Let's go, Izzy. Why are you staying at home with the women? It will drive you crazy to be in the ghetto all day. Come, let's go, we'll all work together for a while."

Izzy was very anxious about it and finally answered, "Well, boys, I just don't know, something doesn't seem right to me." He put his coat on, kissed my cheek and said he was going to walk to the Central Council to find out what was happening there. The other men just stood around waiting to make the full count.

When Izzy got to the Central Council, he encountered another good friend, Itzhak Borstein, a policeman at the Council, who grabbed him and said, "Let's go, they're short some men. You're the right man they need." Izzy brushed him aside and walked away.

Izzy told me later that he had a feeling the men didn't go to work. He was even surer of it when none of them came back that evening or the next. Parents began running around looking for their children. They were crazy with worry. Izzy has always been haunted by the memory of Oszinski, who owned the flour and lumber mills, looking for his two sons. Oszinski took off his Star of David, ran out of the ghetto, and went all over Kaunas crying, saying he didn't care what happened to him; he just wanted to find his sons. After he looked for nearly two weeks, some Lithuanians finally told him that all of the men had been taken to Fort IV and shot. Izzy, once again, had eluded death.

We were barely able to catch our breath before another edict was posted on September 3, another order issued by SA Captain Jordan. This time all ghetto inmates were instructed to immediately deliver a host of articles, all listed individually on the piece of paper. Everything was to be brought no later than 6 p.m. the next day to the Jewish Council, which would orchestrate the delivery to the respective authorities.

You've never seen such a ridiculous list of things, including any money in German or Russian currency exceeding 100 rubles. We were to bring all valuables, including gold, silver, precious stones, precious metals or items made from such metals. Not only were we to hand over any securities, but also receipts of deposit, valuable paintings, and all fur products, except sheepskins or very worn furs. Good carpets, pianos, typewriters, all electrical appliances, including any that could be used for medical or professional purposes, were also listed.

Along with that, we were expected to hand over any good material suitable for making suits and coats. As if that weren't enough, we were also instructed to deliver all cows, poultry, horses with harnesses, carts and even stamp collections.

The order went on to explain that all ghetto inmates were requested to follow this delivery duty as scrupulously and conscientiously as possible, because the fate of the ghetto depended on it. We knew if anyone deviated from the order, not only would the offenders run the risk of the death penalty, but all ghetto inmates, too. Jewish authorities were aware that some items had been buried or otherwise concealed. In view of the risk involved, perhaps even annihilation of the entire ghetto population, pressure was brought to bear on some of those known to be hiding items.

As soon as the order was issued, pandemonium broke out, with Jews running to surrender their valuables to the Central Council. The elderly, afraid to carry anything of value, gave their treasures to anyone who would take them away.

For once, Izzy was scared to death and afraid to even keep his wedding ring. He wanted to give it to the Council, but my father told him not to. My brave father, defying the pressure to sacrifice everything of value, took the few miserable pieces we had left and put them in some places in the wall. He even asked Izzy to act as a lookout and watch out for intruders while he took off one of his heavy boots. Within minutes my father had removed the heel of one boot and hollowed out a cavity inside it. He deftly replaced the heel, pulled the boot onto his foot and smiled as he stomped down hard, securing the nails again.

Many others worked out ingenious places to hide small caches of coins and jewelry. We were all afraid of the time when we might have nothing left with which to bargain for food or other necessities.

My mother-in-law and Izzy's sister had some silver and gold and a few diamond rings. They were so scared they ran to give them to Leibel, Izzy's cousin. Leibel figured out a good hiding place, in a piece of wood where he had knocked out a hole. His mother, Nese, didn't know he put anything into

Jewish partisan unit, which operated in the Lithuanian forests, poses for a group portrait. Many of the group's members had been involved in resistance activities of the Kovno Ghetto.

Courtesy U.S. Holocaust Memorial Museum

the wood, so she put it into the oven for heat, unknowingly melting away their valuables.

Suspense hung in the air throughout the ghetto for a month, constantly fueled by the frenetic, unannounced searching of houses. After one Jew was shot for harboring a few pieces of silver, even those with only a single silver fork ran to the Council, completing the gold and silver "action."

Giving up the valuables wasn't the worst part. When Gestapo officers came searching, they would tear up the living quarters or chop the doors to pieces, and everybody was forced to leave. My mother always made wine for *Pesach*, which she stored in the basement. During a search one day, after some of the German soldiers drank a few bottles, they started breaking up everything they could find. They got crazy, and we were scared to death they would turn on us, but finally, they just stumbled out in a drunken stupor.

Rumors flew like wildfire. We had even heard of Nazi plans for a "Final Solution to the Jewish Question," simply killing all the Jews. When these suspicions coincided with the beginning liquidation of Jews in some other towns, a resistance movement began in Kovno Ghetto. Chaim Yellin, who would eventually lose his life in the effort, began organizing underground activities that would link Kovno Jews with Russian partisans already hiding in the woods and creating havoc for the Nazis. As the partisans gained strength, so did the plan to liquidate the remaining Jews in Lithuania. Word reached us that many Jews, perhaps as many as 25,000, were executed from the towns or labor camps near Telz, Keidan, and Ponary, areas near Vilna.

As tensions mounted, more pressure was brought to bear on all of us. A work permit, referred to as a "Jordan pass," became mandatory. Securing a work permit could mean the difference between life and death, so there were furious fights over them. Workers without permits were shot. Further confusion was added when numbered armbands were also required for workers.

Every morning when Izzy and I woke up, we were torn between going to work and trying to stay home to protect our family members. We were never sure which work detail we would end up in and always afraid to leave Jay and our parents, but working was the only thing that ensured our survival. The young and the elderly seemed to be prime targets. Once, SA Commander Jordan, the man for whom the work passes were named, came into the ghetto and found five people who had stayed home and happened to be in the street. Jordan shot all of them in plain sight. He and his men killed nearly 100 others just to scare us into going to work. Each day, the situation became more intolerable.

I was terribly worried about Jay. Always a picky eater, now he was barely subsisting on meager and tasteless rations. It was hard to believe anyone could survive. Over time, our rations dwindled to less than a third of what we needed to sustain life, another successful way of thinning the ranks. Each one of us was allotted about 25 ounces of meat and small portions, just a few ounces, of beans and grain along with a few tablespoons of flour each week. I don't know how we lived, except for the few slices of bread that were also doled out. Workers were given an extra food ration, if you could call it that, a small allowance of lard and salt. Although food, it tasted horrible. Izzy and I took turns pretending that we didn't want our portions, thereby giving Jay a few extra mouthfuls. We were also fortunate to get a few vegetables from the community gardens. Had it not been for the gardens, I'm sure starvation would have prevailed.

On September 17, the Nazis directed all ghetto residents to gather in Sajungos Square, a public square in a large empty field near Varniu Street. Everyone had to report at 7 a.m., even the small children, the sick, the old men and women. Anyone remaining at home would be shot. A huge group of us started moving toward the designated area while it was still dark. For two hours, a chain of humans shuffled forward, some in carts, baby carriages, and on each other's backs. Lithuanian police and the Gestapo with machine guns, ready to attack, surrounded the whole ghetto and the gathering place.

Inmates of Kovno Ghetto were allotted only about one-third of the calories needed for survival.
Starvation was kept at bay through communal gardens. To reduce theft, the gardens were guarded
by Jewish children.

After we waited two hours, a German came riding up on a motorcycle and spoke to the head of the Gestapo. All of them eventually pulled away, leaving us without a guard. Izzy said the Orthodox Jews believed it was "*Min Hashamaim,*" an order from the heavens as God looked out for us. Everybody shook hands and kissed each other because we had survived our death sentence, but it didn't last long.

The first week of October 1941 marked the beginning of the "selection" in the small ghetto. The Nazis decided they didn't need two ghettos. The Jews who had armbands with numbers were instructed to go over to the large ghetto. The remainder, about 1,800, were taken to the Fort IX and systematically killed.

The Nazis also took away truckloads of nurses and children who were never seen again. Later one of the hospital buildings was boarded up, but not before it was packed with children from the children's home. Many of the children weren't really sick but were being housed in the hospital buildings to try to save their lives after they had become orphans. The building they were forced into, along with numerous surgical patients and others in various stages of recovery, was used to house patients with contagious diseases. The building, which was then boarded up, was subsequently set afire, trapping patients, medical staff, and all the children, burning them alive. The fire burned for almost two days. The stench from burning flesh was unimaginable. As the number of children in the ghetto continued to dwindle almost daily, I became frantic with concern for Jay's life.

The Central Council was soon forced to publish another directive. It, too, was posted on the walls throughout the ghetto, demanding that all ghetto inhabitants, regardless of age or medical condition, gather at Demokratu Square on October 28 by 6 a.m. The directive ordered that all drawers and doors be left standing open. I suppose that was to make sure no one was hiding as well as divulge any foodstuffs or property worth looting.

Before dawn that day, a great horde of remaining Kovno Jews, more than 25,000, came together in family groups. Everyone had to appear for the roll call. Anyone left at home, regardless of physical condition, would be immediately shot. Izzy gathered the members of both our families and told us that we must stick together at all cost. He warned that separation could result in our deaths.

Family members clung to each other, understanding their very lives depended on being able to stand upright. Single women and children tried to attach themselves to family groups, so as not to draw attention to their status. There was little question that some of us, if not most of us, would be doomed before the day was out. We moved at a snail's pace, paralyzed by fear. We understood all too well what was happening. The order stated there would be a roll call, which was necessary to document those who worked at hard labor. They used the ruse that extra rations could then be allocated to those who worked the hardest. No one was fooled by that explanation. By this time we knew the only reason for a "selection" was to thin the ranks.

Some of us, mostly the women, were already crying, especially those who had previously lost family members. As I walked, I began to feel the copper taste of fear in my mouth, an all too familiar happening. While some fell to their knees and retched, overcome with the anticipation that all of us would be summarily executed, the rest walked around the fallen ones, trying to keep families intact. Some were too ill to walk alone. Others dropped dead from the overwhelming fear, their bodies simply crumpling on the ground. The crowd was so thick we could hardly avoid stepping on them. The children clung pitifully to whoever was carrying them or holding their hands. The fear was palpable, even to the smallest ones, but they held their cries within, having been cautioned so many times before to be quiet, lest they draw attention to themselves or their families.

I was almost paralyzed by fear. My knees wanted to give way under me. Jay was walking close beside me, his hand in mine. Each step I took, I wondered if I was leading my son closer to his death. Izzy was walking in front of both our families, a grave look on his face but not showing fear. His straight back and proud presence gave me strength. I felt I could face anything as long as we were together. Some of the women were silently crying, as if they were already mourning their losses. There seemed to be a sea of faces. Although thousands had already been taken from the ghetto and killed, there were still so many people, some of the children got lost and went running around looking for their families. We stood in line for three hours in a cold sleeting rain before the selection process began. It lasted all day, more than twelve hours. We stood shivering and huddled together, moving forward by inches, waiting our turn before the monsters that would decide our destiny.

As the line got shorter, we could see the same Gestapo as in September, with their swastikas and uniforms. They were demanding from the spokesman for each group, "What is your occupation, damn Jew?" As the occupations were called out, the groups were divided. A schoolteacher was sent back toward the area of the small ghetto, where the Gestapo stood in a line, flanking the path with machine guns. A cabinetmaker was motioned to go back into the large ghetto. This was the way it went, all day long, group after group. An accountant was sent one direction; a shoemaker was sent to the opposite direction -- not only him, but his entire family as well.

Master Sergeant Helmut Albert Rauca, a very tall, distinguished looking German, orchestrated the whole operation, which came to be known as the "Big Selection." Rauca stood with feet spread apart, eating sandwiches from wax paper, drinking coffee and smoking cigarettes from daylight until dark, summarily dismissing huge groups to the right or the left with the flick of his finger or riding crop. He looked like a giant standing there. A giant with the power of life and death. From time to time, another German officer would approach Rauca and show him a slip of paper. I surmised it was probably the number of Jews already culled. As usual, they must have had a quota to fill.

Some groups were made up of as many as fifty family members. A singular spokesman who was fluent in German headed each one. In the group next to us was a young man named Mendal Smiskovich, an automobile mechanic. When he said he was a mechanic, Rauca motioned toward the large ghetto, which was to Rauca's left.

Izzy barely spoke a word during the time we were in line, but he just kept observing where the families were sent as Rauca stood making his decisions. Standing in front of Rauca was like facing a firing squad without a blindfold, waiting to be executed. He looked at us for a few moments without flinching. I don't think he even blinked while Izzy was speaking. It seemed like hours before he motioned us back toward the big ghetto. Once inside the ghetto fence, the Jewish police told us to go home. When we were safe at last, Jay ran up to Izzy and said, "I told you we'll be back in our home in the ghetto, that we wouldn't be shot or go to Fort IX. My little heart told me we would survive." Izzy said he was plenty scared. He described his fear to me later that night.

He said, "When our turn came, my mind was spinning a mile a minute. Something stopped me from saying I was a lawyer. Instead, I said I was a mechanic, even though I was scared to say it. When Rauca saw that I was wearing tall boots and a leather coat, I must have looked like a mechanic to him."

The selection was a death trap for thousands. Leibel, Izzy's brave cousin, was able to get his family through somehow. I remember looking back and hoping they would survive. After his family group was detained for a brief period, I saw Leibel acting a little agitated. For some reason, he gently pushed Sheina, his sister-in-law, to the side. I don't know if he was pretending to be her husband or what, but he suddenly grabbed the baby carriage Sheina was pushing with Sara in it and led them all to safety back into the large ghetto. His *chutzpah* as a teenager never ceased to amaze me.

So few made it. We lost the most educated Jewish people of Kaunas. While the Germans orchestrated the madness, they depended on the local Lithuanians to keep order. I still couldn't believe that these Lithuanians, the ones now helping to kill us, used to be our good friends, our neighbors. Finally the selection ended. When it was over, they had taken away about a third of the Jews living in Kovno Ghetto. That night,

Jews look through abandoned property in Kovno Ghetto, probably following a deportation action.

sleep was impossible. We were so exhausted and drained from the ordeal that all we could do was huddle together in our house. For once, the smallness of the house didn't matter. We were just relieved to be alive.

The next morning those herded back into the little ghetto, more than 9,000 Jews, representing more than one-third of the ghetto population, were marched past us toward Fort IX where they were all shot. We were so close to death. Izzy always relived that day with agony and remembered seeing his Uncle Berl, his wife, Revel, and their son and two daughters, all together holding on to each other, walking arm-in-arm. Izzy would sit sometimes and describe how helpless he felt as our relatives and good friends passed by. Leib-Itzik Span was the president from our synagogue who owned a hardware store, a nice looking man, six feet tall with a nice beard. He had walked proudly with his spine straight as a board, to his death.

It was impossible to tell who survived. After that, we just became like vegetables. Life meant nothing to us. We were numb and did everything mechanically, with no feeling at all. The community was torn to pieces. Suddenly the ghetto seemed awfully big. Piles of furniture and vacant houses stood like ghosts, looming as reminders of the once vibrant families who lived inside them.

Later in our life, people would ask Izzy, "Why couldn't you run or resist? Why couldn't you do something?" How could we? The Lithuanians and Gestapo surrounded us, waiting only to kill us and take away what was ours. One wasn't any better than the other. There was nowhere to turn. The only ones who managed to escape were the young ones who had gone with the partisans into the woods.

Although the ghetto community was decimated, reporting for work was the only salvation for those who remained. One day a German officer found Izzy and said his truck needed repairs. While Izzy had some passing knowledge of how motorcycles were mechanically constructed, his wisdom of trucks and automobiles was negligible. Afraid to admit his limitations, Izzy tried stalling for time by telling the officer he was already behind in his work schedule.

The officer insisted Izzy give his attention to the truck immediately, since he was afraid to drive it any farther due to the noise it was making. Izzy told me about it when he got home that night.

"Eta, I was scared to death," he said. "Here was a job to be done, and I didn't know how to do it. I told him, though, that I would lie down on the ground while he drove slowly past me and I would take a look. When I looked under the pickup truck, I saw a large pipe pulling on the rear wheels, and I asked him to stop. I took the pipe in my hands and I saw that it was loose, and then I noticed where it was hanging, at the universal joint. I got out from under the truck and told the German that I could probably fix it by the next afternoon. He said if I fixed it sooner, he would give me a couple of slices of bread. I told him I would do my best.

"I had no idea how to do the repairs," Izzy explained. "When the man left, I got under the truck to start figuring out how to fix it and I saw that the needle bearings were out of the universal joint. I had to take out eight little bolts in order to get the pipe loose. I figured a pipe wrench and a screwdriver would do the job, so I went to the stockroom and asked for the tools. I was so scared I could hardly hold the wrench. When I tried to take out the universal joint, I couldn't even come close; the wrench was too big. I was so scared. I think knowing that German might get angry and kill me helped me gain some power in my fingers. I finally wrenched all the bolts out with my fingers and then the universal joint. I went to the stockroom and asked for a replacement. I also got the correct wrench, a box wrench. When I replaced it, the banging stopped. I couldn't believe I was so lucky.

"When I told the German his truck was ready, he had a hard time believing it as well. He was so happy that he went to the superintendent and told him that I was the best mechanic he had seen in all of Kaunas because I really knew what I was doing and I was also fast. He recommended that I be made foreman. Can you believe that, Eta? But, the very best part is that the soldier gave me a loaf of bread. That was worth all the risk. Now Jay will have bread to eat tonight."

6

Riga Selection

J oy was practically nonexistent in the ghetto. Tension plagued us because selections continuously thinned the ranks. One of the greatest fears for a Jewish worker was to return to an empty house and find toys left unattended. While thousands left the ghetto, only a precious few ever returned. To forestall the hysteria during a selection, Nazi guards, aided by the Jewish police force, always gave excuses of how workers were needed in other areas. Even with the plenitude of European Jews, there never seemed to be enough to meet the demand for slave labor.

Selections were usually done according to age or the number of family members. Gender was irrelevant, except when young girls were singled out for rape, which was sometimes referred to as "peeling potatoes." There was always the ominous fear of selections, especially during a time of relative quiet. When the peace sometimes stretched into months, hope slowly crept back in, only to be dashed when the next selection occurred. Selections notwithstanding, Jewish homes

Jews gathered at an assembly point in Kovno Ghetto during a deportation action. The woman and child to the left of the pole are Eta and Jacob Ipp.

were always subject to surprise inspections, coupled with constant destruction, unmitigated insults and humiliation. Against those odds, some families had managed to hold on to a few valuables at great peril to all concerned.

As inspections escalated, my father decided to collect the few valuables he had hidden and relocate them in a central place. One night he stayed up after everyone else had gone to bed. I was already in bed but wasn't really asleep when I saw him lighting a single candle. I watched as he carefully scraped away the supporting cement from around two of the firebricks in the oven and removed the bricks. He then gathered the few miserable pieces of jewelry we had left and some coins, which he had previously stored in different places in the house. He put most of the bounty behind the firebricks and gently tapped the bricks back in place. He then placed Izzy's watch inside his hollowed-out boot cavity for safekeeping and tapped the heel back in place. It was a beautiful watch with iridescent numbers — a really special piece. My mother had given it to Izzy as a wedding present.

I'm sure my father was exhausted from the tension and fear of the possibility of being discovered. He finally went to bed just before dawn. At best, he would have only an hour or two to sleep before rising for work. I heard him as he walked past us and wanted to reach out to him, but I didn't. He didn't sleep much. I could hear him fitfully turning over and over. I was restless as well and was awake when he finally got up and quietly made his way to me about dawn. He touched my shoulder and waited until I sat up on the side of the bed.

"Eta, I have hidden the treasure," he began. He whispered the rest of the information to me and told me to keep it to myself. I just listened quietly and marveled at his strength. Daddy then exchanged his boots for Izzy's makeshift shoes, went outside and took his place in line at the work detail.

Not many days thereafter, Jewish police officers began to herd large families out of their homes and into lines alongside the barbed-wire fence. They said Jews were needed to work in Riga, Latvia. The officers ran from home to home looking for families with at least four members. They needed about 1,000 Jews to make their quota.

The Jewish police came into our house and told my parents to bring my sister, Minnie, and their sons, Fievel and Chaim, for the selection. When my father refused, all of them were dragged from our home and forced into the lines. I knew they were in dire peril, and although I didn't have to, I took Jay by the hand and stood in line with them. I don't remember where my in-laws were that day. They may have been on work details because they escaped the selection, but I can't be sure. Either way, they weren't in the house when the Jewish police arrived.

Screams of anguish began to penetrate the air as trucks

arrived and stopped beside the line of unwilling passengers. Suddenly a Jewish ghetto police officer grabbed me by the arm and pulled me out of line. When I turned around, I recognized the man as a friend of Izzy's who always enjoyed bouncing Jay on his knee during previous visits to our home. I tried to pull away from him to no avail.

"Eta, get out of line," he hissed, tightening his grip on my arm and shoving his face close to mine. "Hurry. Go back to your home. Izzy will be there soon from the airport. Go home and fix his dinner. You'll see the others again tomorrow. This is just a temporary thing," he said, shoving me a little.

"You're *meshuggah.* I can't let my parents go alone," I said, trying to pull free of his rough hands. "I must be with them. My mother will need me."

The officer grabbed me again and shook me really hard this time before saying, "Izzy needs you more. Listen to

Jews in Kovno Ghetto are boarded onto trucks during a deportation action. The man staring into the camera is Chananya Butrimowitz, Eta Ipp's father.

Courtesy U.S. Holocaust Memorial Museum

what I'm telling you and stop that damn crying. Don't you understand? You must go back. Leave now."

Jay had been quietly holding onto my hand during the altercation. Suddenly, when I loosened my grip of him somewhat, he dug his heels into the ground and began pulling against my arm, forcing distance between my parents and us.

"Mother, I'm not going on the truck," he said. "Come with me. I want to go home," he insisted. "I'm going to wait and see my father."

Although he was slightly built and usually no match for me, Jay suddenly seemed to have superhuman strength. As he held his ground, I realized I couldn't budge him. I knelt down and began talking quietly, attempting to persuade a change of heart. I paused just long enough to look back trying to glimpse my family. I finally stood erect and stopped struggling with Jay when I saw my father helping my mother, sister and then my brothers into the belly of a crowded, canvas-covered truck. I then watched my father climb aboard and stand off to the side near the back. Other Jews were shoved in beside him as he struggled to keep his place by holding on to a flap of canvas with one hand. His stance still proud, his legs spread apart, he began scanning the faces searching for Jay and me among the milling throng of terrified people.

For some unknown reason, I suddenly noticed the stubble on his chin. His beard was so heavy that he always had a shadow on his face, even in the morning right after he shaved. As I watched, those dye-stained, work-worn hands, the ones that had fashioned the very boots I was now standing in, dropped listlessly to his sides.

Chananya Butrimowitz, my stepfather turned father, finally found me in the swarm of others. As I began to sob uncontrollably, he looked at me only briefly then turned his gaze toward Jay, his only grandchild. After staring at Jay for a long time, he looked toward me once more. He nodded, raised his hand in farewell and silently mouthed the words, "Don't forget where it is."

He took one last drag from his cigarette and flicked the minuscule butt to the ground. He always smoked his cigarettes until the coal practically burned his mouth. As usual, a tiny piece of the rolled paper stuck to his bottom lip. Instinctively, he removed it with the tip of his tongue and spat it into the wind. The drivers started the truck engines as he nodded to Jay and me one last time and lifted his hand in a final wave.

Days later rumors came back to the ghetto that Jews taken in the Riga selection had been drowned in the Baltic Sea. I was inconsolable. Try as he might, Izzy couldn't convince me that I was not somehow responsible for my family's deaths. It's a burden I was never able to relinquish.

While I couldn't save my family, I was able to salvage the Russian rubles my father was referring to in his last mouthed message to me from the truck bed. When the trucks pulled away from the ghetto, I ran home to make sure the booty was safe. Although it was still daylight, I frantically removed the two bricks, dug the quarter-size coins out of the oven pit and took them into my bedroom. I quickly cut cloth into small circles, covered the coins, drawing the cloth around them and twisting the thread underneath. Within minutes, I had securely affixed them atop the five buttons on my sweater. From that day on, I rarely took the sweater off except to sleep, and then I kept it within reach. It was the last vestige of love I could hold close to my heart from my beloved father. Touching the buttons not only gave me a sense of worth and hope, it bolstered the faith I had in surviving. Someone had to. Someone had to tell the world of what we had suffered. I resolved once again that my faith would sustain me. No human could take that away from me.

For a few minutes, I allowed myself to be lost in memories of my grandmother, whom everyone lovingly referred to as

Frumme Leah. My *bubbe* had become gravely ill in the ghetto and had died, although I had used most of my meager money to purchase medicine for her. She was a stalwart example of our faith, and whenever I was in the pits of despair, I would conjure up the memories of how *Frumme* Leah used to read her prayer book or pray over the *Shabbat* candles just before the Friday evening meal.

I thought back to how her body had been laid out on the floor of my mother's house in the ghetto, surrounded by white candles for a little while before her burial. Jay, who was especially close to his *elderbubbe*, told me how *Frumme* Leah had appeared at the foot of his bed the night after her death. Jay vividly described what he had seen. He said that *Frumme* Leah was dressed completely in white and that she had comforted him by saying all would be well.

I thought again of Rabbi Shapiro, who used to be the chief rabbi in Kaunas, and what he had offered in a message just before he died. He said that if one person survived, then that person was a *tzaddik*, like a righteous man or a saint. The rabbi also said if no one survived, then the saints would become martyrs. While I knew I was no saint, I was sure my family members were martyrs.

7

Planning the Escape – 1943

T he ability to work in Kovno Ghetto was the deter-
mining factor between life and death. While the Hitler
regime had decided Jews were to be treated as sub-
human and a danger to society, even they could see the benefit
to having a slave-labor work force, especially with regard to
the war effort. On the other hand, Jews were considered an
expendable and replaceable commodity; therefore, even work
assignments didn't necessarily guarantee another day of life.

Some days when I came home from work, I would pass
empty houses with all the furniture thrown out in front
for anyone to pick up. It seemed that some of the ghetto
inhabitants were only vapors. Sometimes I had to stop and
remind myself that I wasn't dreaming, that there really had
been human beings living in the now-vacant houses I had
passed that very morning. I felt so sad for the sick and elderly.
They were easy targets, along with the mentally or physically
handicapped, and especially young children. Any children
under the age of twelve were in constant danger of being

summarily dispensed with, as they were considered a drain on ghetto resources. The ultimate goal was to achieve the maximum result with the least investment. We were really lucky with Jay. There were enough of us to always keep an eye out for him, and he listened when we cautioned him not to stray too far from home.

Young and physically strong, Izzy had been singled out as a good worker from the first days of the ghetto. He had worked in several brigades, but his favorite assignment, of course, was any that allowed him to make a *peckel*, a package, to smuggle food back inside the ghetto to share with us. While we knew of the imminent danger, we also learned which guards could be bribed. Once we got past the guard gate into the safety of our home, we quickly ate the food, removing the evidence of forbidden activity.

Like all the Kovno Ghetto Jews, Izzy and I suffered intense mental anguish as we passed by the guards for inspection. I will never forget the night I was trying to smuggle some food into the ghetto and got caught. When I left that morning, the guard I always bribed with a few eggs had been stationed at the gate. When I returned, another guard had taken his place. I didn't have an alternative, because they were searching everyone, and I knew I would be found out. When I offered the substitute guard some eggs to let me pass, he went into a tirade and began to shout, calling me a dog and worse. One of the Jewish police officers came over and got into the fray. I guess he thought he was making points with the Germans. He picked up a rubber hose, a favorite weapon, and began to beat me about the head and neck. I dodged the blows intended for my face, but my back ended up in terrible shape.

The German also smashed my small loaf of bread with his foot and ground it into the mud. As I was being beaten, the remaining eggs were broken and started running down inside the pocket of my coat. By the time I got home that night

I could barely walk from the beating. When my father-in-law learned what happened to me, he went to get my father. Together they found that Jewish police officer, and let me tell you, he never touched me again while I was in the ghetto.

We never knew when the work details were going to be stopped. There was no set regularity to searching the ghetto workers for any tidbit of food or forbidden contraband. While this was terrifying, it was no more so than trying to guess what would set off the guards and send them into fits of indiscriminate taunts and killing.

Izzy escaped such an incident once while loading metal railings at a barge site on the Nieman River. I'd been worried about him all day. Just before he left that morning I had watched him gingerly rub his blistered feet, trying to massage some feeling and circulation into them. The calluses were rubbed raw almost daily because he insisted on wearing a pair of makeshift shoes he had fashioned from a piece of a tire tread. They were awful things, held together with scraps of wire. Izzy was trying to save the one pair of good boots that he had, believing they would be paramount if we ever had the opportunity to escape. Izzy described his terrible experience to me that night after he got home.

"I was initially assigned to work at the harbor where barges brought in cement for the airport," he began. "They issued me a cutting torch and told me to cut up old trucks, tanks, and large pieces of metal into small pieces. While I was doing that, a group of other Jews had to load the metal, as well as used railroad tracks, onto the barge for its return trip. The men were trying to balance the metal on their shoulders. It made for treacherous and very painful work."

"How could they manage?" I asked Izzy. "Some of them are just bones and can barely walk."

"It was terrible, Eta. They were so weak from not eating. That's why they got behind. To make matters worse, it turned out that an especially cruel German guard was on duty today. He seemed to take pleasure in beating the workers as they carried tracks across that thin plank board to the waiting barge. He laughed like a maniac when one worker lost his bearing and slipped into the river. He beat the man unmercifully while he was trying to climb out. Somehow the guy managed to get back to shore and started working again.

"They kept falling behind schedule. Finally, I was enlisted to help load," Izzy explained. "It was almost impossible. The weight of the metal had caused the barge to sink into the water, making it harder to load. The board from the shore to the barge was actually sloping downhill," Izzy said, holding his hands in an inverted prayer position to indicate the slant.

"On top of that, it was drizzling cold rain, and I was so tired and afraid I'd fall with each step I took," Izzy continued.

"You should have worn your good boots today instead of those dreadful tire-tread shoes," I said. "I don't know how you can even walk in those things."

"You're right," Izzy said. "Those shoes were so slick that they caused me to lose my balance. I had to either drop the piece of railroad track I was carrying or fall into the water myself. The place I would have fallen in was very dangerous. There were pieces of sharp metal sticking up out of the water where the men had missed the barge with their throws. When I dropped my piece of metal and jumped onto the shore, the guard came running at me, screaming, 'You saboteur, you want to see Germany lose the war with the Communists. You're a Communist. You deliberately dropped the metal in the water so we wouldn't have it to make bullets.' "

Izzy said he had never seen the guard before, and since he had just been assigned there, he had no way of knowing what the man might do. Izzy decided just to stand there as the guard started beating him with a stick.

"The first two or three licks were painful, but after that I didn't seem to feel anything," Izzy said. "All I wanted to do was spit in his face, but of course, I couldn't, so I just stood looking at him without flinching. The more he beat me, the angrier he became. I was determined not to flinch or give him the pleasure of seeing me in pain. When the German grabbed his Luger, some of the other men started yelling, 'Run, Ipp, run; he's going to kill you.' At first, I was too stunned to move; then I just started running for my life. I kept zigzagging between the broken pieces of metal from the old trucks and tanks as bullets flew past my head with a zoom."

Izzy managed to stay hidden until he could locate another work group returning to the ghetto. Work brigades were constantly going in and out of the ghetto, even at night. Individuals trying to escape certain work assignments or smuggle contraband into the ghetto often tagged along with another brigade just to pass beyond the guard gate. Most workers, realizing that someone needed a place to fit in, would carefully ease over to make room. Others, fearing they might lose their place in a coveted work detail, wouldn't budge and left the lone worker to fend for himself.

Izzy was reassigned again, this time to the airport work detail, the most dreaded work assignment for the entire ghetto. Workers were forced to run the five miles there in any weather while their guards rode along taunting them from bicycles. Once the work brigades arrived, a cup of water the color of mud, a poor substitute for coffee, was issued as breakfast. They spent the next ten to twelve hours in drudgery, many times without eating. If food was supplied, it was some form of sauerkraut or clear broth soup, which, at times, contained flecks of cabbage, but never any meat. Jews were often executed when they fell from exhaustion or stopped to rest for a few seconds. They were killed randomly at other times, seemingly as sport for the guards.

The runway at the Kaunas airport was a plain green

field, and when it rained the water would stay there in puddles. The Gestapo decided to dry up the water to make a better runway. One of Izzy's jobs was to cut long sheets of wood into twelve-inch pieces, put them on the ground and then shovel gravel on top, thereby helping to turn the water-soaked area into a runway. The local airport was the closest to the Russian front and was very important to the war effort.

All day long Izzy stood in one place, making the monotonous cuts with an electric saw. After a couple of weeks, on a day when he must have been especially tired, he accidentally cut off half of the first two fingers of his right hand. I got sick to my stomach when Izzy showed me the bloody stumps that night. Then he told me something that made me shiver even more. He said he remembered holding his hands up in the air to try and stop the bleeding. As he did that, he suddenly realized the wound made him unable to be a soldier. Now he couldn't even pull the trigger of a gun. Even after Izzy cut off his fingers, he couldn't stop working but reported for the airport drudgery every day.

Eventually he was switched to digging rows and tunnels. The men lifted backbreaking loads of wet mush over their shoulders, throwing the dirt from the trenches where water drained every day from the runway. Three women were stationed along the tops of the trenches. They, in turn, shoveled the wet slop farther away in a never-ending cycle. The only time they stopped was when they were told to move so the small railroad cars could come in and dump gravel for the runway work.

Izzy worked at the airport for a couple of months with my father before he was taken in the Riga selection. Several thousand Jewish people from Kovno Ghetto went to work at that airport and other job sites every day, with very little or no food. The mind-numbing work was unimaginable.

Workers tried everything to avoid being assigned to the airport brigade, where a day never seemed to end, but simply ran into the next. Izzy would get up, run the long distance to work, spend the day in a ditch above his shoulders with his feet screaming in pain, starving, shoveling the same mud he had shoveled the day before. Besides the grueling drudgery, he never had an opportunity to buy or trade anything. The workers were under constant guard in a big field surrounded by the Germans and Lithuanians.

Izzy said he tried to take his mind off the monotony and hunger sometimes by watching the sun and estimating the hours until he could return to the ghetto to see if Jay and I were still alive. Other days he passed the time by counting the wagons of Lithuanian farmers who sometimes also brought loads of gravel to the airport for the construction.

Izzy was peeping out of the ditch one particularly dreary day when he glimpsed a farmer whose features looked vaguely familiar. Saying he needed to go to the bathroom, Izzy slipped out of the trench and dared to take a chance of speaking to the Lithuanian Gentile whom he thought he remembered meeting before the war. After a few minutes, Izzy discovered he was right.

"Kolascus, it's good to see you. Tell me, how is it outside the ghetto?" Izzy asked. "Do you by chance know anyone who lives in Semeliškes?"

"Well, I know many," the man replied. "That's where I live. Who are you looking for?"

"I wondered if you might know Itzhak Kalamitsky or know what has happened to him. He's my wife's uncle, and we don't know if he's alive or dead since he never brought his family to the ghetto."

"Know Itzhak?" Kolascus asked with a broad grin. He lowered his voice and looked over his shoulder before stepping closer to Izzy.

"Itzhak was my neighbor before all this ghetto stuff started. He is very much alive and so is his family. In fact, I saw him just a few days ago. All the other farmers who lived around him convinced Itzhak to go into hiding with his wife and children. We were afraid he'd be killed if he went into the ghetto. He has been staying in barns during the day and moving from farm to farm at night. All of us have been feeding him as best we could for the last two years, ever since the ghetto was formed. He will probably return to my barn before too long."

Izzy was overwhelmed at this news and used a scrap of paper and pencil that Kolascus had to hastily scribble a few lines telling Itzhak that the SS had taken away his sister, Chai Esther, and all her family during a selection. Izzy ended the note with a final sentence of encouragement.

"But Eta, your favorite niece, is still alive. Our family is together and we all remain in Kovno Ghetto. I am overjoyed that you live. Would it be possible for you to find a place for us to also hide?"

About a month later, Kolascus returned to the airport and signaled Izzy by removing his hat. When Izzy found an opportunity, he quickly slipped out of the ditch and ran to get the long-awaited letter.

Uncle Itzhak said he was happy to hear from us but was very upset about losing his sister and her family. He said, "There's nothing we can do. Today it's them and tomorrow it will be us." He wrote in the letter that since I was the last one left from his family, he would like to have me close to him.

He wanted us to come to his place in Semeliškes. Since he was born and raised there and knew all the other farmers, Itzhak said he might be able to find a hiding place. He instructed us to seek any way we could find to get there.

While we began dreaming of how to escape and get to Semeliškes, life went on as usual in the ghetto. Each day was a recurring struggle. Wondering whether we would be caught up in the next selection was never far from our minds. I think many people died simply because they didn't see a need to keep breathing. Izzy and I tried to encourage each other and find a way to subsist.

One day my father-in-law came into the house so excited because he had made arrangements with a former Lithuanian friend to trade a suit for a pound of butter. He was so joyful, thinking of how he would share it with all of us. My mouth watered in anticipation. I couldn't remember the last time I had tasted butter. The next evening my father-in-law rushed out to meet his friend at the designated place and shoved his suit through the barbed wire fence. In exchange, he received a package wrapped in brown paper. Once inside the house, with all of us gathered around, he opened the package to find two bricks. It was another reminder that we could trust no one.

Izzy's job at the airport came to an end, finally, and the labor department assigned him to another work detail in Slobodka, by the Jewish cemetery, where an ammunition shop had been established for the Germans. A Gestapo captain, the overseer there, made it a practice to go into Kaunas for dinner, leaving his office open. At every opportunity, Izzy entered the office and dared to turn on the radio, while five or six other men acted as lookouts. Izzy would then relay the news happening on the different fronts, like Stalingrad. When he returned to the ghetto, dozens of inmates were already waiting to crowd around him and hear the news. In a back yard with a fence around it so no one could see in, Izzy would whisper all that he'd heard. It was a few moments of relief among a catastrophic existence, like water in the desert to the imprisoned Jews.

As the fighting came closer to Lithuania, we ghetto inhabitants could barely contain our excitement. We became hopeful and spent our days wondering how long it would take the Russians to push the Germans out. We talked about Hitler's fall constantly, knowing the war would come to an end and hoping some of us might survive.

While the war news may have been encouraging, news of other ghettos was not. We heard that the nearby ghetto at Vilna was liquidated entirely by October 1943. The news came that there had also been a *kinderaktion*. All the children under 12 years old were deemed "worthless" and killed. Since Vilna wasn't too far away, Kovno Ghetto residents surmised our ghetto would be next. Many of them risked everything to smuggle their children out to sympathetic Gentile friends, and several were saved that way. Leibel Gillman, Izzy's brave cousin, managed to smuggle out Sara, his brother's little daughter, to a Christian couple to keep her. They brought her back, but miraculously Leibel was able to get her out a second time.

Izzy didn't want to believe the terrible rumors about the children in other ghettos. The only things he had left were Jay and me. We were in bed one night, and Izzy suddenly turned over toward me and gathered me into his arms. He said, "It's not going to happen. They're not going to take Jay. I have already given a daughter. If I lose Jay, I'll lose you, too."

"Izzy, what are you talking about?" I asked, not quite understanding.

"This time it will be over my dead body," he said in a low voice. "I'll take the boy away and I'll just fight, and the Nazis can kill me before I let them take him. We have to have enough courage to run away from the ghetto," Izzy whispered. "Somehow, we have to escape and make it to Semeliškes."

Izzy continued to exchange messages with Itzhak, and I even smuggled a few out to him as well when I was assigned to work with a coal detail. Soon arrangements were made.

After a day of forced labor, a group of women wait to be searched by German and Lithuanian guards at an entrance gate to Kovno Ghetto. Thousands of Jews assembled every day for labor brigades outside the ghetto, the largest being sent to construct an airfield in the suburb of Aleksotas. Slave labor, inside and outside the ghetto, was the justification for its continued existence.

Courtesy U.S. Holocaust Memorial Museum

A Gentile farmer named Marchuk, one of the farmers also engaged in helping Itzhak, was to meet us on a certain dark night on Paneriu Street near where the bridge used to be. Izzy chose that particular place because Leibel, his daredevil cousin, lived nearby and ran an extended smuggling operation right under the noses of the Nazi guards. While others were afraid to smuggle anything into the ghetto, fear meant nothing to Leibel. As a motorcycle mechanic, he was very useful to the Germans. He used his position to do all kinds of business, bringing butter, meat and other things into the ghetto.

Izzy told Leibel that we had decided to run from the ghetto to save Jay. He shared our plans about going to be with Uncle Itzhak. Izzy asked Leibel if he could help us through the barbed wire to Paneriu Street. At the outskirts of Paneriu, Marchuk would be waiting with a wagon. Leibel

Announcements for Jews were posted by The Jewish Council in a display box in Kovno Ghetto.

agreed to get a final letter to Uncle Itzhak with instructions for Marchuk. After the letter was delivered, Leibel and Izzy talked numerous times over the next few days, planning everything down to the minutest detail. Finally, the escape date was set for the next day.

Izzy and I barely slept that night. We kept trying to decide if we were doing the right thing. So many of our friends had been killed either trying to escape, through selections or simply for the Nazis' entertainment. We talked about Nahum Meck, a young Jew who was hanged publicly about a year ago. Somehow he had been able to smuggle a gun inside the ghetto. During an escape attempt, he fired the gun into the air. He was immediately arrested and hanged a few days later. His body was left hanging for 24 hours as an example to keep the other ghetto inhabitants in line. As if we needed another example, Meck's mother and sister were taken to Fort IX and executed as well.

I think Meck's hanging and how Jay described it was one of the things that scared Izzy so much. Izzy had been at work when Meck was hanged, but Jay and I were forced to witness it. That night Jay told Izzy that seeing Meck's body twitching at the end of a rope reminded him of a minnow on a fishing hook. The horror of that statement, coupled with the murder of my family, was enough to inspire Izzy any time our resolve to escape began to weaken. And then the word came that Kovno Ghetto was to become Concentration Camp no. 4, Kovno, on November 1. That could only mean one thing — more death.

Nothing, absolutely nothing, could ensure our survival. At least on the outside, with Uncle Itzhak's help, we might have a slim chance of escaping the daily brutality. Now all Izzy could do was pray he had made the right decision. He finally gave up on sleep that perilous night. Instead, he sat

Foot-bridge that connected the larger part of the ghetto with the smaller part. On November 26, 1943, the Ipps escaped Kovno Ghetto by going through a barbed wire fence near the location of the bridge on Paneriu Street.

Photo provided by the U. S. Holocaust Memorial Museum
Courtesy of YIVO Institute

on the side of the bed and held my hand. I knew he was counting the hours until the appointed time when we would meet Leibel, the Little Lion, beside the barbed-wire fence.

8

Ride to Freedom

With Leibel's help we escaped the ghetto and joined Marchuk on Paneriu Street. Even though we were outside the ghetto confines, I knew there was no guarantee we would survive. It seemed that we traveled for an eternity. I was terrified each time we passed someone on the road. We had only stopped a couple of times to rest the horse, fearing to push him too hard but eager to get to safety.

It was barely dusk by the time we arrived at Marchuk's house. Although we were almost frozen, we had to wait until dark before hurrying inside; otherwise we might have been seen. As soon as the door was securely closed, Marchuk lifted Jay up onto a compartment, a type of shelf just above the big hearth where there was a lot of room, a place reserved for company to rest. Izzy and I crawled up beside him and stretched out. Exhausted from our long journey and from fear, we fell asleep immediately.

A short time later, a creaking sound woke me. I listened as Marchuk eased open the door. I became so afraid that I almost forgot to breathe. I heard a man's voice say, "Ah, Marchuk, you're home. I'm freezing." He must have stepped inside because I could hear him stamping the snow from his feet.

I imagined the man looking around before he asked Marchuk, "What's that funny smell? If I didn't know better, I'd think you had city folks in here. Have you had company?"

"No. No company," Marchuk explained quickly, raising his voice so we could hear him. "Just a man from Kaunas. Somebody I don't even know. He stopped by this afternoon looking to buy cattle. He was smoking one of those cheap cigarettes, the kind with a strange odor. He didn't stay long, but we'll be a month getting that smell out of our house. Don't you go spreading rumors that I've had unusual company. Here, have a cup of hot coffee. That'll hold you until you get home."

Itzhak Kalamitsky, Marchuk's neighbor and my uncle, arrived two days later, dirty and wearing ragged clothes. He went crazy with joy when he saw me. He kept me in his arms for at least ten minutes before he began shaking Izzy's hand. Our joy at reuniting eventually gave way to grief. We came from a large family; now only two were left. We clung to each other and cried, inconsolable for a short while.

Itzhak was pitiful looking. Formerly somewhat plump, he was now gaunt and barely able to keep his trousers from falling down. He explained that almost everything he ate, even bread, made him sick. He had always suffered from such terrible heartburn and could eat only veal when the stomach pain was really bad. There had been few opportunities for that in the last two years. He and his family had been in hiding ever since the ghetto was formed. Itzhak's neighbors, farmers like he was but Christians, had come to him when the decree for the Jewish ghetto was first posted. Fearing for Itzhak's life, they agreed to help feed and harbor his family, but they dared not ask for medicine for his stomach.

Overcoming the continuous pain and constant threat of death, Itzhak told us how he and his family had lived like animals on the run. His mother-in-law and his two sisters-in-law, Sheina Berkman and Raja Shlom, along with her two-year-old son, Emmanuel, had subsequently joined them, adding to his responsibility and increasing the ever-present demand for food and shelter. They had all hidden in barns, eating whatever Itzhak could scavenge from the fields or what the poor Gentile farmers could spare.

When we could finally get our emotions in check, Itzhak held me at arm's length, trying to realize that I wasn't an apparition. Talk of safety finally ensued. Marchuk agreed with Itzhak's suggestion that our family should stay with Marchuk for a while. Marchuk's wife had other ideas.

"What's wrong with you, old man?" she demanded of Marchuk. "Should we all perish over a few Jews? Turn them out, or we'll surely die."

Walking over to me, she stuck her face close to mine and continued with a sneer, "I might turn them in myself. We don't even have enough food for us." Glancing back at Marchuk again, she added, "Your brain has a hole in it."

Marchuk turned his back, ignoring the hateful protestations of his wife. It was useless trying to explain that, as farmers, the land had bonded him with Itzhak.

Finally breaking his silence and turning to Izzy, Marchuk quietly said, "My sister lives nearby. She has a barn. It really isn't safe here. Someone might have followed us."

When darkness fell, I slowly pulled on my sweater, placed my arm around Jay and instinctively moved to the door, an action that gave much relief to Marchuk's wife, as well as to Marchuk's ears.

A week of relative quiet passed at the sister's house, where we stayed in the loft of a stable. Itzhak came often to bring scraps of food, but primarily to talk with me, I think. It seemed to help us both just to sit for a few minutes, hold each other's hands and remember our former lives and lost loved ones. Itzhak, always a deeply religious man, never failed to encourage me. His faith was immovable. He was convinced God had kept us alive for a reason.

Marchuk's brother-in-law came running one morning. Almost before we could sit up, the man was climbing the ladder, yelling at us to leave. He was so excited I thought he was going to throw us all out of the loft. He was screaming that the Gestapo would come and kill his family for hiding us. Izzy quickly grabbed Jay, jumped the rungs down the ladder and ran out into the cold December day with me close behind. We slipped on the ice and snow but managed to stay standing as we hurried to meet Marchuk, who had also come running. Marchuk confirmed what his brother-in-law was saying. He had also heard the Gestapo was coming to their village and feared for our safety as well as his sister's.

Marchuk held up his hand for silence, dropped to his knees and laid his ear to the ground. After a few minutes he said he could hear people walking and dogs barking. He guessed they were about a mile away, which meant we had a little time to plan. While we were trying to decide where to go, Marchuk suddenly remembered a kindness my mother had done for a neighbor who lived near the lake.

"Eta, I have often heard one of my neighbors speak of your mother, Chai Esther, and how kind she was to visit her in the hospital when she broke her leg. Chai Esther's kindness might now be rewarded. I'll take you there."

The walk seemed interminable. The snow was deep, forcing Izzy to carry Jay on his shoulders while also trying to steady me. One of my lasting memories is of how Izzy carried Jay that night, holding on to him for dear life and stomping his feet through the deep snow to get his footing. Jay kept his breath from freezing by burying his face inside Izzy's coat collar.

I knocked on the window shutter at about one o'clock in the morning.

"Who is it?" a voice asked through a crack in the window.

"Chai Esther's daughter," I responded.

"Who's Chai Esther?" the voice demanded.

"The woman who helped you when you were in the hospital."

"How did you find me?" the woman asked, opening the window just a tiny bit more. "Don't you know it's dangerous for us to even talk to Jews?"

In a very quiet and respectful voice, I began, "I remember stopping here with my mother when I was a little girl. We always bought fish from you on our way to my grandfather's house. My family and I have just run away from Kovno Ghetto. Please, will you help us? There are just three. We will only stay until my uncle can find us another place. Please, can we stay a few days?"

"It's two weeks until Christmas," the voice said. "My daughter's family is coming for the holidays. You can stay in the loft of the barn, but if we hear a sound, you'll have to leave," the woman said, slamming the window shut.

We managed to find our way to the barn and stumbled around in the dark until we discovered the ladder leading to the hayloft. For once, more exhausted than hungry, we fell asleep in each other's arms, wrapped in the comforter from home.

For days, Izzy and I watched through little openings in the loft. The farmwoman would slip into the barn at night and bring us some small portions of food. It was meager, but it kept us alive. Since we couldn't do anything but lie still, we slept a lot. We soon lost track of time but assumed it was Christmas when we could see a strange man walking around in the yard and heard young children playing in the snow. We were so jealous of their freedom and how those children could jump and run without any worries while we had to constantly silence Jay, making him terrified of moving and almost afraid to breathe.

The night after the company went away, Itzhak came and talked the family into keeping us a while longer. I don't know how he managed, but he was such a persuasive man. The Gestapo had already been in town looking for Jews. The family's son-in-law was a policeman, and that gave them some protection, but they were still afraid to be involved. Itzhak proved so persuasive, though, that they couldn't turn him down. Itzhak returned about four weeks later, saying he had found a Catholic farmer who had agreed to harbor us. Vaclovas Paskauskas lived about thirty or forty kilometers from Kaunas with his wife and teenage stepson on a meager farm near Kaišiadorys. Arrangements were made for Marchuk to take us there as soon as possible.

Itzhak's description of the farm proved expansive when compared to the actual site. The farm animals consisted of only a single cow, a horse and a goat, along with three or four sheep and two or three pigs. There were also a few scrawny chickens running around between the barn and the yard. The house had a straw roof but no chimney and only one door, which made it necessary to leave the door standing ajar to let the smoke from the cook stove escape. The house, which had a dirt floor, was furnished with a table and two benches but only one bed, which the farmer, his wife and son all slept in together.

We originally hid in a little place adjoining the living quarters, hovering between the horse's stable and where the ewes gave birth. Although austere to the extreme, we found comfort in our new surroundings. At least it was warm, and we believed that few visitors would come to see such a poor family.

Eventually we moved into a big shed where the farmer kept the wheat he raised in the fields. Mr. Paskauskas and Izzy would sometimes dare to go out in the daytime. One day, when it was raining, they went to the barn to thresh some wheat. The farm implement they used was funny looking, with two sticks attached on either end of a short chain. They could each hold the end of one stick and swing the other stick over their heads to beat the wheat. Their rhythmic beating muffled the noise of a wagon pulling up outside.

"Vaclovas," a man's voice called out, "why is your barn door locked?" Mr. Paskauskas went to unlock the door and let his neighbor in as Izzy quickly ran outside the back way and slipped inside the pen with the sheep.

"That latch keeps falling," Paskauskas said as he opened the door. "I've got to fix it. Always something to do."

"Who was in here? I heard you threshing. It takes two to do that."

"It was my son, Stasuk," Paskauskas answered quickly.

"Well, where is he now?"

"Oh, you know how boys are. He got mad at something I said and up and left when he heard your voice."

As Izzy hid under the lean-to with the sheep, he said he could hear the man questioning Mr. Paskauskas. Oddly enough, the sheep huddled quietly around Izzy, somehow understanding that he needed protection.

Later that afternoon, Mr. Paskauskas brought the wheat into the house where his wife had two round heavy rocks, one on top of the other, with a little hole where the wheat was poured in to be ground into meal by moving the rocks. Mrs. Paskauskas used the meal for making bread. It was beautiful dark brown bread, so different from the pauper's bread we had been used to and so delicious. During those rare times when Izzy got to work, I think he was very happy to be able to use his muscles. Nights when he was tired and lay down in the shed, Izzy told me he hardly noticed the mice running over his face.

A few times Izzy went into the fields to work, but he stayed nearest the side where the woods were growing. He probably began to feel almost like a free man again. The fieldwork was not nearly as demanding as his work at the ghetto airport, and he was, after all, contributing somewhat to our family's survival by providing manual labor. Even I helped in small ways, especially after Mrs. Paskauskas discovered that I could sew. One day she came just inside the stable and quietly said, "Eta, don't be afraid. It's Ona. I have a favor to ask. Can you sew?"

"Why, yes, I can," I replied from the stable loft. "I even have a needle and some thread."

"All right. Wait a few moments until I go back inside the house, then bring the little boy and the needle with you. Be very careful."

About twenty minutes passed before I dared to venture out to the farmhouse with Jay in tow. Once inside, I saw that Mrs. Paskauskas had laid a pair of her husband's work pants on the table. The hem had been ripped out, and there was a jagged hole in one of the knees. I threaded my needle and set right to work, with Jay standing at my elbow. Mrs. Paskauskas watched out the door as I worked silently, intent on repairing the pants as quickly as possible.

"Eta, that is such a pretty sweater you're always wearing," Mrs. Paskauskas said, finally breaking the silence. "I was wondering. We're going to church on Sunday. Would you consider allowing me to borrow it? I hate to ask, but it's better than anything I own, and I don't get to go to church very often. I would feel so dressed up. I'll take really good care of it," she said, her voice trailing off.

I blanched under the question, knowing full well that all the family's money was sewn atop the sweater buttons. Jay instinctively knew what I was thinking and moved to put his arm around my shoulder, as if to protect the treasure.

What could I do? I had no choice but to give up the sweater. After all, the farm family was risking their lives to save us. How could I refuse? I hurried through the sewing and reluctantly unbuttoned the sweater. I handed it to Mrs. Paskauskas and waited for an opportune moment before returning to the barn with Jay. I felt naked without the sweater and terribly vulnerable again.

A few days later, Mrs. Paskauskas returned the sweater, with all the buttons intact. I fairly grabbed it from her hands and immediately put it on Jay. I had already prepared him for the responsibility. From that time forward, Jay wore the sweater, especially if we went into the farmhouse. Mrs. Paskauskas always treated Jay with such tenderness, I knew she wouldn't take the sweater from him and chance him catching a cold.

A few days later, when we were all in the barn loft, we heard the door open.

"Izzy. Izzy. It's Itzhak."

Izzy crawled from under the hay and said, "Itzhak, how wonderful to see you."

"How do you feel, Izzy?" Itzhak asked as we came down from the loft. "How is the little boy? Does he have any lice yet?"

"Yes, plenty," Izzy answered. "Without a bath and lying in the straw — how can we avoid it? Just today, we stood by the little door where the sun comes in and held the 'Hour of Delousing,' " Izzy said, actually laughing. "Jay is also learning his numbers by counting dead lice. At least they're good for something."

Itzhak came often, and one day he asked if Izzy wanted to go out with him to beg food. They managed to trade a pair of shoes for half of a calf. Itzhak slaughtered the calf himself, leaving part of it for the farmer. That night they came back to the farm, carrying the veal along with a sack of potatoes. The sack was heavy, and they had to walk about ten miles through the woods, since they couldn't go over the main highway for fear of being seen. While they were resting in the woods, Izzy said he remembered something.

"You know what, Itzhak? I know how a horse feels," Izzy said.

"What sense does that make?" Itzhak asked. "Your brain is frozen."

"I was just thinking about a horse I used to have," Izzy explained. "It used to make me angry when it couldn't pull a wagon uphill. I would beat him with a stick trying to make him pull the load. Now, I realized how hard it was for the horse."

Before returning to us, Itzhak and Izzy had stopped where Itzhak's family was hiding for a day. Izzy said that Itzhak didn't talk much, but it was comforting to see his family and know that some of them still lived. Izzy especially enjoyed seeing Itzhak and Ida's two little boys, Jacob and David. Jacob was born just one day after our Jay, with each of them being named after their grandfather.

Izzy and Itzhak could not walk in the daytime, so they stayed until nightfall before setting out again to return to our hiding place. Mr. Paskauskas must have felt rich. With judicious use, his family would have enough veal for a month.

Moving from one place to another was not simple. Itzhak would always go in front of Izzy. He knew every path well enough to follow it in the dead of night. They always carried long sticks because in certain places, dogs would attack them. Like spies, they listened to every little move, every little scratch. Izzy said they walked on their toes, trying to be quiet, and stayed back in the brush, trying to avoid the lights that were turned on in the houses to examine them. When a full moon was out, they could see the way the people who stood in the windows watched them. Itzhak and Izzy were daring everyone's life by moving around. But it was either that, starve or be caught by the Gestapo.

Itzhak was on the best of terms with most of the farmers, but there were a few who didn't always appear supportive. Once, when one of them grumbled about having to help feed extra mouths, he implied to Itzhak that someone just might turn him in to the authorities. Itzhak had been afraid that might happen and was prepared. Itzhak told the farmer that he should make sure that there were no reports to the Gestapo. Itzhak said, "As soon as anyone tells the Gestapo about me, I'll be arrested and I won't have any choice. They will beat me, and I'll have to tell them all the places I've been, and you'll be in trouble just as much as I am."

Some of the farmers became so scared that when they heard somebody had been talking about Itzhak they would tell them to shut up and not say anything. Over time, I think they even became afraid of each other.

Itzhak and Izzy continually made their rounds of begging and gleaning in the fields. They hiked through the woods loaded with supplies in backpacks, in constant danger and afraid for their lives.

Izzy soon decided that we would settle permanently at the Paskauskas farm. It was close to the woods, and there were no houses nearby. Izzy knew he had to find a place, a new home, where we could stay in hiding, especially since it was getting colder and colder. Izzy saw two pits where the farmer kept potatoes for the winter, so he asked Mr. Paskauskas how much he would rent them for. Izzy said the farmer just smiled and said, "You don't have anything. What are you going to give me?" After a moment, Mr. Paskauskas said, "I'll tell you what I'll do; give me your coat." Izzy traded his nice leather coat in exchange for rent on the two potato holes. Mr. Paskauskas said he wouldn't need the pits again until September.

9

The Maline

Izzy began working laboriously to excavate a place for our family to live, since we had no idea when the war would end or how soon we could leave the *maline*, or hiding place. Izzy's plan was to dig an underground hole between the two potato pits and join the hole to the pits by digging tunnels between them.

Izzy's mind wandered during the many hours he spent digging alone. He told me once that he often thought of Masha, our little baby daughter who had died, and the other children in the ghetto who had either died or had been taken away. Izzy said he wondered if Masha's hair would have been wavy and brown like his or if her eyes would stay the same beautiful sky blue as mine. Those are his words, not mine. He was always partial to my eyes. He said there were times when he couldn't help but think of how I should be making little dresses and bonnets for Masha rather than repairing clothes for the Paskauskas family or trying to keep Jay quiet in the nearby loft.

Izzy said that sometimes he was so plagued with exhaustion and fear, he just stopped his work and wept, especially when he remembered his mother's last words to him. She had kissed him and said, "Go. Save yourself and your family. Don't be afraid — God will take care of you." Digging in the dark at least protected him from always having to be strong in front of me, I guess. It allowed him a respite, a time to escape into his own emotions.

I'm sure thoughts of his mother always saddened Izzy at first, but then her memory had to bolster his courage. My mother-in-law, Toni, had been such a serious person and always given to doing things just right. That's why her sewing skills had been in such demand. The stitches on the hems of dresses she made were like an artist's signature on a painting. Her attention to detail and fastidious ways had certainly influenced Izzy. I believe her admonition to always strive for perfection was one reason Izzy had been such a good law student.

Law school was only a distant memory now. Izzy probably wondered if he had ever actually attended university. Digging a hiding place for us to live underground was surely never a part of his plans. As he dug, he said, he wondered if his parents might have already been hauled off to an unmarked grave during a selection. The possibility of their deaths made him even more determined that we should live. He had to find a way for our son to survive. The family history had to be kept going, no matter the cost. Izzy even confessed to me that he often wondered whether Jay and I would even survive until he got the hiding place ready because we had grown so thin from lack of food.

The work was very slow going. Uncle Itzhak helped when he could and a few times Mr. Paskauskas helped Izzy during the day; at others, he stood watch. When Mr. Paskauskas wasn't there, the family dog, a German shepherd named

Rexxyx, kept a vigil from his chain. The farmer had tethered him there for that purpose. The dog never made a sound when Izzy or any of us were around, but he barked furiously when other strangers happened by, a good alarm system that allowed me time to gather Jay and hide under the straw in the barn loft until it was safe to come out again.

Izzy worked alone in the pit at night, bringing buckets of dirt to the surface, carrying them a distance from the hiding place and spreading the dirt around evenly near the potato field, not too far from the house. His progress was extremely slow, and I wanted to help him, but I didn't dare mention it. My job was to take care of Jay. Sometimes, when Izzy would creep back in the loft at dawn, he said he would see Jay wrapped up in the comforter and that the sight bolstered him when he could barely drag his body above ground one more time.

During those dark hours, I ached from the agony of losing my family. Izzy would often hold me close to his chest and just let me cry. Even though he always tried, sometimes it was impossible to comfort me. I think Izzy marveled that I had the capacity to cry so much. He never scolded me but rather just held me whenever he had the opportunity, sometimes rocking me like a baby, while Jay slept beside us, curled up in his comforter. I knew that thoughts of his parents and sisters were never far away. When he left the ghetto with us, he had no option but to accept their doom. Given the frequency of the selections and the fierceness of the monsters who guarded the inmates, there was little chance they would survive. Still, he couldn't give up hope for their safety.

One night Izzy was lying exhausted on the straw in the hayloft, and I was trying to encourage him when Mr. Paskauskas came to tell Izzy that a visitor had come to see him. My heart began to race as Izzy jumped up and ran into the house. He found Leibel Gillman standing just inside the doorway. I'm sure Izzy breathed a sigh of relief to see that it was only his cousin. Leibel was likely to turn up anywhere. Like a cat, he could come and go at will, not even leaving his scent behind.

Much admired for his black market skills, Leibel had been the one to secure the three guns and a hand grenade that Izzy kept hidden in the barn loft just within reach. He had also been the one to repair the ghetto fence once we made our escape. Leibel must have felt exceptional pride in helping us get away. Sometimes at night Izzy still marveled at how Leibel had been able to slip Sara Gillman, his two-year-old niece born in the ghetto, to a Christian couple. He risked his life to try and save hers. Izzy described his meeting with Leibel later that night as we lay down again in the loft.

While relieved to see Leibel was still alive, Izzy wondered why he had come. Leibel had managed to get out of the ghetto that morning and rode a bicycle all day to get to the farm. He wanted us to know there were rumors about the ghetto being liquidated. He said Izzy's parents, his sister, her child and husband had all been taken to a suburb of Kaunas in the east, an area where Jews were locked up under the pretense of being closer to their workplace.

"The Germans must be planning to kill a whole group," Izzy told me. He asked Leibel if there was another reason he had come here.

Izzy said Leibel cleared his throat and began talking in a low tone, choosing his words carefully, saying, "Izzy, you're by yourself here and it must be very lonesome. Would you allow me to bring my brother, Lola, to be with you? It's my job to find hiding places for my family. I have managed to get Sara, Moshe's daughter, out, and I have to get my brothers out next. This is a good hiding place. It would be much better for you to have others, so you would not feel so bad."

Unable to hide my aggravation with Leibel, I said, "I can't

believe he was saying that to you. After all, he knows how much responsibility you already have."

"I had the same reaction at first, but I guess I can't blame him. He wants his family to live as much as I do, but I told him it was very dangerous. People could start snooping around, and we could all get in trouble. I'm afraid if Lola comes, people would be suspicious. When I voiced my concern, Leibel said I shouldn't worry, that he would bring Lola at night and nobody will know about it."

Izzy said he tried to stay calm before answering. Finally, he said, "Leibel, I'll tell you what. Can you at least bring my mother, my sister Dvoira and her little boy, or my sister Golde? Bring one of them with Lola and I'll be happy. You have my approval, but please, don't bring Lola alone. Bring even my father, but I'm not so worried about my father as much as I am about the younger ones."

Leibel promised to do as he was asked. In less than a week, Leibel returned, slipped inside the barn and called Izzy's name. Izzy climbed down from the loft with great expectation of seeing his mother. The next thing I heard was Izzy practically shouting. It scared me to death. I hadn't heard him raise his voice above a whisper in months.

"Leibel, what have you done to me?" Izzy demanded. "Who is this stranger?"

When I heard that, I dared to peek down from the loft and saw a woman I had never seen before standing very close to Lola.

"This is Sheina Veinstein, Lola's girlfriend," Leibel explained. "Lola loves her and would be very lonesome without her. Don't worry. You'll like her."

I knew Lola, but not very well. He had always been a loner and kept pretty much to himself. Now that he was here with a girlfriend, right away I thought this would be trouble.

Izzy was trying to control himself, but I could see that he

Sheina Veinstein (1940).

was having a very hard time of it.

"Why have you punished me so?" he managed to ask Leibel. "It's too dangerous to bring strangers here."

Leibel started talking really fast, hoping to calm Izzy down some.

"Don't worry, Izzy," he said. "I'll go back now and I'll bring your mother and your sister next time. Then, I'll come myself with my mother. Don't get upset. You know me. You know I can take care of myself."

Izzy just stood there twisting his hands and not knowing whether to believe Leibel or not, but it would be on his conscience to send Lola's girlfriend back to the ghetto, where her life would surely be in danger. What could he do? Izzy was so upset he just climbed back into the loft and didn't even speak to the girl. Lola and Sheina found a spot in the barn loft and kept very quiet. Accepting the situation, Izzy went back to his digging the next night, now with added responsibility.

Two weeks later, Leibel was back, and this time he brought his older brother, Moshe, and his wife, also named Sheina. At least his brother was a cousin to Izzy, but his wife was almost like another stranger.

By this time, Izzy couldn't stand it. He shouted, "Leibel, what's the matter with you? What's going on? Where is my mother?"

"Well," Leibel began, "I have some terrible news. Preidl, your father, was at home one day last week. Your mother, Toni, was at the sewing machine working when she looked out the window and saw trucks coming. There had been rumors for days that trucks would be there soon for the old ones and the little children. Guards burst into your parents' home and pushed Preidl out the door. Then they grabbed Jacob, Dvoira's child. Toni snatched the child from the guard's arms and jumped into the truck bed beside your father. She was covered with bruises where she had fought to hold on to the baby. The Gestapo guards nearly strangled her before they finally managed to pull her out of the truck, still holding on to Jacob. They yanked Jacob from her and threw him back into the truck toward your father."

Izzy stood frozen for a moment without speaking. I suppose he was trying to imagine the horror of the scene. I could almost hear my heart breaking for him. That news was bad enough, but it was magnified by the fact that Leibel said Izzy's brother-in-law, Berkman, little Jacob's father, watched it all and did nothing. Berkman had deserted Dvoira and the baby months earlier, had found another woman and was living with her in another part of the ghetto.

Leibel also explained another problem. While he was trying to take Toni and Dvoira through the gate on another day, a Jewish policeman arrested the women. Izzy's mother and sister were locked up for trying to escape, but Leibel was able to get away somehow. It was hard for Izzy to judge whether Leibel was telling the truth.

Leibel did say he tried to bring Izzy's sister, Golde, but she refused to leave without her boyfriend's family. That would have been three more. Leibel couldn't risk taking such a large group, even though he was a fearless young man with nerves of steel. Just a teenager, he didn't believe anything could happen to him.

Izzy just stood there seething, not saying another word. After a very long silence, Leibel finally said, "I'm going now, Izzy. I'll bring your mother and sister."

The next evening Izzy started digging in the pit to make it even larger. I think his anger helped him work harder. He worked every night, enlarging the square pit to accommodate all the extra people. I often wondered why none of the others helped him, but Izzy was so angry that they were probably afraid to even offer. The hiding place would eventually become twelve feet long, nine feet wide and four feet tall. While none of us would be able to stand erect, Izzy said he thought it was more important for the families to have a few inches of privacy, since we would be lying or sitting down most of the time. Izzy told me one night that he was almost finished with the tunnels on either side of the hiding place and that they would be about four feet long. He grew quiet for a moment and then started talking of his parents and how much they had meant to him. He even teased me a little, calling me *Tzipke* Fire. It was a pet name his father gave to me not long after we were married. It was supposed to mean "firebird."

It comforted us to gather our memories close to us. For all

we knew, that was all we would ever have of our parents. However, we had to put that aside and think of the present. There were seven altogether now — two of Izzy's cousins, one with his girlfriend and the other one with his wife, Jay, Izzy, and me. We had been hungry before, and now I couldn't imagine how Itzhak would be able to take care of all of us.

Izzy told me later that he was so disgusted that he felt like tearing his hair out. He was helpless to save his own family. Here his flesh and blood had been left in the ghetto looking for ways to survive, and Leibel had brought people that we had little connections to.

Izzy finally got back to being himself. Eventually, after several days, the digging must have diverted the anger, and he seemed a little more relaxed. Although he was mechanically inclined, Izzy knew little of the finer points of excavation and construction. While digging in the pit one night, he failed to make allowances for the mixture of sand, which shifted suddenly as he worked, burying him up to his neck.

Izzy was afraid to call out, for fear of endangering the rest of us. Unable to lift the weight of the dirt, he lay there for hours, struggling to breathe as the pressure on his chest mounted. He couldn't understand why he was facing yet another death sentence.

"My arm and legs were pinned down, and breathing got very hard," he said later. "I tried to stay calm and pray. I was afraid to move, afraid I'd become completely buried. I couldn't yell for help because if someone had heard, that would put everyone in danger. Although I never made a sound, Rexxyx sensed that I was in trouble. He kept running up to me and began licking my face. I knew it was futile, but I kept whispering, "Doggie, go and bring somebody. Help me! Save me!"

Finally Rexxyx started barking.

"I was terrified. Rexxyx never barked except when

strangers were around. I must have been there two hours, but it felt like years. You can't imagine how relieved I was when I heard Stasuk's voice, asking me if I was all right."

Stasuk had been walking up the path on the way home from a hoedown where he played the fiddle that night. It was about three o'clock in the morning. When he heard Rexxyx barking, he became alarmed as well. That's when he discovered Izzy's head barely above ground.

"Stasuk looked like an emissary from heaven at that moment," Izzy told me. "When he couldn't dig me out, he ran to get his father. Together they freed me, while Rexxyx stood watch."

Mr. Paskauskas had insisted Izzy go inside the house, have a cup of tea and rest awhile. He and Mr. Paskauskas talked about the cave-in and what Izzy could do to prevent another one. It was decided that the farmer would start dropping small pieces of timber near the hiding place. In that way, Izzy could begin to shore up the sides of the hiding place, thereby preventing another cave-in. In the end, Izzy said they managed to laugh about the problem, especially when he told Mr. Paskauskas that his training as an attorney certainly didn't prepare him for excavation work. Mr. Paskauskas started leaving the boards the next day, and slowly, slowly the hiding place became a reality.

During daylight hours, Izzy would lie in the loft and braid ropes from long strands of straw and wheat. In the evenings, he carefully took the braided pieces into the hiding place and used them to tie the boards together, making sure to turn the split side toward the wall. In this way, we could avoid splinters. Eventually Izzy reported that the four sides were secure, the wood creating a substantial wall that looked something like a flattened barrel. However, there was no way to secure the ceiling or the tunnels.

Some days Izzy told me that he had been working underground for so long that the hiding place had begun to take on a feeling of security. It was also rather warm, but constantly damp. There was nothing Izzy could do about the dampness, even though he was able to shove a pipe from the hiding place to the surface for ventilation. The pipe, which was four or five inches in diameter, would be the only source of air except for what seeped in around the covers over the potato holes and made its way through the tunnels.

Even though Izzy said he tried to light matches several times while he was working, it was to no avail because of the dampness and lack of oxygen. Everything had to be done by feel, unless he managed to slip inside the hiding place during the day. There was a very short period of time when the sun would shine through the potato holes and provide a bit of light. Izzy used that time to dig the tunnels trying to prevent the dirt from falling into his eyes. When Uncle Itzhak came to bring food, he would also dig in the pit. I don't know how he managed to stay so strong. The risk and responsibility, especially for my uncle with so many mouths to feed, was terrible.

After a week or so, Leibel came back with his mother, Nese, whom he left at Marchuk's home. From there, Leibel came with Marchuk to see Izzy in the barn. Leibel told Izzy that he had brought Nese but had been unable to bring Izzy's mother or sister.

Izzy exploded at the news. I thought I had seen him angry before, but this time he was livid.

"Leibel, how can you do it to me? What kind of harm have I done to you? I want to speak to Nese and ask her how she could come here without my mother, her own sister."

Izzy was probably talking too loudly, and until his death he felt terrible when he thought about what happened next. Leibel must have felt very guilty. He avoided Izzy's eyes and didn't say anything. Without a word, he turned around and walked out. He took his horse and wagon, along with Marchuk and his wagon, and went back to the ghetto to get Izzy's mother and sister. Nese went with him. Perhaps she insisted on going back so he wouldn't be alone.

On the way to the ghetto, they were a few miles from a little town called Zezmer. It was sometimes called Ziezmariai and was about 35 kilometers from Kaunas. Marchuk said that Leibel's horse lost a shoe and, of course, he could not travel. Marchuk offered his horse and wagon, saying he would stay to fix the horseshoe and catch up with them later. Leibel took Marchuk's wagon and horse and went on.

That was market day, and it was the wrong day to be in town. When Leibel came closer to Zezmer, he saw some Lithuanian policemen, and he must have gotten frightened. He and his mother jumped out of the wagon and ran into a field where they hid in a big haystack. The soldiers chased after them and eventually locked them in the Zezmer prison.

While in prison, Leibel offered a drunk a piece of gold to buy a saw once he was on the outside. Leibel probably planned to cut the steel bars, escape out the window and go get Izzy's mother. But the drunk told the police, and they took away everything Leibel had.

Marchuk came to Izzy later and described how he arrived in town not long after Leibel and Nese were arrested. The next day Marchuk also learned the Lithuanians had taken Leibel and Nese to a small forest and shot them. It was April 26, 1944, another date I'll never forget. What a terrible thing to happen on a beautiful spring day. Neighbors said they went naked, arm-in-arm, kissing each other. Izzy blamed himself, but what could he do? He didn't understand why at least one of his family couldn't have come with Leibel. Izzy said he felt like killing himself. He kept saying, "What have I done? What have I done?" Then his cousins started yelling at him, saying because of him they lost their brother and mother.

Leibel Gillman (date unknown).

Nese Gillman (date unknown).

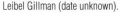

Izzy didn't know what to say. He said he felt so bad that he wished he could find another pit and cover himself alive. He thought it would be better for him to die than have to face these men and blame himself for the murders.

Before that horrible event, Itzhak and Izzy had already gone to Marchuk, trying to work out some way to bring Izzy's family to the hiding place. Izzy had arranged to go with Marchuk to the ghetto and leave Jay and me in hiding. In the end, nothing could be done. Not only had we lost Nese and Leibel, but now there was no chance of saving Izzy's parents, his sisters and nephew, all of whom were very dear and close to him.

For all of the ghetto life, this was the worst time for Izzy. Nothing was more miserable or painful for him than those moments, hours, days, and nights lying in hiding and thinking of nothing else but what had happened. Izzy told me many times that it was the biggest tragedy of his life.

10

Life Underground

Finally the hiding place was complete. It was another terrifying time, another excruciating move to more uncertainty. In the barn loft, the families had been able to spread out and have a few feet between us, which allowed at least a modicum of privacy. Privacy, such as it was, would be left behind as we made our way through the dark night to a hole in the ground that would literally entomb Moshe and Sheina Gillman, Lola Gillman, along with his girlfriend Sheina Veinstein, Izzy, Jay and me. We had no way of knowing when our existence in this new underground world would end.

While it was surely a hiding place, I wondered if it would be any safer than the barn. Once underground, we would be like animals trapped in a dark cage. At least in the barn, we had been able to tell when it was night or day. Our chances of escape from the loft were also somewhat higher. The two potato holes were innocuous enough, but they had little protection except makeshift wooden trap doors.

Potato holes, or food pits, were common in Europe. The bitter weather made it necessary for farmers to dig several feet into the ground to construct the storage pits. Once constructed, with the entrance usually dug on a slant, the pit was lined with straw or leaves to separate the fruit and vegetables, thereby keeping spoilage to a minimum during the months of constant freezing snow and ice. When Izzy constructed the hiding place, there weren't many potatoes left in the hole, just enough to camouflage the trap doors and tunnels leading to our world underneath.

Izzy went into the hiding place first, followed by Jay and me. Izzy slid in with ease, now accustomed to lowering himself into the hole. He had even constructed a small ladder to assist his entrance and exit. Once everyone was inside, Izzy planned to draw the ladder in behind us. He believed that situating the hiding place between the two potato holes would provide us at least one route for escape if we were discovered. It really wasn't much of an advantage to have a second exit, since both holes opened into the same field, but somehow it gave me comfort to know there was a second way out. Maybe we wouldn't all be killed if we had to run for the woods nearby.

While Uncle Itzhak tried to bring food to us sporadically, and Mrs. Paskauskas baked bread and cooked field peas and sometimes potatoes for us when she could, there was no guarantee we would even eat, much less live, in the dank and dreary hole. Going beneath the earth to live like moles was another retreat, a further drawing into our-selves with absolutely no idea of our future. I felt as if I were entering my grave.

Once inside, each of us began to feel our way around. Jay hovered close to me, afraid in the dark. Izzy had suggested a way for us to share the floor plan prior to going into the hole. He suggested that our family be near one of the tunnels leading to the potato holes, but not because it would be a quicker exit from danger. Izzy knew he would be responsible for scavenging for food, and being close to the entrance would allow him to leave the hiding place without having to crawl over the others. Because of his proximity to the outside, the duty of emptying the chamber pot, our makeshift bathroom, would eventually fall to Izzy as well. It seemed there was a price to pay for everything.

Each family more or less found a space to occupy. Exhausted from the tension, we fell into an uneasy sleep. The first night, Izzy had trouble sleeping. He said he stayed awake for a while listening to the breathing and snoring of the others, thinking of the walls and wondering if his construction plan would hold. He had put Jay between us and wrapped us in the comforter. It not only felt like a safe cocoon, it was another fortress, albeit a soft one, built around our family's lifeline.

Uncle Itzhak came to us a day or two after we went into the pit. He brought a few raw vegetables and some leftover scraps of meat from his neighbors. It was a joyful, but sad, reunion. The scene was repeated each time he came during the long months that followed. The elation at seeing him and knowing that he still lived would disappear shortly thereafter. With each departure, we wondered if he would ever return. Every exit was a reminder that life was perilous outside the hiding place, that there was no guarantee for tomorrow, or any day for that matter.

Like any eight-year-old boy, Jay set about exploring and finding ways to occupy himself. He crawled around the perimeter of the hiding place until he had memorized the space and set a mental picture about where each family's line of demarcation was located. He entertained himself by discovering how fast he could scoot back and forth in the tunnels but he didn't spend a great deal of time away from me at first. Although he wasn't a large child, even he couldn't stand completely erect in the hiding place or the tunnels. Every move had to be made on hands and knees, except when he entered the potato hole. When they dared, he and Izzy would crawl through the tunnels and stand up in one of the potato holes to stretch their cramped bodies. The muted light was just enough to expose the lice that continuously infested them. As they picked the lice off each other and squashed them, Jay's knowledge of numbers grew over the months, along with the amount of blood accumulating under his fingernails from the louse execution.

Mice turned out to be another source of entertainment for Jay. They would wait until everyone was still at night and then would begin to rummage around, looking for scraps of food. They were disappointed more than not and over time became brave and crawled over our bodies, over everyone except the three of us. When Izzy would lie down at night, he would put his arm around Jay and me, pulling us as close as possible to him. The iridescent numbers on his watch must have looked like cats' eyes to the mice. For whatever reason, we were glad to be free of at least one plague.

Try as he might, Jay wasn't able to catch a mouse. I was horrified at the idea but didn't have the heart to discourage him. After all, there were no toys for him to play with. Before coming into the hiding place, he and Rexxyx had always chased each other a little inside the barn during the early morning hours. I sometimes laughed at them poking around in the hay trying to find where the chickens had indiscriminately laid their eggs. Jay became quite astute at finding them. When he did, there was no sharing with Rexxyx; he simply cracked the shell, held the shell over his head and swallowed the raw egg as the dog ran circles around him and barked. Sometimes he teased Rexxyx by allowing him to lick the empty shells. Jay even managed to preserve some of the shells, using a string Mrs. Paskauskas had given him. With painstaking care, he pricked tiny holes in opposite ends of the eggs. After sucking the contents through a hole, he found a safe place to allow the shells to dry completely before threading them onto the string, forming a necklace. In time, it fell apart, much like his clothes did as the days turned into months in the hiding place.

Another short-lived toy was a ball Mrs. Paskauskas constructed for Jay, whom she was particularly fond of. After her husband had killed a hog one day, she managed to save the pig's bladder. While it was still moist and supple, she blew it up to form an odd-shaped ball. Before tying it off like a balloon, she dropped a few field peas through the opening into the bladder, thinking the peas would provide a nice rattling sound when the ball was bounced. She laid the makeshift ball in the sun and waited for it to stiffen before presenting it to Jay, who was thrilled with the new diversion and bounced it constantly. A few days later, the noise became so irritating to Lola that he slit the ball with his penknife. Jay didn't utter a word of protest but rolled up in the comforter for a while beside me. Izzy remained silent during the entire episode, but I could feel him breathing heavy for a long time after it happened.

Toys and food weren't the only scarcities. Water was at a premium, and not a drop was wasted, rendering tooth brushing, baths, and laundry as unnecessary amenities. Mr. Paskauskas and his wife would occasionally bring a small pail of water outside and leave it near the potato-hole entrance. They were afraid to make the trip too often, because they also had to leave bread or other food at different times. They had staked Rexxyx near the hiding place, thinking he could be their excuse if ever questioned about carrying food or water so far from their house. I often wondered if Rexxyx drank from the pail before we did.

One of the most degrading things we had to endure in the hiding place was having no privacy, especially for bathroom privileges. A single bucket held everyone's waste and leaves or whatever we could find to use for toilet paper. It was usually stored near the potato-hole opening, as much to keep someone from turning it over as to have it close to the entrance for Izzy's convenience in emptying it.

The lack of bathroom privacy proved minor when compared with medicinal needs. Since my parents had been taken in the Riga selection, I had suffered with unrelenting migraine headaches, especially when I cried a lot. Sometimes they lasted for days, and I couldn't bear to even lift my head or sit upright. Again, God bless him, Itzhak provided relief. He was able to sketch the area of my head that hurt and, on rare occasions, bring medicine from one of his friends. Izzy was also plagued, but with another malady. He was in dire need of a dentist, and ultimately began suffering from an abscessed tooth. Mrs. Paskauskas was able to make him a tea and garlic poultice that drew the infection out of his gums and finally gave him relief after weeks of suffering. My monthly cycles had already ceased due to lack of nutrition, and now it seemed that I would have even less to eat. It made me wonder if I would ever be able to conceive, or do anything normal, again.

Some nights we were able to recapture a hint of our former lives. When we dared, on very rare occasions, a few of us ventured outside the hiding place. We didn't all go out at once. When we did go above ground, we were careful not to push too hard on the trap doors that kept the few loose potatoes in place over the tunnels. We would inch the door forward and crawl over the few remaining potatoes. It was very awkward, but it was worth it to be able to stand up and stretch. I was always amazed to see that the stars and moon were still in place. It helped me feel almost normal, even if it was for only a few minutes.

A couple of times I went into the farmhouse, but none of the others did. It wasn't that they weren't welcome, but it would have been another way of endangering the farm family even more. Over the whole time we were there, I couldn't have gone inside more than two or three times. Once I took a few pieces of clothing to wash. All the others had no extra clothes. Even though it was dark, they didn't want to stay naked while I laundered their clothes. I would have had to stay outside the hiding place for hours in order for them to dry on the hearth. I was the only one who had any extra clothes, and all I had was a second dress and apron. I wouldn't wear them. Instead I waited for the day that I could dress in them after our liberation.

I remember one night in particular. I was coming back to the hiding place from the house, and suddenly I heard a noise. I fell to the ground and held my breath. It took me a long time to realize that the sound wasn't the dreaded Gestapo but a fast wind blowing through the trees. I finally managed to crawl back to the potato hole and wiggle myself inside it.

The hours spent in complete darkness seemed endless. We all seemed to be in a coma. Days and nights became synonymous. The only way we knew the seasons had changed was when Izzy or Itzhak told us the trees had begun to sprout again or brought apples for us to eat.

When we first entered the hiding place, we tried to carry on conversations, even though they were stilted at best. There was still lingering animosity over Lola's girlfriend being there instead of one of Izzy's family members. Sometimes we spoke of Leibel and Nese, the Gillman family members who had been executed. Discussion of that topic was rare, though, and when it was broached, there was always a heated discussion followed by a tense silence for several days. After a few months, no one dared to speak of them any more or of hardly anything else. It seemed as if we turned all our attention toward just breathing, just existing for another day. I was almost relieved when we stopped talking. Tempers were so short that I was really afraid things might get out of hand. When we went into the hiding place, Izzy had given a handgun to Lola. Sheina kept the bullets in her dress pocket. Izzy kept the hand grenade near us. I guess Izzy reasoned that we would be better able to defend ourselves if there were two men with weapons. Maybe each one could leave through a different exit.

As time dragged on, there was nothing to say, nothing to do but endure the dark tomb-like existence, wondering if we would just lie there and starve to death. Sometimes I passed the hours by imagining what Jay's bar mitzvah would be like and which synagogue it might be held in. I even planned the menu for the meal that would be served afterward. At other times, I just hoped to live to see another sunrise. The worst times for me were when Izzy was gone. While he was out foraging for food with Uncle Itzhak, he sometimes heard radio reports and, just as he had in the ghetto, he would bring word back to the inhabitants of the hiding place. Like the ghetto inmates, we hung on Izzy's every word, hoping for an end to the war but afraid it wouldn't come in time to save us.

Itzhak came to fetch Izzy often. Sometimes they stayed gone for days, gleaning in the fields or begging food from farmers. When they returned, there was always a short span of lifted spirits, depending upon the amount of food and news they brought with them. At times, though, the scarcity of food caused the family groups to huddle away from each other, guarding what precious morsels we were able to save.

Somehow we adjusted. Our bodies settled for less and less food. Dirt piled up in layers on our arms and legs. It became so unbearable that I tried to scrub some of it off. When I rubbed it, the action would set off a firestorm of itching that nearly drove me crazy. A few times of that taught me that it was best to leave the filth alone. We women managed to bite or tear off our ragged fingernails while Mr. Paskauskas would, on rare occasions, leave a straight razor so the men could shave.

Nothing, not even food, could give us a modicum of cleanliness. While we didn't dare discuss it, we all longed to feel water cascading across our bodies. I ached to wash my hair until it squeaked and feel the tingle of toothpaste in my mouth. I sometimes fantasized about brushing my teeth and actually eating the toothpaste. I would have been more than happy to swallow it, just to have the taste in my mouth for a few moments.

Even under these dire circumstances and virtually starving, Izzy and I clung to our faith, refusing to eat the small portions of pork sausage the farm family offered to share. We did, however, allow Jay to eat the sausage, simply because we felt duty-bound at least to do what we could to keep him from dying.

Mrs. Paskauskas baked bread constantly and tried her best to sustain us. She would also soak the hard field peas for days before cooking them. Even so, the peas proved too difficult for Izzy and me. When I tried to chew them, it sounded like I was eating marbles and made my head throb harder. Izzy, poor dear, continued to have problems with his teeth. Sometimes, after the small pail was passed around and everyone had taken a portion from the wooden spoon, Izzy and I would simply swallow the peas whole. The rough black bread that Mrs. Paskauskas baked was something else altogether. It was most edible and proved to be the one constant in our diet. No wonder bread is considered the staff of life. On occasion, Mrs. Paskauskas managed to make us some weak potato soup. Moshe Gillman would quickly slurp up his portion and declare it delicious. In one of the rare moments of mirth, Moshe's wife, Sheina, would laugh at him and say the soup was terrible but tasted good because of our starvation. Either way, it must have been an interminable task for Mrs. Paskauskas to try to feed seven extra mouths when her own family was practically destitute.

Nothing, including raging hunger, could drive the constant thoughts of Leibel and Nese out of Izzy's mind. Although it was unspoken most of the time, Izzy knew Lola and Moshe blamed him for their deaths. Their absence added to the tension of living underground. Sometimes, though, we would speak of them. During one of those times, Sheina described how knowing Leibel had saved her life. It seems she was caught outside the ghetto but was left unharmed by the guards after insisting she was Leibel's girlfriend, not Lola's.

Another time, Lola told a story that gave us all a good laugh. He described how a German officer had come to the ghetto and wanted Leibel to work on some motorcycles. No amount of cajoling would move Leibel. He told the officer he couldn't possibly concentrate on motorcycles when his mother had been recently moved to Fort VI. When Leibel wouldn't budge, the officer gave up. However, he came back the next day with a gun and invited Leibel to get on the motorcycle with him. Leibel felt obliged to do as he asked. Lola said he would never forget seeing Leibel, the officer balancing a gun and Nese all atop that motorcycle when they returned to the ghetto.

While that image brought levity for a moment, Izzy constantly mourned Leibel's and Nese's loss. He couldn't help but wonder whether his parents and sisters had suffered the same fate. If so, he could only pray that their deaths had been swift.

11

Raja's Story

After Izzy came back with food one time, he whispered to me that Uncle Itzhak was coming to stay in the potato hole on his return visit. I was astonished. We had barely survived; with new mouths to feed, how would we hold out? And where would they stay? It was such a small place, we already felt like we were suffocating.

"Itzhak has provided for these people for a long time, Eta, along with us," Izzy reassured me. "He has many friends among the farmers; everyone loved him in the old days, and it has paid off. He will continue to scavenge food for all of us. But the German patrols are going through the woods and farms more often now and you know many of the Lithuanians hate Jews and would turn them in if they caught them. It's getting much more dangerous out there. We have to make room for them."

Then he told me that not only Itzhak but his wife, Ida, whom I had never much liked, would be coming with their two boys, Jacob and David, also Ida's sister, Raja, and her son, Emmanuel. I had always loved Raja. She was such a bright spirit, so very smart, pretty and happy all the time. At least it would be good to be with her again.

"We will do what we have to do, Izzy," I told him. "God will see us through as he has all along."

Now we would be thirteen in the cramped hole. I dreaded thinking about what might happen with so many in such a small, dark space. As it was, there was not enough air to burn a candle.

Izzy seemed to read my mind. "We can leave the doors open at the bottom of the potato hole at night to let in fresh air now that it's warm enough. But we will have to watch the children and keep them quiet."

A few nights later Itzhak brought in his little troupe of refugees. Everyone hugged each other and tears flowed. In the end, we all praised God that we were together again. Itzhak, who had always been the religious leader of the family, led prayers of thanksgiving for our reunion. The sound of his voice brought calm to my spirit.

Raja crawled over to sit by me as soon as she could. Her son, whom we all affectionately called Mannie, was about five years old, the same age as Ida and Itzhak's David. Mannie was a sweet child, I could tell, although I could not really see him. He and his family had been on the run since he was about two. Jacob and our Jay, both eight, were all getting acquainted and playing quietly in the other corner.

"Eta, Eta, oh, I am so glad to find you alive!" Raja said. "So many have died. So much has happened."

"It has been worse than a nightmare, Raja," I said. None of your romance novels you used to love would begin to match the stories we have to tell."

"Now don't make fun of me, Eta," Raja laughed. It was good to hear laughter in this place.

"Oh, I know, you read all sorts of things. But this is a hard story to match."

Raja did, indeed, read everything. She spoke many languages, some of which she learned because she wanted to read books in that tongue. She even learned English as a young girl by reading a series called *Nat Pinkerton, Detective* at night by flashlight. Her mother always blamed her bad eyesight on her reading after dark.

"Tell me, Raja, if you can. Where is your dear mother, Bluma?"

Raja grew silent. Finally she spoke. "She hid with us in the woods for a long time. It was very hard, of course — we moved 74 times in the past three years, if I counted right. One night she went into the woods to relieve herself." Raja paused for a minute and then said, "She must have thought she heard a patrol or something, became frightened and had a stroke. She was breathing when Itzhak found her, but she couldn't move or speak. Itzhak managed to carry her back into the barn. She lay motionless in the hay for three days and finally died. I felt so badly for Itzhak. I'll never forget seeing him put her body over his shoulder and carry her away. He went deep into the woods and buried her."

"I'm so sorry, Raja. I know that was terrible. We have all lost so many," I said as I thought again of my mother, my father, all the loved and lost ones.

"I will tell you soon about my husband, father-in-law and my father," Raja added. "I can't do that today. I'm too exhausted."

Raja curled up beside me and was instantly asleep. I felt her clothes, barely hanging on her body they were so worn, and stroked her hair, once wavy and vibrant and now greasy and coarse. I remembered what a lovely thing she was. I wished with all my heart that this war was over, and we could all be ourselves again.

In the next days, we established some rituals that allowed

us to live together more comfortably. We set turns and times to empty the bathroom bucket, always in places where it wouldn't be noticeable. Itzhak found some carrots that night, along with a few potatoes, and we ate them raw and dirty, with greedy appreciation. Mornings, Itzhak instructed his sons in the *Torah* and taught them a little about numbers in the light from the entry to the hole. I was delighted that Jay crawled over to see what they were doing, and he stayed to learn some things. Mannie joined them as well. Itzhak's voice was so rich, so encouraging. Raja sometimes entertained the children by telling them stories. She had a great imagination. She told me that she had used that skill to entertain Mannie for hours while they were hiding. When he tired of that, she used straws to teach him numbers and how to write.

Ida continued to be her old self, putting Raja and me down, talking only to Lola's girlfriend and complaining all the time. She insisted, for example, that her boys get the first share of food. Raja and I knew from the past that the best defense was to ignore her.

Several days later, when Raja was more rested, and when we were lying side by side in the hole, I asked, "Do you want to tell me about your family, what happened to you all?"

"It's a long story, Eta. It's not a happy story, either. So many terrible things … I will try. It may take me a while."

"I understand. Don't rush. Just as you like—"

At this moment, Ida's voice hissed across the space between us: "Some of us are trying to sleep. Can't you girls keep it down?"

"Come with me," I said, pulling Raja's sleeve. We crawled through the tunnel to the entrance of the potato hole. I pushed up on the wooden cover and raked back the potatoes that disguised it. It was always hard to tell what time it was in the hole without Izzy's glow-in-the-dark watch, but it was dark outside, no starlight even, and seemed safe to come out.

I had pulled Jay's comforter with me, in case it was night and chilly. "Let's sit here on the edge of the pit," I suggested. We climbed the little ladder to the top and sat on the rim, huddled together with the comforter around us. The night was cool, but the air was wonderful to breathe outside the dank hole.

"Now tell me," I said.

"I guess the last I saw of you, I was teaching at the gymnasium in Kovno, at Dr. Schwabe's school."

"Yes, I remember when you got that job, how proud you were."

"Oh, it's a wonderful school, very famous, but mostly it was fun to teach there. I taught the lower grades Hebrew, but I really enjoyed organizing the plays and pageants for the holidays because of the singing."

Raja had a lovely voice. I could feel the smile in her voice as I squeezed her hand.

"The school-sponsored tours were best of all, so I got to go to Finland and Berlin. I really wanted to go to Paris. I had been saving for that."

Raja grew very quiet. I knew what had happened. Itzhak had courted Ida, Raja's older sister, and Ida needed more money for her dowry. Their mother had asked Raja to contribute her savings, and she had done so.

Suddenly animated Raja said, "But now, look! Itzhak is keeping us alive with his foraging, and so it was a blessing!"

Raja could always look on the sunny side.

She went on. "My dear Moshe — you remember Moshe, don't you?"

"Of course," I said. Her husband was involved in business in South Africa. He had a tearoom there, as well as other enterprises. He had been terribly sick when he came from there when he was courting Raja, but he studied natural medicine diligently and on his next return, the effect was quite obvious. He was a fine-looking man, humorous and smart and could sing as well as Raja. It was always a treat to hear them together.

"Emmanuel was born in February of 1939. I will never forget how cold it was that night. We were so happy. We were talking about where we would live. Moshe had a British passport, and we could have gone as a family to South Africa, or he even suggested Australia, since the world was becoming such a frightening place. Moshe was so dedicated to his parents, you may remember, and he kept putting off leaving. And then suddenly, the Russians moved into Lithuania, so we were stranded. Then the Germans invaded. Moshe managed to get us on one of the buses headed for the Soviet border. ..."

"We tried to escape, too, in a buggy Izzy got for us," I told her. "It didn't work, and we had to come back to Kovno."

"Well, it didn't work for us, either. The Germans were strafing and blowing up the buses. We got out and ran for the woods, dragging our things. The woods were full of Germans and Lithuanians looking for Jews. We decided to act like we were unafraid and just walk down the road naturally. I went to a farmhouse to try to get some milk for Mannie and was stopped by a German on a motorcycle, but since I spoke good German I talked and flirted with him. He winked at me and flirted back. He took delight in telling me that in six weeks the Germans would be in Moscow. Then he rode on. We hid in the woods for several days, buying food or begging it from farmers. We saw the German and his men later, from the woods, as they were retreating. They didn't look good, believe me. The Russians had taken their toll.

"Moshe had friends in the area and found us a horse and buggy, and we got home. But things were bad there, too. The Lithuanians, who were so anti-Semitic, were treating us badly everywhere. We had to walk in the gutters instead of on sidewalks, with people pushing and shoving us because of the awful yellow stars we had to wear."

"The last thing I did before we escaped was to rip mine off my clothes," I said.

"Me, too. Disgusting. Anyway, there were these awful Lithuanian extremists, and then the Germans searching us all the time and making life hell. But we kept together and tried to avoid conflict.

"Then, on August 17, 1941, all the men over sixteen were rounded up. This included my dear Moshe, my father and my father-in-law. I remember as they left, I held Emmanuel in my arms, and he called *'Papeh! Papeh!'* and waved good-bye from the window. Of course, he had no idea what was going on. I actually moved away from the window before Moshe got out of sight. I was afraid they might come back and shoot Mannie.

"I cried for a while, then I got mad and started asking questions. I found out they had been taken by forced march to Kashidar, which isn't too far away, and held as prisoners there. After about a week or ten days, I couldn't stand it any more. I didn't know if they were alive or dead, and I wanted to find out. So I got the women of the family together, and we cooked up two huge pots of macaroni with cheese — we didn't have much else. I slung a wooden stick across my back and neck as a yoke and put those pots on the ends and started out. It was about nine kilometers, and I thought I would never make it. I kept thinking about Moshe, and that helped me. I managed to sweet-talk the guards into letting me in."

Raja burst into tears. "Oh, Eta. I can never forget that place. It is always going to haunt me. The men were packed in like sardines, and there was no room for them to move. There were no sanitary facilities, and it smelled horrible. No one seemed to care. My father, to my horror, had had half of his beard ripped away by the guards as an insult, just raw flesh showing and blood clotted on his face.

"My husband's father was lying on the floor, too weak to get up. It was so awful. He had been trampled into the filth. When I came in with the food, he was so hungry he stuffed the macaroni into his mouth with both hands. Others fell on it like wolves. As soon as some of them ate, they threw up. I realized these men probably hadn't eaten for a week.

"Moshe was horribly depressed. He had no hope for himself but just kept saying, 'Protect the boy. Just protect the boy.'

"I'm coming tomorrow with a razor and women's clothes and I'll get you out of here. Don't give up hope!" I said. "In front of all those men, we kissed...."

By this time, I was crying along with Raja. How she had stood all this was beyond me.

"Anyway, Eta, I left, and I was just stunned. I walked a short way off — I could still see the buildings. I sat down on a log to get myself together and try to plan for a return trip. As I sat there, I saw trucks full of German SS and Lithuanian collaborators come driving up. They went into the prison and came out in no time with all the men pushed before them, weak as they were. There were other men packed inside the trucks. They were dragged out of the truck to join Moshe and the others. While I watched, all of them were forced to march into a group of trees nearby and stand alongside a big ditch.

"And there...." Her voice caught, and she took a minute to recover. "And there they shot them all. I could see it. I watched the bodies as they fell into the ditch, and the Germans and Lithuanians shoveled dirt over them. And Eta, they weren't all dead. I could hear the cries and moans before the dirt covered them. I could only hope my Moshe had a merciful and swift death."

I held Raja close while she sobbed. After a minute she said, "Eta, if I had stayed ten more minutes I would have been shot, too. I thought for a minute that would be good. But God has saved me, and Moshe's words encouraged me. I determined I would avenge my husband's life and our fathers' lives by saving me and Emmanuel."

After that night, Raja and I would try to get away to go "up on the roof," as we called it, to sit and talk quietly, and sometimes laugh into each other's shoulders and sometimes to cry. It was so good for me after all that time of near silence down in the hole. Raja, worn thin and exhausted as she was, was still full of her spark of life. I was so tired sometimes I could hardly speak, but "on the roof," my voice came back. Once Rexxyx let out a low growl, and we slid like water to the bottom of the potato hole, freezing in place, not even daring to open the door to the tunnel. After a very long while, Raja whispered, "I remember once when my sister Sheina and Mannie and I were hiding, and we were in a hole like this. Sheina saw a silhouette at the top of the hole and made us all duck down and be quiet. It was a German, walking right by the edge of the hole. If she hadn't seen him, we would have been shot like fish in a barrel."

The next night Raja explained that her sister had separated from Uncle Itzhak's group. Sheina had slipped away one night after saying she had decided to join a man she had fallen in love with. Raja wasn't sure where she was, though, or if she lived. Finally, she asked me the question I was hoping she would never ask.

"Gdalia, my brother, was there in Kovno Ghetto with you," Raja started. "Do you have any idea what happened to him?"

"Oh, Raja," I said. "You didn't know." But of course, the way I said it, she knew now.

She sucked in her breath and said, "Tell me."

"He was so eager to do right. Soon after we were in the ghetto, they called for 500 young men to do archival work, and he thought — as they all did — that this was a great opportunity. He volunteered for the detail. Right before he left, he rushed into our house, because we lived right near the gate where they were gathering. He asked me to make him a sandwich, and I did, and he hugged me and ran out the door." I paused. "All those young men were killed, Raja."

"One more of us gone. Poor Gdalia...."

Raja didn't even cry. She just put her hand in mine and gripped it.

Then, "Eta, why didn't Izzy go with them?"

"It's a miracle. Izzy must be blessed with some sort of sixth sense. He felt there was something wrong with the whole thing, even though his friends urged him to go with them. He has been saved by his intuition many times."

"Well, thank God, because he is keeping us alive now. I don't know where we'd be without him or Itzhak." She paused and then added, "or the blessed farmers."

Another night we talked about the ways we had both escaped from the ghetto. I told her about slipping out to meet Marchuk. "Yes," she said, "Marchuk helped us, too, but that's another story." She told how she and little Mannie, who was still in diapers, and her sister Sheina and their mother had tried once to escape but had been found by the SS and brought back to their village to be taken to a death camp. She and all the women and children were searched, their valuables taken, and they were herded onto carts to be taken away.

"We went twenty or thirty kilometers to Semeliškes and were shoved into the synagogue and a few houses nearby. There were hundreds of us. We weren't allowed to use the lavatories or anything. There were guards, each with two guns, at the exits. I had been to this synagogue before and was familiar with it. I kept thinking of escape plans and then discarding them. To get us all out would be difficult. I knew there was a field nearby, then some woods below it and then the river.

"The guards came in all night long with flashlights and picked out young women to drag out and rape. Some returned, sobbing. Others were tortured and didn't come back. There were screams all night long, and I almost gave up hope. But the next day, I recognized one of the Lithuanian guards. I talked to him about escape, and he said, 'Now's your chance; the next guard won't be here for a while. You have to go immediately. When you run, I'll shoot in the air.' I rushed back to the others and told them, but they were afraid and dithered, and before long, that guard was off-duty. Oh, Eta. If only they had had the courage then. Most of those women never lived through the next days.

"My mother and my sister Sheina were in a house close by. I spoke to the guard the next morning and asked if I could take Mannie and go to be with them. He agreed and took me over to the house they were in. It was as bad as the place they had held Moshe: stinking, packed with people, some dead or dying on the floor.

"It took me an hour, carrying my boy, to find my mother in a far corner and then my sister. Between us we managed to carry our mother out into the yard. Sheina had been talking to a guard she knew, who thought she was a great beauty and said he wished he had taken her out to save her for himself. Sheina used his attention to get information. When she told him that we had another sister, Ida, who was married to Itzhak Kalamitsky, he grew very excited. He told her Itzhak and his family had fled from their farm, were hiding in the woods nearby and that friendly farmers were taking care of them. He went so far as to beg her to get out fast and find Itzhak, as he was her only hope. He said, 'Wait until tonight, little one, and I will help you.' But Sheina didn't trust him, and our mother refused to try to escape. Learning that Itzhak and Ida were safe in the woods gave us hope. Itzhak had helped all the farmers around him for years, and we knew he would be all right."

"So what did you do?" I asked.

"We simply walked off in the middle of the next day. My friend came back on guard duty, and I spoke to him. He told me where to dig a hole under the fence that circled our prison. We had to do it before 2 p.m., when the guard would change. No one paid the least bit of attention, either. We slipped under the fence and across the field, three women and a boy. Then we got to the river — a stream, really — narrow but deep. There were local women washing clothes on the other side. Police actually passed us at this point but ignored us. They probably believed we were Gentile Lithuanians like those washing. Some of the women had extended planks into the river so they could reach the clearer water. I asked them to put out another plank, and then we could make our way over the little bridge, but instead they pulled out all the planks and walked away a distance and watched us. I felt like they were waiting for the show when our weakness would lead to a tragic performance.

"We jumped into the water. I was the only one who could swim, so I got my mother across, which wasn't easy because she refused to take off her fur coat. Sheina had Mannie on her back, and I went back and dragged him, then her, ashore, and we all lay there a minute, shivering with cold. We climbed the hill beyond, and suddenly there were guards who began cursing and chasing us. One old peasant standing nearby said, 'Quick. Get into a trench and they can't see you. You can get to the forest that way.'

"The trenches were for drainage and were muddy at the bottom and had bushes on either side. They were hard to travel in, but no one could see us, although we heard shots and voices. I had Mannie in my arms and I fell several times, but we got to the woods by night. We were so cold. We found a hut, and the woman there, with five children, said her husband was away, so she allowed us to come in. She gave us food, and we dried out a little, but her husband came back early and was furious. He opened the door and threw us out.

"For several days we wandered, cold and hungry. We were even robbed by people who offered to help us. They took everything but the clothes on our backs. We heard the SS in the woods often, but they never found us. Then, quite by luck, we happened on the house of the caretaker of that forest. He gave us food and led us to where he thought Itzhak might be. It took us two weeks, staying in the woods, cold and hungry, begging what food we could, until we ran across a man who had herded sheep for Itzhak, and he took us to a place a distance off where he thought Itzhak might be hiding. As if by a miracle, we stepped into a trench one night and there was Ida buried under some leaves. What a reunion! What joy we had in all being together again."

"Oh, Raja, that's so amazing! You were so brave!"

"God watched over me every minute, Eta. Believe me."

"Was Itzhak there?" I asked.

"No, but he came soon and was overjoyed to see us. He had heard that all the women and children at Semeliškes were killed and was convinced we had died. We have wandered with him in the woods for about three years and spent months with no roof over our heads. Other times, we have lived in a little outhouse on some property, like a smokehouse on Marchuk's place, where we stayed four months, and then two months more later on. He liked us, but his wife and child hated Jews. I think she was jealous, too." Raja paused. "Marchuk was — um — too fond of me."

"Did he molest you?" I asked.

"No, but he kept looking at me and saying, 'After the war is over....' He frightens me a little." She went on. "Once I remember keeping Mannie quiet when we were lying in a pea field and Germans were patrolling nearby. I took peas and shelled them and gave them to him one at a time and made a game of it. Mannie kept me going. I remember countless nights, walking, always walking, with Mannie's little hand in mine. The only sound in those nights was the creak of the handle on the white enamel chamber pot that Ida always insisted on carrying with her. Somehow the sound was comforting.

"Whenever we were hiding with the farmers, I told them they were perfectly safe, because we had Emmanuel, which means, 'God is with us.' I truly believed that, too. One time Itzhak fell on a stob when he was out foraging for food. We didn't have any way to dress the wound and Itzhak's leg swelled so big I thought it would burst. He couldn't walk for several days, and we were facing starvation. Finally, though, Ida said she believed that ammonia would draw out pus. She urinated on a rag and applied it to the wound, which brought the infection out.

"There was a time — I counted — that we could not wash for seventeen weeks. The winters were terrible, but we lived through it. I don't know how we kept from freezing. Eta, we made it this far, and I believe — I truly believe — God will take us all the way."

"I do, too, Raja. I do, too," I said. And I did.

12

Jacob and David's Lesson

Before my Uncle Itzhak and the others came, I would think about them in order to pass the time in the potato hole. Itzhak's older son, Jacob, had already shown signs of being a serious farmer when he was still a very little boy. We had been to visit them not too long before we were forced into the ghetto. I remember thinking that Jacob was wise beyond his years, already helping Uncle Itzhak do small chores around the farm. That wasn't surprising, really. He was following in his father's footsteps.

I remember my mother telling me stories of how Jacob Kalamitsky, Itzhak's father and my grandfather, had died when a wagon turned over on him. At the time, my Uncle Itzhak was only about twelve years old, but he assumed the responsibility of the family farm just the same. Little Jacob's seriousness came naturally, I guess. Jacob even looked like Itzhak, a little stocky boy with an air of independence. He even took on the responsibility of looking after his brother, David, who was three years younger, because Ida was sick so much of the time. Yes, Jacob grew up knowing responsibility. Later, when Itzhak would bring food into the hiding place, I always pressed him for details about Jacob and David. I savored each little morsel of information as much as the food my uncle brought.

At first I thought it would be unbearable to have so many more in the hiding place, but their presence actually proved comforting. It was really sweet, too, that Jacob had a comforter with him. Just like Jay, he had carried his comforter through all their trials and wouldn't let go of it. To hear Uncle Itzhak teaching Jacob and David the *Torah* was a semblance of normalcy, an anchor to reality. Jay and Mannie always grew quiet and listened, too. Uncle Itzhak was such a learned man, quite a scholar, really. It seemed strange for such an educated man to be a farmer, but the fact that he was a very dedicated Jew, as well as a good farmer, is really what saved all our lives.

One morning I asked Jacob to recite some of the *Torah* for me. It must have reminded him of an incident that happened while all of them were hiding in the countryside. Although I couldn't see Jacob's face very well, I could hear the awe in his voice as he began describing an incident that happened sometime earlier in the fall during *Yom Kippur*, the day Jews customarily celebrate the holiday of atonement and forgiveness.

"*Mameh*, *Papeh*, and David and I moved one night to a new hayloft," Jacob began. "*Papeh* had already found a place for Aunt Raja and Mannie to hide in. It was another building not far from the barn where we would be staying. The next morning I heard a voice. When I woke up fully, I saw *Papeh* praying. He had his prayer shawl over his head. Suddenly the farmer who owned the barn came running in screaming that the Lithuanian police were coming to arrest us."

"What did you do?" I asked.

"*Papeh* put David on his back and climbed down the stairs. *Mameh* and I followed quickly and ran after him into the woods. Aunt Raja and Mannie also came running from their hiding place. Just inside the trees, *Papeh* stopped so suddenly I almost ran into him."

"Stopped? For what?" I asked.

"I don't know. *Papeh* didn't say anything, just handed David to my mother. He lifted his prayer shawl over his head again, gathered us close to him and began to recite the prayers out loud.

"*Papeh* prayed louder and louder as the Lithuanian police were coming up the hill. They were chanting something I couldn't understand at first. As they drew closer, I heard them singing, 'We're going to kill some Jews today. Hooray! Hooray! We are going to kill some Jews today. Hooray....'"

Jacob grew silent for a minute. I held my breath trying to envision the terror of that scene for a little boy. I finally asked, "What did your father do?"

"He turned his back to them," Jacob finally said. "I wanted to be brave, too, but I looked past *Papeh's* elbow and saw this big man coming closer and closer. As he got closer, I thought I recognized him. He reached us first and grabbed *Papeh's* prayer shawl off his face. The man jumped back and said, "Itzhak Kalamitsky! I thought you were dead. How have you managed to stay alive?"

"Did you know this man?" I asked Jacob.

"I thought so, but I was so scared I wasn't sure. The man tried to hand his gun to *Papeh* and said, 'Here — protect yourself. You'll be killed.'

"*Papeh* said, 'God is my protection. Keep your gun. It is you who has need of it.' *Papeh* turned his back to the man, covered his head and started praying again. I turned my back, too, but I could still see the rest of the men getting nearer out of the corner of my eye. The man stepped in front of *Papeh* and started back toward the others. He stretched out his arms real wide and waved them back. He said, 'Go home. Report nothing. You have seen no Jews today.' "

"Did your father run away then?" I asked.

"No," Jacob said, with such satisfaction that I imagined he was smiling. "We stayed in the woods until dusk and then my father started leading us to another hiding place. When we got to our new hiding place, *Papeh* began our lesson from the *Torah*. He always taught David and me every night, even some nights after he had been out gathering food. That night *Papeh* told us how God's instructions commanded a farmer to plant his crops so that one portion of land remains unplanted every seven years. *Papeh* said a time of rest is necessary, even for the land."

"What did you learn from that?" I asked.

"Well, my father says in order to be a good farmer, you must learn to honor the land. He told David and me how God always blessed him with good seed and how he had followed the teachings of *tzedakah*, helping those who are less fortunate. I remember seeing *Papeh* measure out seed for our Christian neighbors many times. Some were so poor they had to take other jobs and never repaid it. But *Papeh* said on that day, that *Yom Kippur*, one neighbor repaid his debt in full."

13

Liberation at Last — 1944

E arly one morning Izzy suddenly sat bolt upright and said, "Eta, do you feel that? The earth is shaking. Maybe it's a tank."

Izzy's words jolted everyone out of their sleep. We held our breath and huddled together as Izzy cautiously crawled through one of the tunnels to the opening of the potato hole. My heart was beating so hard I was sure everyone could hear it. I grabbed Jay, pulled him close and wrapped my sweater around him. In just a few seconds, Izzy shouted back to us, "I can see a tank. I can see the Russians."

We sat in stunned silence for several minutes, trying to take in the meaning of Izzy's words. We were afraid to believe what he was saying. It was too much too quickly. We all sat frozen in place until Izzy came halfway back into the hiding place and started calling impatiently, "Hurry. Come out. Come out. It's safe now."

Izzy ran up the ladder again and turned to offer his hands to Jay, who was scrambling close behind him. About the time

I got to the top of the potato hole, Mr. Paskauskas ran out of his house waving his arms. He was yelling, "You're free! You're free! The Russians are here! The Russians are here!"

As Mr. Paskauskas helped the others crawl out of the pit, Izzy and I watched in amazement as several Russian tanks came into view in the distance. The fields were ripe with Russian soldiers, all carrying guns and running as if they were on fire.

Standing there I felt like I was part of a dream. From the ghetto until now, we had been waiting almost three years for this moment, but we just couldn't take it in. It was happening at a whirlwind pace. Finally realizing it was true, Izzy and I grabbed Jay's hands and began to dance around in circles. Our legs were so stiff from lying down that we could hardly stand up straight, but we danced anyway. I ran back to the potato hole to wait for Uncle Itzhak and Ida to come above ground, hugging and kissing them when they stepped into the open. We were overcome with emotion, and all of us began crying with joy, even the men. It was overwhelming to understand that we had survived.

At first, we had to shield our eyes from the light, although the sun wasn't fully up. Daylight was foreign to us, causing us to blink repeatedly. The children were able to adjust much more quickly than the adults. Within minutes, they were running around in circles jumping and yelling and playing tag with each other. They began to shout, drunk with the wonder of their own voices and freedom.

The Russian soldiers paused to look at us. They were laughing and cheering as we were dancing around. They hardly slowed down, though, before continuing their pursuit of the Germans.

Suddenly David saw a butterfly. We all grew very quiet and watched it flit from a flower to a bush. Its wings looked like a rainbow, with the sunlight shining through them.

Ona and Vaclovas Paskauskas (date unknown).   Stanislovas "Stasuk" Krivicius (circa 1951).

Photos courtesy Virginia Holocaust Museum

I wondered for a moment if this was how Noah felt when he first stepped on dry land after the flood. After the first few minutes of elation, we turned to the one thing we hadn't dared to voice while lying in dirt all those months. Other than not having enough food to eat, the one thing we had missed the most was bathing. We asked Mr. Paskauskas to help the men with the four boys. Mrs. Paskauskas ran back to the house to gather towels and soap for us.

Mr. Paskauskas beckoned the men and boys toward a big pile of rocks not far from the house. While Stasuk started placing small sticks of wood under the rocks, Mr. Paskauskas got ready to set the wood on fire. Next he brought several buckets of water, which would turn to steam when he poured it over the heated rocks. Izzy and the other men and boys, went behind some blankets hanging there on sticks to take a steam bath. We could hear them laughing as they stripped off their filthy clothes. Mr. Paskauskas and Stasuk tore small branches from the bushes to help scrub their backs, while we women began ladling water over each other's heads just beside the house near a little patch of trees. We were too excited to wait for the water to be warmed.

I reached for the comb that I'd had in my apron pocket all

the time but hadn't used. What good is a comb when you can't shampoo your hair? I was actually afraid to wash my hair at first. I thought it would all fall out. I was happy to see it was still attached to my scalp, even though the water running off my head was filthy. And, while I was terribly thin, probably weighing less than 100 pounds, I felt even lighter after a bath. It was an indescribable feeling. It was another step toward realizing we were human again.

Mrs. Paskauskas did her best to find us some decent clothes to wear. I was the only one with an extra dress and apron, plus my sweater, of course. I had been saving the dress and apron just for this day. The underwear we took off was only rags and smelled so bad that I wanted to gag after looking at it when we finished bathing. Each of the women put on a housedress. The men looked really funny in Mr. Paskauskas's trousers and shirts. He was a bigger man than they, and we were all so thin. Izzy's and Itzhak's clothes hung on them, making them look like scarecrows standing in a field. They finally laughed and began teasing each other about how they would have to "grow" into their new clothes.

The boys fared a little better. Mrs. Paskauskas was a very sentimental woman and had kept a lot of Stasuk's clothes for years. Sometimes she used the especially worn ones for patches. It's a good thing she held onto them. They certainly came in handy, although we had to cut the pant legs off so the boys wouldn't trip on them. I could put a hem in them later. It didn't matter. We were just so glad to be free of the filth.

We had to practically hold the boys down long enough to shave their heads to rid them of lice. They hadn't run in such a long time, they were only interested in chasing each other, stretching their legs and climbing trees.

Later that night, when we had finally settled down a little and eaten some potato soup and bread, we were all sitting in the barn marveling, almost drunk in our freedom. It was so wonderful to be in a dry place and comforting to hear the cow making a soft lowing sound to her calf. My whole body still tingled from the bath and the hard scrubbing I gave it with the towel. I felt like I was on fire with anticipation. Each noise seemed electrified. Everything was so new and took on a heightened sense. I thought my nose was going to explode from the scent rising from the fresh hay, and Jay couldn't stop sneezing from the chicken feathers.

During a quiet moment, Izzy started laughing out loud. He said, "I wish all of you had seen the faces on those soldiers when they first saw me coming out of the potato hole. They were so funny. That's one time I'm really glad I could speak Russian. I wouldn't have wanted to miss that. They kept asking me, 'How many are in there? How long were you in that hole? How did you live? How did you keep from going crazy?'

"They couldn't believe that seven of us had survived in that dungeon for some two months and for another month there had been thirteen altogether. They kept asking, 'How did you keep four boys quiet?' Now it even seems impossible to me. I tell you it was funny."

"No, I tell you what's funny, Izzy," I said, interrupting him. "It's thinking how those soldiers probably mistook you for a rabbit when your head came popping out of that hole. They didn't expect humans to be living in a pit this far back in the country — only animals. Don't you know they're telling stories about us tonight, just like we're talking about them."

We took turns listening to each other into the early morning, languishing in the freedom of speaking aloud. One by one the others drifted off to sleep. I was too excited to close my eyes. I wanted to remember everything about this day. But, eventually even I became drowsy. I put my arm around Izzy's waist and snuggled up very close to him. I pressed my face to his broad back and breathed in the clean smell of his

Jacob Kalamitskas *(left)* and David Kalamitsky (circa 1944).

neck. When a shiver went through me, I almost laughed out loud. Now I knew I was really alive. Suddenly I was hungry for Izzy's love, for the joy of knowing him as a man. I almost got dizzy thinking about how it would be to make love again after all this time. Still, I knew it wasn't possible, at least not yet. Instead, I looked at Jay as he slept under the comforter.

And then, without warning, I began to cry. I hadn't thought of Masha, my little baby girl, in such a long time. I didn't dare think of her when we were underground. It was too much to remember her death and the loss of my family at the same time. But now I had an overwhelming desire to hold Masha and rock her again. I wanted to see her sweet smile as she gently suckled my breast and feel her tiny hand wrap around my finger as I sang to her.

Thoughts of Masha brought back memories of Izzy's little nephew and all the other Jewish children who had been hauled away and murdered. So many parents had been robbed. I couldn't believe I was so fortunate, that God had spared my son. For the first time in my life, I had hopes of becoming a *bubbe* one day. The thought of grandchildren in my arms helped me finally fall asleep.

It took a week for us to get our nights and days straight. We finally stopped sleeping during the day. We had lost all sense of time. Our world seemed almost right again the night Uncle Itzhak called us together. He and I had talked earlier that day, and he told me we were going to do something special that evening. We were going to celebrate the Sabbath. We had much to be thankful for.

Mrs. Paskauskas let me borrow a couple of candle stubs and a towel to use as a tablecloth. I also asked her to leave the loaf of bread whole instead of slicing it as she usually did. Once she had brought those things to us, she quietly left. The barn door was standing open a little, and we could see the streaks of sunlight beginning to fade into evening. Uncle Itzhak motioned for us to gather around him and said, "This is a *Shabbat* of special significance. We have survived just like Jews have survived for centuries before us and will do so for centuries after us. We're alive because we refused to give in or deny our faith and because we helped one another.

"Each of us was spared for a purpose, that we should forever remember those who have perished — shall their memory be blessed — that we should always be proud of who we are and what we believe in."

I waited until Itzhak looked at me to signal the lighting of the candles. This done, the women moved closer to the table, which was really a bench, lifted our hands above the flames and began to say the prayers to usher in the Sabbath. After Uncle Itzhak made a prayer over the bread, he broke it and ate the first piece before passing the rest around.

The boys sat on either side of the bench. Jacob and Jay had spread out their comforters so that Emmanuel and David could sit close to them. They had all grown quiet and sat very still. It was the first time they had stopped moving since our liberation. Their eyes seemed to grow rounder and bigger as they watched the flames. We had been in the dark for so long that to see light was almost hypnotizing to them. Even as children, they understood this was a holy time. Neither of them moved or said a word until the prayers were offered and the food was passed around.

Itzhak took time to say *kaddish* for the ones who were lost and to pray for the safety of those still living. I have been in many *Shabbat* services before and since, but none quite so meaningful. At last, we were Jews again, able to live and worship in the open. It might have been held in a barn, but to me it was a beautiful banquet. I went to sleep that night thinking of my mother and her mother and all the times I had seen them pray over candles. Somehow, I felt their presence. The feeling stayed with me far into the night.

14

Izzy Returns to Kovno

T he first thing Izzy wanted to do the next morning was follow behind the Red Army and see what had happened in the ghetto. I begged him not to go.

"Izzy," I said, "stay with me and Jay and the others for a while longer. You'll be in danger, even now. I am still so afraid. Even though we're free, you know there are Nazis everywhere. And, you know they will kill any Jew they can."

Try as I might, I couldn't remember what it was like to be free. I was afraid of every shadow, every noise, the sudden appearance of a chicken or even hearing Rexxyx bark. I couldn't stop jumping from every sound or thinking someone would suddenly come running out of the woods and shoot us. I'd been afraid for so long, and now Izzy was talking of leaving me. I didn't want to be without him watching over us. Izzy stayed for several days, but it wasn't just to appease me. He knew it was dangerous to venture out while the fighting was still so close.

During that time, he would turn to me intermittently and

ask, "I was not human and how can it be that I am human again? Am I the same man, the free man? How could I be free? It's unbelievable!" Every time he asked me, I'd just throw my arms around his neck and say, "Yes, Izzy darling, God spared us, and we're alive because of you and Uncle Itzhak."

"You left out the Paskauskas family," he said once, teasing me a little.

Evidence of the war still surrounded us. As we were bathing, Russian planes had flown overhead. One came so low, I was afraid he might start shooting.

"Quick, Raja, grab a towel and throw it to me," I had said. "What do you think that crazy pilot is doing up there, spying on us? He must think this is a free show."

Raja threw me the towel and grabbed one to cover herself. The plane was so close that we could actually see the pilot and co-pilot in the cockpit. Raja and I exchanged fearful glances at first while we stood huddled together. After the plane passed over, we both started laughing at the same time.

"Isn't it crazy?" Raja asked. "We've had no privacy for years and now all of a sudden we're modest again. I guess that means we're almost normal."

We were liberated on July 14, 1944. It took several days to realize that freedom didn't mean life was going to be good. Slowly, slowly, the misery, pain, and hopelessness began to sink in. We were no more than paupers. We had nothing but our hands to fend with and didn't know how we'd survive, but at least we were all alive. It didn't seem possible.

We had been liberated about two weeks when Izzy left for Kaunas behind another wave of the Red Army. It was August 1, 1944, just fourteen days shy of three years since the ghetto gates closed behind us.

Moshe and Sheina set out walking almost immediately. They desperately wanted to find their daughter, Sara, to see if she had lived. Lola and his girlfriend left on Leibel's bicycle within a few days. I don't know where they were headed, probably back to Kaunas. Uncle Itzhak's family went back to their home. Raja and Mannie went with them. My uncle was convinced he could return to his farm and take up his old life.

With Izzy gone, too, I was alone again and terrified. All I could think about was that day when my family left the ghetto, and now Izzy had to find out if he had any family members alive. I hoped his mother and sisters were safe, but I dreaded what he might find. I also worried that he might not come back, that he'd be killed far away and I'd never find his body, either. I tried to pass the time with sewing for Mrs. Paskauskas and helping her to make bread. Still, there were so many hours with nothing to do. And the nights were terrible. I kept Jay close to me. My sweater, the comforter, and my son were all I had to call my own in that barn.

After Izzy left, my mind wouldn't leave me alone. I had constant nightmares of my parents being taken away in that awful crowded truck. Sometimes the nightmares didn't wait for dark to show themselves but would reappear in the daytime as well. I found myself hoping that my sister, Minnie, hadn't been raped before she was killed. That had happened to so many young girls. At least they usually shot the boys outright, so maybe Fievel and Chaim, my little brothers, didn't suffer too much. Maybe they were even in my parents' arms when they died. Or maybe they all drowned together in the Baltic Sea, which is what I heard at first. I don't know. It was the not knowing that was so maddening. If I could just find a place where they were buried, I could move their bodies to a Jewish cemetery and say *kaddish* for them. I tried not to think about it. Every time I did, the headaches returned.

It was about thirty or forty kilometers from the Paskauskas farm to Kovno Ghetto. Izzy was gone for almost two weeks.

Jay and I were so happy to see him coming down the road that we ran to meet him.

At first, all he could do was weep. Every time he started to tell me what he found, he would begin to cry again. It was terrible to see him broken that way. He had been so strong for all of us during the last few years, but now he didn't seem to have any strength left. He finally managed to tell me how he ran with all his power to reach the ghetto after he learned the Red Army had liberated Kaunas. I don't know how Izzy ran that far on foot, although he did say a Red Army truck with soldiers in it allowed him to ride with them for a few kilometers.

Between wiping his eyes and blowing his nose, Izzy described what he had encountered.

"All we could see on the highway were soldiers from the Red Army," he began. "The only other person I saw was one German soldier at the edge of a forest. I could see him from my vantage point on the truck bed. It was actually funny. That 'no good' started running away from me. For once a Nazi was afraid of me."

Izzy's hopes for his family were dashed; Kaunas was deserted, except for Russian soldiers.

He continued, "There was nobody there. The streets and houses were all empty, with doors standing open. The only ones alive were soldiers. I ran across the bridge into Slobodka where the ghetto had been. The gate was standing wide open there, too. Everywhere I looked, it was just burned houses and bodies. Some of them were still smoldering. Do you remember where Monge's house was? He lived near your parents' home."

"Where you thought your mother and sisters were hiding?" I asked.

"Yes. It took me a long time to get to their house because I had to keep stepping over bodies. When I finally got there, the home was all burned out just like the rest. I jumped into what I thought was the basement, their hiding place. I looked around and dug in the ground thinking I might find some clue, something to identify them like a piece of paper, but there was nothing. I was so desperate. I felt like a wild animal and just started running, looking for someone alive."

Izzy began to cry again, which nearly tore me to pieces. Finally I said, "Come, Izzy, darling, let me fix you something to eat. You can finish telling me tomorrow."

Izzy seemed almost in a trance and didn't even respond to what I had said to him. He looked straight ahead and continued describing what was left of the place we used to call home.

"A few steps farther I found the Waintraubs' basement. It was also a hiding place. There were charred bodies lying at the front entrance, and I recognized one of the men. It was Fievel Sydrer's uncle. He was an accountant who came with his family in 1939 when the Nazis took Poland. You remember Fievel, don't you? They were such a nice family. Fievel's uncle was lying in front of his wife and their teenage daughter, like he was trying to protect them to the end. There were around twenty other bodies there, all burned alive where they had been trapped. I couldn't recognize anyone else.

"Then I saw an old Lithuanian woman poking around with a stick, not paying any attention to the bodies. I screamed at the old bitch, 'Murderer, what are you doing? Get off that holy place! This is no place for you! I'm going to lock you up.'

"She looked at me like I was crazy and said, 'Why? I'm just looking. There were a lot of Jews that had a lot of gold and maybe I'll find it.'

"I told her to run before I tore her to pieces. She saw that I was very serious and kind of wild. She threw a sack over her shoulder and ran away. I don't know what she had in the sack."

"Izzy, I don't know how you stood it. Why didn't you just come back to the farm?"

"I had to stay," he continued. "I hoped I might find something that belonged to one of my family members, but I couldn't walk without finding more bodies. There was only death. I just kept running around like a wild man turning over the bodies. I just wanted to find one person alive. Finally I gave up. I wanted to bury the dead, but there were too many and I didn't have a shovel. I needed help to do that. I was so tired from all the walking that I could barely stand up."

My heart broke as I listened to my dear Izzy. Here was a man who had done everything to try to save others, yet his own family had all been destroyed. Now we were both orphans. All of Izzy's siblings were dead, as were most of mine. I wondered how we could stand this much pain.

Izzy went on, "I was desperate to find somewhere to stay away from those corpses, so I finally went to the ammunition factory where I used to work."

"Isn't that where the Wilsons lived?" I asked. "Weren't they the ones who used to give you food and let you listen to the short wave radio?"

"They're the ones," Izzy said, nodding his head and barely smiling.

Then he began remembering the ghetto years and his face darkened again.

"I used to hear the Archbishop of Canterbury on the Wilsons' short wave radio. He appealed again and again for someone to help the Jews. He also appealed to the pope over and over, but the pope turned a deaf ear."

"Yes, Izzy, I remember how you used to tell us the news. I remember how excited we got the night we heard about the uprising at the Warsaw Ghetto."

Izzy continued his story.

"After the Wilsons got over the excitement of learning that we had lived, they gave me a slice of bread with butter and a cup of coffee. I tell you, it was a feast. Then they started telling me that there in the factory, my friend Mendelson had just been killed a few days earlier."

Mendelson worked with Izzy in one of the brigades. He was a young man, strong, tall, and very handsome, only twenty-four years old. Wilson told Izzy that Mendelson ran into the ammunition factory to hide the last day before the ghetto was liquidated. He thought all of the Germans had already retreated, but there was one left. The Nazi discovered Mendelson, and even though Mendelson begged for his life, that madman shot and killed him in the last minutes before the liberation. Mr. Wilson buried him in the Jewish cemetery.

Izzy told me he stayed with the Wilsons overnight and went back to Kaunas the next day to see if he could find a place for Jay and me to live. He described walking by his parents' home.

"Here was the place where I was raised in Slobodka. It looked like our home was standing with its head down weeping. I thought I heard it speaking to me as I passed. There was my youth spent with my two younger sisters. There was the place where my mother had done all her fine sewing and where my father used to come home for dinner from the brewery. Here is the place where you and I lived behind my parents' home, where Jay ran back and forth from our house to my parents' home. It was the place where I had spent all my life from the age of five until we left the ghetto. There, just three years ago, I saw Meir Abel Meller with the *Torah* being chased by the Lithuanian Home Guard and the Nazis."

Izzy began to sob so loudly that I couldn't stand it. I took him by the hands, pulled him to his feet and said, "Come, darling, let's walk a little into the sunlight. It will help you feel better."

Izzy stopped crying only briefly. He seemed compelled to get all the agony out of himself. After a brief pause, he sat back down and began again.

"I started saying over and over to my family members, 'Where are you? Where are you?' And then I suddenly remembered my sister Dvoira's furniture. She gave it to the Lithuanian woman who lived in the first-floor apartment of my parents' home. You remember her, don't you? She's the one who protected us before we were forced into the ghetto. After we moved into the ghetto, I heard the woman had moved to Krevos Street. While I was trying to find her house, I had to go through Laisves Aleja, 'the Street of the Free.' When I thought of that, I began to feel better. That name was describing me. I was free."

Izzy said he finally discovered the house he was looking for, but an old woman, about eighty years old, was living there. She must have moved in after the house became vacant.

"I knocked and knocked. Finally, the old woman stuck her head out the window of the third-floor apartment," Izzy said. "I described Dvoira's furniture and told her I had come to reclaim it. When she finally opened the door, I walked in and locked the door behind me. Then I took the key. I told the old woman that I would take care of the house and she didn't have to worry. I promised that no harm would come to her and she could continue to live on the third floor as long as she wanted. I could have thrown her out, but I thought of my own mother and hoped someone was kind to her before she died."

"But, did you find the furniture?" I asked. "Was it broken into pieces like ours?"

"I'll get to that in a minute. First I have to tell you about all the food I found. It was unbelievable. The Germans, who had been living there, left coffee that they didn't finish. Butter, cake, and eggs were still on the table. Whoever was there had just started eating breakfast and they left it all and ran. I opened the closet and found smoked ham, salami, flour and sugar. There was enough food for a family to live there for three months while the ghetto inmates were starving to death on the next street."

"But, where was Dvoira's furniture?" I asked again.

"I found it in the bedroom, every piece was in perfect condition. I sat down in one of the chairs right away. It gave me comfort to touch something that had at least belonged to my family. I know Dvoira would want us to have her furniture. I moved it onto the first floor of that house so it would be in place when you and Jay arrived.

"When I went back toward the center of town, there was a group of Jews gathered there. It was so terrible to see them. There were about ten of them. They weren't saying a word but were either just standing or sitting. They were in shock, I think, and didn't know what to do with all the pain. Everywhere I turned, there was misery and everyone crying because they had lost their families, and so many of their homes had been destroyed. I gathered a few of the men together, and we went to the Red Army and told them we wanted to bury the dead who were strewn about in the ghetto."

"How did you and all the others have the strength to do that much work?" I asked.

"The Red Army gave us a group of Germans with a Russian soldier as a guard. We went into the ghetto and buried all the dead in the cemetery. I never thought I'd live to see the day that Germans would bury Jews."

"What did you do after that?"

"I waited a day or two because I wanted to see if other Jews would come. I just couldn't leave some of the survivors. Many of them clung to me because I was younger than they. Some of them were so distraught that they didn't even remember to eat. Gradually, more Jews came out of hiding until there were about thirty or forty altogether. They were coming from the woods a few at a time, where they had served with the partisans or from other hiding places. They looked like walking skeletons. Some were so crippled they could hardly walk. Everybody tried to help each other. They all found themselves a living place finally, most of them staying with complete strangers. That's when I decided it was safe to return for you and Jay."

15

Leaving Safety

S omehow Izzy managed to secure a horse and wagon before he returned for Jay and me. The wagon was in disrepair, and the horse was very skinny, just like us, but Mr. Paskauskas came to our rescue once again. He had an old wagon wheel that he and Izzy used to replace the one that was about to fall off the wagon, and he also gave Izzy extra grain and hay for the horse to try and build up its strength.

We made plans to leave the farm in about a week. I had such mixed emotions. I knew we couldn't stay with the Paskauskases forever, but I really hated to leave, especially since I had begun to enjoy myself a little and not be afraid for the first time in so many years. And Jay was having such a wonderful time with Stasuk, even though Jay was about eight years younger. Stasuk never complained when Jay followed him everywhere. He would make a special effort to come and get Jay in the mornings before he chopped wood. Jay would often just sit nearby on a tree stump with his chin in his hands and watch Stasuk as he split the kindling and cut the wood that Mrs. Paskauskas needed for cooking. Sometimes he would help Stasuk stack the wood or pick up the wood chips and add them to the kindling pile.

He also enjoyed watching Stasuk milk the cow, something that always fascinated him. After the milking was done, Stasuk would let Jay hold onto the handle of the pail and help bring the milk to the house, as if he were somehow responsible for the work. Stasuk seemed to delight in doing anything that included him. In the afternoons, when Stasuk had finished his chores, he would often play his fiddle. While he was playing and tapping his foot, Jay would jump and spin around as if he were dancing. Sometimes he got dizzy from the spinning and would laugh just as he fell down. It was wonderful to see him enjoying life and being a little boy again instead of having to be afraid, hide and remain silent.

I could hardly get used to the sun coming up again. It felt really strange the first morning I woke with a semblance of hope. That day I remember wondering what Izzy would do for a living. I also gave some thought to how Jay would need to attend Hebrew school. Because we had been in the ghetto and in hiding for such a long time, Jay had never attended formal school more than a few days. He did learn his numbers in the potato hole when he and Izzy were killing and counting lice, but you couldn't count that as real education. And he seemed so interested in what Uncle Itzhak was teaching his two sons those few weeks when everyone was together just before our liberation. He would have to work really hard to make up for lost time, especially with his Hebrew studies. He had only a few years before his bar mitzvah.

I think Jay was the main reason I survived those terrible years. Without him, I'm sure I would have given up hope and died, as so many other parents did after their children were taken. In the ghetto, he always ran out of the house to meet me when I came home from work. I lived for that moment every day, when he would put his little arms around my knees and tell me that he loved me. It seems I drew strength from him instead of the reverse. It was hard for me to realize that those dark days were finally behind us.

Mrs. Paskauskas and I didn't talk a lot. She was a quiet person, like her husband. When she did say something, it was in short sentences, as if she had to pay for each word. We talked once about the similarity of our losses. Of course, her first husband's death, like my father's, was natural, but it was still a big loss for her, especially since she had Stasuk to look after at such a young age. She, like my mother, had been fortunate to find another good and kindhearted man who not only became her husband, but a father to her child. I thought about the irony of that some days, how both Vaclovas Paskauskas and Chananya Butrimowitz had been stepfathers but that it didn't seem to matter to them or to the children they loved.

After much thought, I decided to ask Mrs. Paskauskas about their decision to help us. It was such a personal question, but one day my curiosity got the best of me. I can still see her standing by the cupboard near the window with her hands in a bowl mixing flour and milk, her apron tied loosely around her waist.

"Ona, I've really been thinking about something for a long time," I started. "I hope you don't mind, but I wondered why you and your husband took such a terrible chance to help us."

"Well," she started, "we did think about it and wondered what we would do if the Germans came looking for you."

"That must have been a really hard decision for you," I interrupted, unable to hold the words back any longer. I had wanted to say it for a long time, but had been hesitant. "When we were in the potato hole, sometimes Izzy and I prayed that you wouldn't be harmed. We knew that all of you, even

Stasuk, would be killed if we were discovered. Since you're Catholic, we wondered why us, why perfect strangers?"

Ona wiped her hands off on her apron, brushed the brown hair back from her eyes and sat down beside me on the bench. She was a small woman, not much taller than I was, and had beautiful eyes with long dark eyelashes. When she smiled, which was often now, her eyes seemed to dance. She didn't say anything for a few minutes, just watched as I hemmed and inspected my sewing.

Finally, she said, "Sometimes I wondered myself, Eta. I really did. I was terrified every time someone came to the door or whenever Rexxyx barked," she added, shivering a little at the memory. "He only barked at strangers, and I think he could sense danger better than we could," she said. "Even the nights were no better. Vaclovas and I used to talk in the evenings, too, after Stasuk was asleep. There would have been no escape, only death for all of us, had you been discovered."

She paused for another brief moment and shyly put her arm around my shoulders and hugged me ever so lightly. "It was by the grace of God that any of us survived," she said, with her voice trailing off.

I had always understood that their lives were in the balance, but hearing her say it took my breath away. I couldn't say a word for fear that I'd completely lose my composure. When the silence continued for another minute or two, she started talking again.

"I think it all began a long time before Marchuk brought you here," she continued. "Vaclovas came home from going to the market one day. He didn't say anything for a long time, just sat at the table with his head in his hands. He wouldn't even eat. I finally asked him what was wrong.

"He told me he had watched some Jewish children being marched away from the Kovno Ghetto, and he thought they were going to be killed. He said there were Nazis everywhere. The children were being forced to march in rows, like a little regiment. The women inside the ghetto were screaming and crying. He said the children and their guards passed in front of his wagon. He told me how those children looked starved, dressed in rags, and many didn't have shoes. Some of them were so weak that they kept falling down. They didn't say a word, just looked at him. He said he couldn't stop seeing their eyes."

Ona hesitated for a minute and wiped her own eyes before going on.

"I'd never seen him like that," she explained. "Vaclovas said the children seemed to walk without making a sound, like they were already dead. Some of the older ones were carrying the young ones. My husband didn't know what to do. What could he do? All he had was a horse and a wagon. He said he kept seeing little boys about three years old, the same age as Stasuk when we were married. I tell you it was terrible. He said he felt so helpless."

She paused again, as if trying to find just the right words. Just then I realized that we had lived in close proximity to each other about half a year, and this was the most I had ever heard her speak.

"Not too long after Vaclovas told me about the children," Ona continued, "Marchuk came to see us. He said that Itzhak Kalamitsky had some family members — just three — who needed a place to stay. Vaclovas came into the house, and we talked about it with Stasuk for a little while. Stasuk encouraged us to take you in. When he learned that he could help save a little boy, regardless of whether he was Jewish or not, he was ready to help. He loved children so much and had always wanted a little brother. Maybe that was his way of finding one. I don't know.

"Vaclovas and I prayed about it, too. We didn't understand

why it had to be so hard for Jews. The only Jew we actually knew was your Uncle Itzhak, and he had always been such a generous man, always willing to help anyone, Christians and Jews alike. We couldn't help but think of our faith and believed we had an obligation to other human beings. Either way, you were here in no time, and look how it has turned out."

Suddenly smiling again, she added, "The first time I saw Jay, I knew we had done the right thing."

Ona stood up after that and returned to her bread making. A few minutes later, she looked at me as if she'd had an afterthought. "We wanted to help Itzhak," she added, "but we didn't bargain for all the others that came later."

"I know," I said quietly, thinking of how hard it must have been on her to try and make bread every day for thirteen of us, plus her own family. "It's a miracle," I said. "We owe you our lives."

Neither of us talked for a while. I just sat at the kitchen table and continued my mending while she finished forming the loaves. It was warm, and we could leave the front door open as she baked. That way the heat and the fumes from the hearth could escape, since there was no chimney in their house. I couldn't help but think about how poor they were as I sat there looking at that dirt floor and the one bed the three of them shared. They barely had enough to eat themselves. I wondered if other Jews had been spared because of other good Catholics like them, people who were willing to risk everything for another human being.

Ona and I would laugh sometimes as we watched Jay playing with Rexxyx. We would bet each other whether Jay or the dog would be first to discover the hen eggs each morning. They used to go scavenging for the eggs inside the barn before we went into hiding. For the two of them, it seemed there was no break in time. When we were liberated, they just took up where they left off. I don't know which one enjoyed the game more, the dog or Jay. The only difference was that now Jay would carefully bring the eggs into the house, holding them just out of Rexxyx's reach in his shirtfront, so as not to break them.

Now that he wasn't starving, Jay could understand that we'd use the eggs for cooking and they'd go further. That was hard for him to realize until I used a few eggs to make cookies one day. He was so overjoyed that he almost choked from shoving several cookies into his mouth at the same time. I'm sure it was hard for him to realize that the food wouldn't run out now. At times, it was even harder for me to believe it.

Izzy came inside the barn one evening and said we were leaving the next day. He could see the immediate apprehension on my face. Before I could protest, he said, "It's time, Eta. Time we went back to Kaunas." He said it rather sternly, too. "I hope that old woman hasn't left the house. As long as someone is there, the furniture should be safe. You'll like the house. I promise. There's plenty of space. Jay can have his own room."

"Well, space is one thing, Izzy," I replied. "But, how can I go back where my parents used to live? How can I walk down the street where my sisters and brothers and I grew up and went to school? They're all dead. Murdered. Everything is gone. How can I bear it? I have nothing but a few rubles from my family."

"And do you think I have any more?" he asked. "At least you have rubles. They're worth more than furniture. What's the difference? Neither rubles nor furniture can replace our families. Don't you see that it doesn't matter what we don't have? We must go on. You can't just keep crying all the time. It's not good for you and it's not good for Jay, either."

His words were so cutting that I felt like I was being flogged. I couldn't stand the tone of his voice, which was uncharacteristically harsh. I just turned my back to him and cried harder.

"Oh, Eta, don't you see," Izzy said, his voice becoming tender toward me again. "There are only three of us, but three is a family. We have to look forward. Nothing can be done about the past. We must plan for Jay's future. It will be better, you'll see. Time will help."

"Izzy, Izzy, I'm sorry," I said, hugging him very tightly around the waist. "Sometimes I can't be as strong as you. I just can't help it, but I'll try. Maybe I'll feel better once we're back in Kaunas and I have my own house and can cook in my own kitchen again. That would be so nice. I could get busy making Jay some new clothes, and maybe Uncle Itzhak and his family will decide to come and be with us. I miss him so much."

"I do, too," Izzy said. "I'm really afraid of what he'll find when he returns to the farm. He thinks he can live the way he did before the war. But I don't think that's possible. If he were with us, perhaps I could help him now. We owe him so much."

Izzy suddenly pushed me away and held me at arm's length. He looked right into my eyes and said very matter-of-factly, "We're going to have very different lives now. Come on. Help me put a few things into this bag. I got it from Mrs. Paskauskas. She has already put a pot, a bowl or two for us and some honey for Jay in here. Just look," he said, holding out the sack for me to peer inside.

"I know one thing," he said with a grin on his face. "I'll bet she is going to miss your sewing. You'll feel better once we're in Kaunas. I know you will. Let's plan to leave first thing in the morning."

I woke up dreading the departure. We would be trading the only safe haven we'd known for so long for the charred ruins of homes and factories. And, there, it would be a daily reminder that my family was gone and was never coming back. Where would we get shoes or boots now that my father was dead? Who would make the *lokschn kugel* my mother used to make for the holidays? Hers was so good I never bothered to learn the recipe. And, who would attend Jay's bar mitzvah? Yes, we had been forced to live like animals in a stall, but at least we were all alive then and together in the ghetto. Now there were only three. The loneliness overwhelmed me.

"Eta, Eta, don't cry," Izzy said gently, putting his arms around me. "Where is my *Tzipke* Fire, my 100,000 litas woman? I know she's hiding in there somewhere," he said, carefully wiping the tears away. "I know we won't have everyone, but we'll have each other. I've got a little surprise for you. I was waiting until we got to Kaunas to tell you."

Curious about his words, I looked up and said, "Tell me now, if it will make me feel better."

"Just before I left Kaunas, I found Moshe and Sheina."

(left to right) Sheina, Sara, Liuba and Moshe Gillman (circa 1949).

Courtesy Sheina Gillman and Dr. Sara Pilamm

Although fearful, I asked, "Oh, Izzy, did they find Sara?"

"Not only did they find her, now she holds onto her mother's hand and won't go anywhere without her. It seems they had quite a time convincing her that she was their child."

"What do you mean?" I asked. "She wasn't with the Christian couple that long."

"I know, but they didn't think Moshe and Sheina were coming back. They had done a pretty good job of convincing Sara that she was a Christian and that she belonged to them. In fact, when Sara first saw Moshe and Sheina, she called them 'Jews' and refused to go with them. She even told them she wasn't a Jew, and if they had been her real parents, they wouldn't have gone away and left her."

"That must have been terrible to hear," I said.

"Moshe was so overcome by her words that he fainted dead away, but finally Sara remembered the red and white polka-dot dress Sheina was wearing. Now she won't leave her mother's side. Sheina is excited about us coming back. Now get ready."

It was really hard to say goodbye. I think Stasuk actually cried after he hugged Jay. Izzy attempted to thank Mr. Paskauskas, but he just waved away the words. After all, how could Izzy express a debt we could never repay? Mrs. Paskauskas had baked an extra loaf of her good brown bread for us to have for the trip. She wrapped it in a paper sack and brought it out and handed it to me at the last minute. We embraced without speaking.

Just as Izzy was helping me onto the wagon, Stasuk lifted Jay, set him on the seat beside me and quickly backed away.

Finally, Ona reached her hand up to touch my arm and managed to say, "God be with you," and I said, "God be with you as well."

Izzy flicked the reins, and the horse started down the road. Jay turned around and waved until they were out of sight.

I'll never forget Stasuk standing there in the sunshine with Rexxyx sitting beside him. It was a far cry from the way we had arrived, in the dead of winter and at night, not knowing whether we would ever live to see another springtime.

16

Starting Over

I zzy was right. The house he had found was big, and I did
feel more at home, especially with Dvoira's furniture. It
gave me comfort just to dust it. The house had belonged
to our former friend, but I surmised she must have abandoned
it when the ghetto was burned. Izzy quickly found work at
the Prom Corporation, which was really a group of cartels
where he had worked previously.

We hadn't been in Kaunas very long before we heard from
Uncle Itzhak. When my uncle returned to his farm, he found
his house and barn ransacked, most of the furniture and all
the farm implements missing and another farmer working
his fields. It would have been impossible to start over again
with only his two hands. Besides that, he had a family to feed.
Izzy managed to find a truck to use and brought them to stay
with us for a while. Izzy was able to find a position for Uncle
Itzhak as the manager of the flour cartel, one of the groups
that he supervised.

Before long, Itzhak and Ida got a separate apartment and

settled down into their new life as best they could. Raja took Mannie back to Zosli and then came to Kaunas where she taught school for a while. She managed to get them to Poland and then to Germany where they stayed for almost two years at a displaced persons' camp. Amazingly, she eventually got to South Africa and reclaimed her husband's property. I couldn't imagine the kind of courage it took for her to strike off on her own to another country, with Mannie so little, but courage always came naturally to Raja. She wore it like a coat.

It was hard starting all over again, and we had to get used to the fact that the Soviet government owned everything, even our personal lives it seemed. We were adjusting as well

Itzhak and Ida Kalamitsky (1950).

Courtesy Virginia Holocaust Museum

Raja and Emmanuel Shlom (1947).

as we could, but one day Izzy came running into the house. He was so excited I couldn't understand him at first. When I did, I just sat down, unable to believe my ears.

"What do you mean, you have to go into the Red Army? That's insane," I finally got out.

"Here it is," Izzy said, holding up a paper for me to see. "This is the announcement saying I have to serve in the Red Army. Here I have survived the ghetto and lived in a hole, and they're going to kill me at the front?"

It was too much for me to take in. I was speechless. Izzy didn't say anything else for a few minutes. After finally composing himself, Izzy sat down beside me and took my hands in his. He finally said, "Eta. I'll do something. Don't worry. Be quiet now. I need to think."

The next day Izzy spoke with his supervisor, Stacis Mickevicius, who was in the Red Army, and was probably a Communist. He told Izzy that they would list him as a dispatcher, a raw-material supplier, and too important to release for army duty. Mickevicius contacted the army and asked that a deferment letter be sent to Izzy stating that Izzy was free from being drafted. I didn't sleep a wink until that letter arrived, but finally it came. Once again, we were safe from harm.

Izzy eventually worked with other men to set up cartels for candy and cookie production, as well as others making everything from textiles to suitcases. Izzy was the dispatcher for nine or ten of them, as well as the flour mill, where he found the job for my Uncle Itzhak. Izzy was doing all that he could to help the other Jews. Some of them were so pitiful. He told me about Meir Krieger, who had once been in the textile business.

"Eta," Izzy said one evening. "I think I'm finally making some headway with Meir. He is talking a bit now, since I found him a position in the textile cartel. I hoped being busy would occupy his mind and he'd snap out of his depression. It's been about a month or so now. He still gets upset and cries sometimes, and I don't blame him. Do you remember how his wife was killed in the big selection in October of 1941?"

"Wasn't she the one who was sick in bed and the Nazis just barged into their house and shot her, right in front of her husband?" I asked.

"Yes, that's the woman. Meir has his son left, but he is still having a rough time."

Suddenly Izzy stopped talking and took me into his arms and kissed me full in the mouth, which was something he usually did in private. It shocked me.

"Eta, I don't know what I'd do if that had happened to you," he said so tenderly it melted my heart. "Do you know how much I love you?"

"Yes, Izzy," I said quietly at first. "I know how valuable

I am. Remember, I'm your fire, your 100,000 litas woman."
That made Izzy laugh, something we always tried to do for
each other with a little teasing. Sometimes we went for days
without laughing, but we were getting better at it lately.

Our lives began to take on a quiet routine, and I was
beginning to go out more and more. I took Jay for a walk in
the sunshine each day. It helped me bear the sadness I felt
over my family and Masha.

Most of Izzy's work centered on the candy and cookie
cartels. Just about every day, he would come home and tell
me that more female survivors had arrived.

"They're the most pitiful creatures you've ever seen," Izzy
said, trying to describe them. "Some of them have had their
heads shaved, and others have teeth falling out or no teeth at
all. Their health is deplorable. They've come looking for their
families the same way I did, but no one is here."

"How will they survive?" I asked. "They must find jobs.
You know what the Russians say: 'The one that doesn't work
doesn't eat.' Today several of them came to our back door.
They heard you were working at the cartels and hoped I
could help them. I gave them some soup."

"I know," Izzy said. "They told me how kind you were.
They're so pitiful. There's no question whether or not to
help them."

"But how can they work if they're so weak?" I asked.

"It's not just that. Food will strengthen them, but there's
such bitterness. Today there was even a fistfight. I finally put
the Lithuanian women in the candy section and the Jewish
ones in the bakery with the cookies."

"Why are you hiring Lithuanians after what they did to
us?" I demanded to know.

"I don't have a choice. My boss keeps saying, 'Look, Ipp.
You'd better get used to this regime. Everybody is equal in
communism, and you have to take in everybody.' "

"Well, Izzy, we have a little money now, since we sold your family home. Thank goodness it was outside the ghetto and didn't get burned. We'll be all right for a while. Can you resign and find another job?" I asked.

"I tried to do that today, but my boss only laughed at me. He said, 'What do you mean resign? You're living under a Communist regime and you can't do anything you want.' He said I'd better start paying more attention to production instead of thinking about resigning."

The German surrender on May 8, 1945, didn't really change our everyday lives that much, but at least we didn't have to worry about being gunned down by Nazis any more or live in a hole. What a blessing to be able to lay my head down at night and go to sleep without fear. I knew we were free, but it was still difficult, especially to walk through the streets of Kaunas and know that only a fraction of people would ever be accounted for. We had no choice but to carry on and do the best we could. Slowly, slowly I began to lose my fear of letting Jay out of my sight.

Several months later — I think it was in the fall of 1945 — a notice was posted at the Prom Corporation stipulating that every worker had to go into the woods and cut wood, or find it any way he could. Each person was expected to provide three meters: one meter for himself, one for the government, and one meter for the cartel. By then, Izzy had sixty workers at the cookie and candy cartels. Of that number, forty were Jewish women still recuperating from the concentration camps. Some of them were still so weak that they could barely stand. To send them into the woods where Nazis in hiding could catch them would mean certain death. After a day or two, Izzy told me he had come up with another plan.

"I decided we would make a big to-do about the day of liberation, the day the Russian Army moved into Lithuania. We would celebrate and give each worker a kilo of candy.

I figured they could take the candy and sell it on the black market, and with the money they could buy wood."

Sure enough, the wood quota was gathered very quickly. It was even announced on the loudspeakers that Ipp's workers had fulfilled their quota of wood. They made a public hero out of Izzy. No more than a week had gone by before Izzy came running into our house again, just as upset as when he received his induction papers for the Russian Army.

"Eta, we have to flee. Pack a few things and be ready to leave quickly."

"Pack for what? Go where?" I wanted to know.

"They are announcing my name on the loudspeakers again, but this time they're saying that I'm an enemy of the Soviets. They've checked my books and found where I gave the candy to the workers to trade for wood. They're going to put it on the radio. Mickevicius said they'll send me to Siberia, and we should run for our lives. He said he would act as if he didn't know anything. Maybe we can pretend to be Poles and get out of Russia. I heard that anyone born in Lodz, Warsaw, and a few other places can now go back to Poland. We'll use your maiden name. A lot of Poles are named Butrimowitz."

The next day Izzy bribed a truck mechanic to come to Kaunas for us. We had already said goodbye to Uncle Itzhak's family. When we were sure it was safe, we slipped through the back bedroom window and ran to the truck. We all escaped to Vilna and stayed in an attic, waiting for the truck driver to bring us forged Polish papers that Izzy paid dearly for. After a week, we knew the scoundrel had just taken our money and would never return. Somehow Izzy arranged a truck ride for us to a little town where the railroad passed through. He located a room for us and, although he was scared to death of the Communists, set out to find out who was in charge of the train station. Later that night he told me what happened.

"I found the manager," Izzy said. "He offered to trade Polish papers for my boots."

He continued, "The next transportation train leaves in four days. I have rented a small house right beside the station. The manager said we'd be safe there. I think it's because I told him we have a little boy. He even offered to let Jay go ice skating on the lake with his son."

"But, Izzy, Jay has never gone ice skating. I don't know. We've never seen this man before. How can you be so sure you can trust him?"

"I just have a feeling he's OK, Eta. How could I refuse him? He said that his little boy didn't have any playmates and that he'd be sure to take care of Jay, just like his own son. I didn't see where I had a choice."

I agreed reluctantly, but as soon as Jay stepped onto the pond the ice broke and he fell into the lake. The station manager couldn't swim, but his son pulled Jay out. We dried him off and put him to bed. I wouldn't let Jay out of my sight after that, no matter what Izzy said.

We went to the station at the appointed time and were really lucky. Izzy was afraid there might be another bribe, although he had provided a bottle of whiskey just the day before as a precaution. We had to ride in a cattle car, but we didn't care, as long as we were leaving. We were some of the first ones to board the train. We arrived at Warsaw on Christmas night, 1945. We then had to take a truck to Lodz. We were able to find a hotel room but had to share it with several other Jews.

We had just settled down when the police barged into the room to arrest Izzy. It had been reported that we were from Russia, not Poland, as Izzy had been saying. I tried to keep Jay calm as Izzy bribed the officers. After they left, we escaped right behind them and found a place in a nearby synagogue. We slept on a big long table in the rear of the synagogue for five nights and hid during the day. Izzy believed we should change our plans at this point and try to get across the Czechoslovakian border. Once again, I felt like I was in no man's land.

17

Escape Across Borders – 1945

I t was an awful, rainy day when we were crowded inside the back of yet another truck with yet another bunch of strangers. We were all trying to get past the Czechoslovakian border police, but they were detaining everybody, asking questions and threatening to lock up every other person in line. I think they went easy on me because I had Jay. Izzy and a rabbi, who was standing with a group near us, took the brunt of the harassment. There were two men doing the interrogation, one with a small build and a second really tall man whose face was so red and veined it looked as if he had been drunk for years. Unhappy with Izzy's answers, the two men started punching him and pushing Izzy out the door. He managed to yell encouragement.

"Eta. Don't be afraid. I'll be all right. Just take care of Jay."

They started hollering at Izzy again and kept pushing him. They grabbed the rabbi as well. Although I could barely stand to see it, I watched until Izzy was out of sight.

Once he was gone, I had my hands full trying to distract Jay. Izzy was released several hours later and told me what had happened.

"At first I thought they were going to kill us, but then I realized they were just looking for money," he said. "They jammed their hands inside my coat pockets and found a few rubles and a train ticket from Kaunas to Vilnius. The ticket seemed to infuriate them."

"The big ugly one said, 'Here's the proof. You say you're a Pole, but here's a ticket in Russian made out to Mr. Ipp. How do you explain that, Mr. so-called Butrimowitz?'

"That's easy," I said. "I assured them that Butrimowitz was a long-established Polish name and that I had bought the coat at an outdoor market in Lodz. I acted angry and insisted they stop pulling on my coat before they ruined it. I told them I had paid a lot of money for it and I didn't want it destroyed. What difference did it make to me what was in the pockets? I was only interested in whether it was warm or not. I said I didn't know anything about the rail-road ticket."

"What made you say that?" I asked.

"I don't know. I just did and I really acted insulted. It must have been convincing, because the ugly one told his partner, 'We're wasting our time. Just see if he has any more money.'

"They found a few more coins inside my trousers and then let me go. When I left, they had started working over that poor rabbi. They had twisted his *tallith* around his neck and were using it to pull him around like an animal. I wanted to help, but I knew if I intervened they would probably kill me for sport. They just laughed when the rabbi tried to explain that his *tallith* was a prayer shawl. The ugly one made some snide remark as I was leaving about sending me back to 'no man's land' because I didn't know where I belonged. He had no idea how accurate he was."

It took a long time to settle Jay down that night. He wanted to sit on Izzy's lap or stay close enough to touch him. Poor thing, he'd been constantly frightened, and there wasn't much we could do about it. But every time Izzy came back to us, Jay got a little more confident that things would be all right. I even overheard him boasting to another child the next day about how smart his daddy was. He was retelling the story about how Izzy was able to get away with his lie about the coat and the train ticket.

We were so weary, and there was still mass confusion. We thought the Jews from Czechoslovakia would come to rescue us, but somehow we were forced to board another train going back to Lodz, along with a lot of other Jews headed for Poland. Even so, we were so lucky. Thank God, Izzy was always looking ahead.

"Eta, I think we can find shelter in the same synagogue at Lodz," he said, trying to reassure me as the train rolled along. "When we were there last week, I heard some men talking about the truck transports to the German border. Maybe we can get to Munich that way."

"I'm so tired of going from place to place," I said. "It doesn't matter to me where we go as long as we can stay for a while."

"It will be all right, Eta," Izzy said in his patient way. "It won't be much longer. I hear there is work in Munich and that some Jews are finding their way to Palestine from there."

Izzy was right, of course. We were welcomed at the same synagogue again and stayed for almost a week. Izzy managed to link up with the Jewish Committee, which had a contact with the Russian Army. Twice a week a Jewish captain crossed the German border to pick up confiscated goods, bringing everything he could get out of Germany: sewing machines, paintings, door handles, anything for resale on the black market. I don't know where he got the things, but in a it seemed justice that some of the Germans were losing their possessions.

We came to Berlin in the middle of the night and got off the truck in the Russian Zone. Since the war had ended, there were different zones occupied by different soldiers, some of whom were willing to help the refugees that came pouring over the borders. As we were climbing down, the captain cautioned us that some weren't so friendly. "You're on your own now. I don't know you, and if anyone asked, I will deny ever seeing you. Take my advice. You should disappear from the face of the earth. The Russian police are prowling around at night, and if they see you, they'll lock you up."

We were terrified and didn't know where to go, so Izzy ran up to the first house we saw and knocked on the door. A big man wearing long-sleeved underwear and pants held up by suspenders answered the door. He began asking Izzy questions in German. Thank God Izzy could speak German fluently and was able to answer him. The man opened the door wider, stepped aside and motioned for us to come inside.

As we were going into the house, Izzy whispered in Lithuanian, "Jay, don't say a word. Pretend you don't understand if he speaks to you." Izzy gave me a stern look. I took it to mean that I was to remain quiet as well.

"Oh, how wonderful to find a man of authority," Izzy said as he straightened up. He was talking really loudly, probably trying to mask the fear he was feeling. Whom had we run into? A policeman. A German policeman. Once inside, we could see his uniform shirt hanging on the back of a chair. Izzy began conversing with the man and learned that although he was now working for the Russians, he didn't appreciate them very much.

"Well," Izzy said. "I can understand that. I'm from Berlin myself, from Hochstrasse 1. Now there's a place where you find very different people, the sort you'd want to have dinner with, not like these unrefined Russians."

That puzzled me for a minute, but I figured Izzy knew what he was doing. In a few minutes, it became clear that Izzy was trying to establish himself as a native Berliner. I'm sure he felt we would be safer that way.

"Would you know any of my relatives?" Izzy asked the man in a nonchalant manner. "My aunt and uncle, name of Neuendorf, lived nearly at the end of Hochstrasse 1. It's a short street."

"No, I don't recall anyone by that name," the man answered, "but I haven't lived there in a good while."

"Well, perhaps you can help us anyway. We are trying to locate the French Zone," Izzy explained. He stopped short of saying that we were really trying to get to the American Zone. I guess he was afraid to press his luck.

For some reason, the man didn't question us further. He seemed very tired, and I suppose he was content with Izzy's German and believed the story Izzy told him. He said he would take us to the train station in the morning. He must have liked children, because he started grinning at Jay and offered him a sandwich and some cookies to eat. Jay didn't say a word but nodded his head to thank him and took the food. He also gave us some food and coffee and was generally very nice, a far cry from other ways we had been treated by Germans. That didn't give us much comfort, though. We were too accustomed to being afraid to relax for even a moment.

When the man stepped outside to use the bathroom, Izzy whispered to Jay that he must answer to the name of Neuendorf, the same as Izzy's relatives.

"Who is that?" Jay asked, looking at Izzy in a quizzical way. "I don't know who I am any more. Every day, I have a different name."

Izzy had to stifle a laugh as he told Jay to be quiet and

finish his sandwich while I spread our coats on the floor for us to sleep on.

The next morning the soldier put on his uniform like a big shot. He didn't even have a gun, only a stick. He took us to the train station and left us at the French Zone. As soon as he was gone, we asked a passerby how to get to the American Zone. Once there, we could breathe easier.

At the American Consulate, we found food and a place to stay. But our hopes of a quick escape were crushed. The next transport to Munich wasn't scheduled for six weeks. Izzy was so nervous; he couldn't even sit down but kept pacing back and forth. Finally, he looked at me, and I could tell he had an idea.

"Eta, I can't just sit around here and wait," he declared. "We could stay six weeks and still be put on a train and end up somewhere else. I'm afraid to wait. Who knows what will happen if we come across any more Russian soldiers. I'm still afraid we'll be sent to Siberia or worse. Come, we'll walk to Munich. At least we can count on our own feet."

Once again, like the vagabonds we had become, we set off, not knowing where the road would take us. The trip from Berlin to Munich was terrible. We had to walk at night through fields, because we were still terrified of getting arrested. The zones were confusing and occupied by different soldiers, all speaking different languages. Thank goodness Izzy could speak several languages. The war was over, but we still didn't feel safe anywhere. Our clothes became filthy again, and our shoes were nothing more than leather pieces tied onto our feet with string. A few times we had to retrace our steps, making our journey even longer. Once more, exhaustion and hunger became all-consuming. Jay got so tired that he just fell down while we were crossing a field one day.

"Jay," I said. "You must get up. We can't rest now. We'll rest tonight."

"I don't care," he said. "Just let them shoot me. I can't walk another step."

I thought my heart would break. Here was my child, ten years old, so tired of life that he was willing to die for a few minutes of rest. I knelt beside him and tried talking, but no amount of persuasion would work. From then on, Izzy and I had to take turns carrying Jay until he regained his strength.

Our meager food supply ran out quickly, but we managed to find springs to drink from. We staved off starvation by begging from farmers or stealing from the few gardens along the way. We slept in the fields, or in barns, which we slipped into after dark. I was always glad when I could cover Jay one more night with the comforter. Besides my sweater, it was the one thing that had been constant for us since we left the ghetto. That and our faith.

We found an abandoned shack one night and slept there. Just as the sun was beginning to rise, Izzy sat up and stretched. He grinned really big and then reached over to hug me hard. I was surprised to hear what he whispered into my ear, that we were close to Munich. After five weeks of torturous walking, we could finally rest our feet.

18

Meeting Mr. Green

I n Munich there were so many Jewish-assistance agencies
on Siebert Strasse that it became known as Jewish Street.
We quickly found a two-room apartment, and Izzy began
looking for work. A few days after we arrived, he came home
around noon, grabbed me by the waist and almost lost his
balance as he swung me up into the air.

"I found a job today, Eta," he finally said. "They remembered me as a good mechanic from Lithuania and Kovno
Ghetto. I guess fixing that German's truck paid off after all.
And the best part is, I can walk to work; the job is only two
minutes from here. I can come home for lunch," he said
dancing around, holding me off the ground.

"If you don't put me down, you won't have any lunch," I
said, trying to pull my dress and apron down. "Go and wash
up. Lunch will be ready in a few minutes."

"Yes, you're right," Izzy answered, gently placing my
feet on the floor again and giving me an affectionate pat on
the rear end. "That means you'd better start cooking better. I

have to eat to keep up my strength for this new job."

I was so glad to see Izzy happy. All we had was each other and Jay, and now a job gave us hope for the future.

Strangers were pouring into Germany from all over the world — America, Australia, and Africa — looking for survivors and friends. Izzy was in charge of around 150 vehicles in the transportation department for the Central Committee of the Liberated Jews. He had trucks, ambulances and jeeps, just to name a few. The main motor pool was right next to Siebert Strasse in a large field, along with a repair shop, which really came in handy. Izzy was doing very well with his job since there were no taxicabs in Munich at that time, only streetcars.

When people came from America, they wanted to see Dachau and the survivors near Munich. The only way to reach some of the former concentration camps was by car or truck. Izzy had plenty of Jewish survivors as drivers. It gave them an opportunity to make a few dollars in tips and regain a sense of self-worth, because now, for the first time in years, they were working at a real job for real wages. Even with an abundance of workers, though, Izzy sometimes had problems with sending drivers out. Some of them would balk at taking anyone but Americans. They thought Americans would give better tips.

Izzy was always telling me some kind of tale about things that happened at work. He had entertained Jay and me for a long time with his stories about a mysterious "Mr. Green" who had come a few months back looking for transportation. The man was always disheveled but was very quiet according to Izzy. He never stayed very long, but always seemed to have appointments with important officials. Since he was kind of frumpy, Izzy was having a hard time getting a driver for him.

One day Izzy left for work as usual, but he didn't come home that night. He often worked late, but it was approaching midnight, and he still wasn't home. Jay had fallen asleep in a chair waiting for Izzy to tuck him into bed. He always insisted on telling Izzy goodnight. I think it was the only way he really felt safe enough to go to sleep.

I finally carried Jay to bed about 2 a.m. As I tucked his comforter around him, the gnawing feeling returned in the pit of my stomach, the very same feeling I had lived with for so long. As the hours wore on, I became frantic. It was so unusual for Izzy not to come home. I was worried that something terrible had happened. The fear was so real that I couldn't go to bed but spent most of the night pacing back and forth, first checking on Jay and then pulling back the curtain at the kitchen door and looking out the window repeatedly.

The next morning Izzy still hadn't returned. I had a hard time trying to explain to Jay why Izzy wasn't at home for breakfast. I just kept assuring him that his father had always come home and that he would be all right. I wasn't so sure myself, but I couldn't let Jay see my fear. On one of my trips to the window, I finally caught a glimpse of Izzy coming up the walk. I flung open the door and went running to him. I cried from relief, even though I could tell nothing bad had happened.

"Here," Izzy said, handing me his handkerchief. "I'm sorry I worried you, but I didn't have a way to contact you. You won't believe what I'm going to tell you."

Once inside, Izzy had me make a pot of tea. While I was busy with that, he took a few minutes to visit with Jay and sent him out to play. Izzy insisted I sit down so I could give him my full attention.

"Do you remember that I finally got Alter der Klinger to drive for that Mr. Green some time back?" he started. "You remember Alter, the taxi driver in Kaunas before the war. He's the one who always told jokes in a loud voice. That's why they called him 'Klinger the Ringer.' The first time I asked him to take Mr. Green to Dachau, Alter refused and said, 'Ah, give me an American. Look at the way this man is dressed. He doesn't have any money. An American would give me a tip. The way he looks, I'll have to give him a tip.'"

Izzy said he argued with Alter for a few minutes, lost his patience and finally said, "Alter, don't argue. I am the boss today. Just go."

As it turned out, Mr. Green really liked Alter, even with his loud jokes and crazy personality.

"Well, Mr. Green came in a couple of days ago," Izzy started again. "He said he was in Munich for a meeting with the executive committee of the liberated Jews. While he was here, he needed transportation to the Nuremberg Trials. Alter couldn't go, and I became very anxious. I couldn't find a substitute for Alter. Then I had an idea. After a few hours, Mr. Green came back, and I told him that I had a good driver for him. He said, 'Who is that?' I said, 'It's me. I'll make you a deal, though. We must return the same day, and I want to go in with you to see the trial.' He said, 'That's good. That's a promise.'"

Izzy didn't tell me about his planned trip. He knew the idea of him going to the trial would just upset me, and besides that, Izzy thought he would be home that night and then he could tell me about the whole day. I was so relieved that he was safe that I couldn't be mad at him. I was really surprised, though, because they didn't let just anyone go to the trial. It took a special permit to gain entrance to the courtroom.

Izzy continued, "When we came to Nuremberg, it was Mr. Green who went into the courthouse. It was David Ben Gurion who came out ten minutes later. I always had a feeling that he was an important man, but I had no idea that he was Ben Gurion, especially since he used an alias."

"Do you mean the Ben Gurion that has been so involved

in the Zionist movement in Palestine?" I asked, almost losing my breath at the thought.

"The same one. I tell you, Eta, I was surprised, too. Anyway, we sat with each other to see the murderers. Ben Gurion was very excited, upset, and kept making remarks all the time. If it had been someone else, we probably would've been thrown out. The trial went on all day and at five o'clock, I told him we had to go because we had a three-hour drive to Munich."

"What did he say to that?" I asked.

"He acted like a deaf man. I couldn't get him to budge or to even pay any attention to what I was saying, but I couldn't leave David Ben Gurion stranded. At seven o'clock, the trial was postponed until the next day. By then it was already dark.

"I was really upset," Izzy continued. "What could I do? After all, he was paying for the transportation, but I didn't want to be on the highway full of Nazis and Germans. I kept driving and driving, but all the hotels had no vacancy signs in the windows. Finally, at the very last one, I decided to try another way.

"I had a couple of packs of cigarettes in the glove compartment," Izzy told me. "I laid one pack on the hotel counter. I kept my hand on the cigarettes and told the clerk, 'When you give me the room, I'll give you the cigarettes.'

"The desk clerk smiled at me and said, 'You know, I just might have one room, but it's on the fourth floor. I hope you don't mind climbing stairs.'

It turned out to be an attic, and there was only one bed, one armchair and a regular chair.

"I told Ben Gurion I would pull the two chairs together and sleep in them, although he insisted I take the bed," Izzy said.

"We both laid down, but Ben Gurion wasn't satisfied. He kept sitting up and insisting I should take the bed."

I said, "'That will never happen.' I didn't realize just how important he was, but I had respect for my elders. He finally insisted we sleep crossways of the bed and put our feet in the chairs."

The "Mr. Green" story became one of our favorite stories to tell.

After a few weeks, we settled into a routine. Izzy would leave for work each day, and I would busy myself with Jay and keeping the house in order. After working in Munich for a year and a half, Izzy began making plans for us to go to Palestine. He started the process by going to Nahum Goldmann, the director of the Jewish agency, and asking for three certificates of passage. Izzy was really excited when he got home that night.

"Mr. Goldmann offered me two certificates, enough for you and Jay, but he said I'd have to stay and work one more year," Izzy told me. "Isn't that wonderful? I'll make arrangements for the two of you to leave, and I'll join you before you know it."

When I heard that, I got very upset. I usually didn't make a fuss about anything, but this time I was almost screaming. I shouted at Izzy, "Hitler didn't separate us. The war didn't separate us. Do you think Nahum Goldmann will separate us? It's all three or none."

When Izzy told Goldmann I wouldn't agree to a separation, Goldmann threw up his hands and said, "Well, you'll just have to go to America. America is also a country."

Izzy was bitterly disappointed. After all we had been through and the times we had escaped, here we were trying to do things legally and the door was slammed shut. I had a secret hope, though. I wanted to see Sadie and Abraham, my sister and brother who had gone to live in America. Besides my Uncle Itzhak, they were all I had left of my original family. I had written to my Aunt Bessie Brown, my mother's sister, in America and asked if we might come to Richmond, Virginia, where my uncle owned Brown Distributing Company, which distributed Pepsi-Cola among other things. I believed he could help us until we got established.

I was astonished at how fast our visas came through. One day Izzy received a letter directing him to report to the American Consulate. Izzy didn't know what it was all about, so I told him that it must be an answer from the letter to my aunt in America. Izzy turned to me and asked, "We're going to America?"

"Yes, we're going," I said. I figured there was no use staying in Munich. We couldn't get the certificates to get to Palestine legally, and Izzy wouldn't hear of us going illegally.

Izzy decided to be stubborn and refused to go to the consulate office. One month later he received another letter giving him another appointment. Izzy didn't really want to go to America, so he disregarded that letter as well. After two more weeks, another letter arrived, stating a final and very firm warning. If Izzy didn't come this time, they would cancel our appointment.

Izzy took Jay and me with him. There was such a crowd; we could hardly walk. There were three men in different offices interviewing applicants in two very long lines and one short one with hardly anyone waiting. Somewhat impatient, Izzy ushered Jay and me toward the short line.

A man approached Izzy and said, "Ipp, don't go into that room. That man will not pass you. When you get to him, you can just forget about going to America." Well, Izzy didn't want to go to America anyhow, so what difference did it make to him? He only came there so I wouldn't blame him if it didn't work out. At least this way Izzy was giving the man in charge of the consular office a chance to reject us. I had a feeling that a rejection would have made Izzy happy.

We could tell the man who would examine our papers was very tough. Not only did he look mean, he really pored over the health certificates and closely examined the ones standing before him, asking all kinds of personal questions. He read the birth certificates very carefully and rejected half of those who appeared before him. Some left his office crying. I couldn't help thinking of Abraham and Sadie. I wished I could run to them right now, but I had to stand in line with Jay and just remain quiet. I had already accepted a long time ago that my fate seemed to be out of my control. Once again, I could only stand and pray.

The examiners were looking for sicknesses like tuberculosis. Bernstein, a man who was a close friend of Izzy's, was acting as the translator for this particular examiner. Bernstein was standing just inside the door. When he saw Izzy coming toward him, he said, "You're *meshuggah*. Get in the other line. Hurry before he sees you."

It was too late. The consular officer had already waved for us to come inside the office. I was too frightened to speak, so Izzy had to answer all the questions. I can only really remember two questions. He wanted to know our names and how old Jay was. Izzy gave him our names, and, for once, Jay spoke up spontaneously and gave his age. I think he had been taking lessons from Izzy on how to be assertive. Also, he was very excited about the prospect of going on a ship to America.

The man brought out our file. When he opened it and laid it on the desk, I could see some stationery with a Pepsi-Cola emblem on it. I couldn't actually read it, but it was one of the most beautiful things I'd ever seen. Suddenly I had hope again. The consular officer looked Izzy over and then spoke to Bernstein. I finally heard him say, "Oh, there won't be a problem with him. They'll have plenty of work in the Pepsi-Cola plant. He can wash bottles." He picked up his big metal stamp and punched a huge "APPROVED" on our papers. That sound reverberated through my head all day.

19

Life in America – 1947-96

I will be honest; Izzy wasn't very happy. Such a miserable look he had on his face. I'm sure he thought everybody congratulating us was crazy.

"What is all the fuss? I wanted to go to Palestine, not America," he said.

I tried to console him by saying, "Well, America isn't Palestine, but it isn't Germany, either. At least we'll have a chance to start over. My uncle will help us. We'll go to Palestine someday. For now, though, we have to leave Germany any way we can."

I had to hide my joy because Izzy just felt so disappointed. He went back to work that day and told his co-workers we were going to America. Some of the men were upset. Many of them had been waiting a lot longer than we had to leave Germany.

Izzy went back to Nahum Goldmann again, determined not to give up his dream. Izzy described their conversation later.

"I tried to talk very respectfully, Eta, and I didn't raise

my voice or anything. I just said, 'Mr. Goldmann, won't you please reconsider? What is the difference? We'll all be leaving Germany anyway. At least I'll feel at home in Palestine and with other survivors. In America, I'll be like a fish out of water. I don't even know one word of the language.' "

Mr. Goldmann wouldn't budge. Izzy was furious. He said Nahum Goldmann was one of the most stubborn men he had ever known. It was really a paradox of sorts. Izzy had been working for months providing ways for Jews to quietly get to Romania, where they were later transported into Palestine illegally, and now we couldn't go ourselves. While it might have been possible for us to go illegally, Izzy was afraid to take the chance with Jay and me.

A month later a letter arrived instructing us to be at the train station in a week. Izzy ignored the letter. Everybody told Izzy that he shouldn't play around, but Goldmann was not the only stubborn Jewish man I knew.

Another letter arrived. Izzy felt he had no choice, so he turned over his office to his dispatcher, and within thirty days we were in Bremerhafen boarding the SS Marine Marlin. It was the biggest thing I'd ever seen and had such a musical name. I learned that it weighed over 12,000 tons and was just under 500 feet long, but it seemed like we could walk for miles on deck.

Once we got over being seasick, it was very exciting. Jay was so thrilled, it was hard to contain him, but I felt very sad for Izzy. Even on German soil, Izzy was happy in Munich after he got a decent job. And even though only a few cousins survived from Izzy's family, he felt more at ease around someone he knew. We both took comfort in the fact that Izzy had been able to get some of the survivors to Palestine. As for me, I couldn't leave Germany fast enough. There were too many bad memories.

The days passed quickly and I was thinking of our

new future when we first glimpsed the Statue of Liberty. Passengers were all crowding to the side of the deck and exclaiming about how big and beautiful she was, but I have to admit to having very mixed emotions. While I was excited about our new life in America, I was also very afraid of what we might encounter. The anti-Semitism had been so unbearable in Europe, and I wondered how we would be accepted in a world where we didn't even know one word of their language. It seemed as if my heart was engaged in a tug of war. One moment I was thrilled with coming to America; the next I was feeling the dismay of having left my beautiful Lithuania, my family's home and the only history I had ever known.

We left May 30 and docked at the New York harbor on June 7, 1947, just two days after Jay's twelfth birthday. That was quite a birthday present. The dock was so crowded that we could hardly walk. It was mass confusion, so many different languages with people pushing and shoving. Some of the men got so upset I thought they would actually fight each other. Jay was terribly frightened by the commotion. Although he felt like he was too old to hold my hand, he stayed very close to me. It seemed we couldn't escape turmoil. It was like a cloud following us.

Finally we were settled on Lafayette Street and stayed there for two nights near the place where they registered us. I was very disappointed that my aunt and uncle weren't already there from Richmond. Izzy blamed me and said it was because I was stingy. I preferred to think I was thrifty, although I did spend one dollar on oranges for Jay.

The Hebrew Immigrant Aid Society (HIAS), the organization that brought us over, and the American Joint Distribution Committee had given us each ten dollars. Izzy had been so anxious to smoke that he went to the ship's little store and bought a carton of Camel cigarettes. He also bought a candy bar and a pair of sunglasses for Jay. When I asked Izzy why he bought a white pair of ladies' sunglasses, he said it was because that was all they had left and Jay wanted to be like everybody else on the ship. I didn't blame him. We had been denied enough, but I was surprised that he spent two dollars on these items. When he returned, he suggested I call Aunt Bessie from the ship.

"Izzy, I have checked into the matter already," I told him. "To call Richmond from the ship will cost a whole dollar. I'm not going to spend a dollar on a telephone call. That's a lot of money. We'll wait until we get to New York to call. Something will turn up. Besides that, I have sent a letter to my aunt." What I was afraid to tell Izzy was that I wasn't sure I had the right address.

I decided I had made a good decision not to spend the money on the phone call. Between the bribes Izzy had paid and being robbed, we were destitute except for a couple of my father's rubles still sewn into my sweater and the HIAS money. We didn't know when we would get any more.

Izzy had explained to the man who registered us, the one who worked for HIAS, that my uncle ran the Brown Distributing Company in Richmond, Virginia, but we didn't have his telephone number. The man could see I was very anxious. He said, "Don't worry. We'll take care of it. We're in the business of finding people."

In no time, my uncle was on the phone. The HIAS man asked my uncle several questions and then handed me the phone. I was trembling so hard I could hardly hold it to my ear. When I heard Uncle Abe's voice, it seemed like a dream. After a few minutes, my uncle, a very sweet man, asked to speak to Izzy and welcomed him to America as well. For the first time in months, I began to feel a little confidence.

The next day I walked into the lunchroom, and who should be standing there but my brother. I ran to him, unable to contain my joy. I kept hugging and kissing him and saying, "Abraham, Abraham." After I introduced him to Izzy and Jay and had settled down a little, he explained that I should now call him Alvin. Like so many Jews trying to fit in with Americans, he had changed his name. My brother now lived in Washington, D.C. A friend of my aunt's had seen our names in the list of immigrants in a New York newspaper and had called her. Aunt Bessie contacted my brother so he could locate us. The next day, Alvin got off the train in Washington, D.C., and we rode it to Richmond.

Arriving at Main Street Station in Richmond seemed like another dream. There was my sister, Sadie, and my Uncle Abe Brown and his wife, Aunt Bessie, waiting to greet us. I remember the day like it was yesterday and for some reason I remember the car my uncle was driving. It was a 1941 Packard. We all got inside, and my uncle drove us to Sadie's house on Cutshaw Avenue, where Sadie had prepared a special room for us. Now we had a room in America and seventeen dollars. Suddenly I felt very rich. Sadie introduced us to her husband, Milton, who had just come back from the Pacific, where he was stationed with the U.S. Army. While he was gone, Sadie had been working at the Pepsi-Cola plant as an accountant.

We took a few days to settle down and walk around the neighborhood. It was all so new for us and so exciting, but very scary, too. The English sounded like so many garbled words. It was terribly frightening not to be able to understand a single word. I was afraid of the police and had run from the first one I had seen. Anyone in a uniform frightened me. That had meant only one thing in Germany. It was going to take a long time for me to get used to seeing police officers actually helping people. I didn't have as hard a time remembering to walk on the sidewalks, instead of in the street. The main problem was understanding the language. One time in particular, it really got Izzy into hot water.

"Izzy," Sadie said one morning, "you need a haircut. Here, take this dollar and go to the barber shop."

"How am I supposed to find it?" Izzy asked.

"Just look for the shop that has a revolving striped pole outside the door," Sadie said. "You won't have any trouble."

I could tell Izzy was a little afraid, but he didn't want to seem ungrateful or disrespectful of Sadie, so he and Jay went out the door and started walking down the street.

Izzy said he decided to try and find my cousin's drugstore, thinking that perhaps a barbershop would be located close to a drugstore. Sure enough, he was right. Izzy said he went inside the barbershop and motioned with his hands that he needed a haircut. Jay described the scene to me later.

"Daddy sat down in the chair, and I sat down in the one next to him to watch. The barber didn't say anything until after he finished cutting Daddy's hair. Then he said a word I didn't understand. I was sure Daddy didn't know what he was talking about either. Before Daddy could say anything, the man leaned him back in the chair and started washing his hair. When he was finished with that, he looked at Daddy and said something else. Daddy just looked back at him and shrugged his shoulders, so the man stretched him out on the chair and began shaving him."

At this point, Jay stopped talking and had a good laugh. Then he continued reiterating his conversation with Izzy.

"I said, 'Daddy, you're in trouble. They gave you the works and you only have one dollar. What are you going to do?'

"Daddy said, 'I didn't tell him to do it.'

"When the barber finished, he held up three fingers. When Daddy gave him only one dollar, the man started getting angry. I told Daddy, 'Ah, ha. You didn't believe me when I said you were going to be in trouble.'"

Izzy picked up the story from there.

"I took my wristwatch off and gave it to the barber and

motioned with my fingers to the door that I would be back."

Sadie had overheard the story from the hallway. When she came into our room, Izzy grew quiet, thinking she might be angry. Instead, she laughed, gave Izzy another two dollars, told him to retrieve his watch and suggested he be more careful next time. That night Milton had a good laugh about it, too.

Izzy and Jay spent their days trying to find somewhere for Izzy to work. One afternoon he came home and said he had gone into several places asking about mechanic's work, but no one there could understand him. Uncle Abe and Izzy talked about it just about every night. One evening Uncle Abe offered to buy Izzy a grocery store, a good business on Canal Street. He said it would only be six thousand dollars.

"I appreciate your kindness, Uncle," Izzy told him. "But, I don't want groceries. My father wasn't a grocery man, my grandfather wasn't a grocery man, and I'm not going to be a grocery man. This is a country on wheels. I want to roll with the wheels."

Uncle Abe leaned back in his chair and laughed out loud. He told Izzy he had better first learn the language before he got run over. It turned out to be good advice. All of us started working on improving our language skills. It came very slowly, through speaking, listening to the radio and trying to read the newspapers.

Izzy, so adept at languages, learned quickly and worked for quite a while at a local garage and then for Uncle Abe as a mechanic at the Pepsi plant. I went to work at Thalhimers, a department store, doing alterations. Thanks to my mother-in-law, I was very good at hemming. We had moved to an apartment and, much to our delight, discovered that I was pregnant. A few months later, though, I was standing up on one of the buses on my way home from work. The bus lurched suddenly, throwing me into one of the seats. Our baby boy was born that night, but he didn't survive. Somehow, it didn't seem fair to have yet another loss, but there was nothing we could do but accept it and go on.

Izzy finally managed to buy a vacant service station where Jay and I helped out. Izzy even allowed me to turn a little room into a kitchen. It was a pleasure really, just to be near Izzy. I would make his lunch, and we'd have a few minutes together. Sometimes I even fixed sandwiches for our customers.

Eventually we began to get a lot of work, including inspections for state vehicles. We all worked long, hard hours. I remember pumping gas in a dress. Ah, those were different times. Izzy even owned a small used-car lot. Finally we began to prosper, and in 1952 Izzy opened our final business, American Parts Company, where he stocked thousands of parts for cars and trucks. We were so proud to be Americans that we painted our trucks red, white and blue and erected an American flag on each of them. In 1953 we signed our naturalization papers and changed our name from Ipp to Ipson, thereby making our transition to this country complete.

The night before our naturalization, just as we went to bed, Izzy put his arms around me gently. He rocked me a little, like he used to do when I was so afraid in the potato hole. Just before he fell asleep, he quietly said, "Edna, tomorrow we'll be true Americans. There were times when I didn't think we'd make it, but we have finally come out on the other side of hell."

Jay worked in the business right along with Izzy, even when he was attending school. One summer, though, he decided to take a few weeks off and go to Canada to visit Lola Gillman, Izzy's cousin who had been in the potato hole with us. Lola had moved to Canada and established a hosiery factory and was doing very well for himself. When

Jay returned, he had quite a surprise for us. He had met a young woman that Lola and Sheina knew, and Jay shocked us by saying he was going to marry her. I laugh about it now, when I realize what my first question almost was. Instead, I asked, "What is her name?"

"Her name is Elly," Jay said. With a wide grin, he added "and, yes, she is Jewish. Not only that, but her father was born in Lithuania."

Israel (Lola) Gillman worked as an employee of the American Joint Distribution Committee as driver of a medical supplies truck in Germany. The American-issued uniform ensured that he could eat in American restaurants and stay in American hotels (1948).

20

A Wayward Letter Arrives – 1997

Some people probably thought Elly Gaffen, my daughter-in-law, was a bit strange when she first came to Richmond from Canada. Instead of taking her time and adjusting to a new country and a new husband, Elly began working at Izzy's business a month after marrying Jay in July 1959.

Since Elly has always been a very serious person, she turned that seriousness toward the family business. It made perfect sense. Her keen memory was a valuable asset, especially after we moved the business from 1903 W. Cary Street just a few blocks down the same street. No one was as good at details as Elly was, and she eventually worked for the company for over forty years.

I'll be honest. I was a little apprehensive about the marriage. Elly married Jay over the objections of her father, who thought she would have a particularly difficult time marrying into a family from Europe. I could hardly blame him. Given the horror the Holocaust survivors had endured, it wasn't unusual for them to commit suicide or be committed to mental institutions.

I was actually more concerned that she and Jay had dated for only three weeks before deciding to marry. Izzy and I wondered whether it would last, but over the years things have worked out well. Elly proved to be a devoted wife and mother and definitely was someone you could always count on. And look what she has given us — three grandchildren and four great-grandchildren already. What's not to like?

Izzy usually went to the office about 7 a.m. each workday. Even if he was busy waiting on customers or taking calls when Elly came in, Izzy always inquired about our precious grandchildren and great-grandchildren. Elly usually had some tale to share, since her daughters, Edith and Esther, often dropped off their children for a short stay at her house before they went to school. And Ronny, Jay and Elly's son, visited them often as well.

Sometimes Elly went home and prepared lunch for Jay, who was in and out of the office during the day. I worked there as well. We all took turns making sure the customers were helped. Jay had decided to give up his duties as a small-airport manager and had become increasingly more active in the business. He had always worked right along with Izzy and had even managed one of the branch offices, but now he was handling more of the day-to-day responsibilities servicing the entire metropolitan Richmond area.

Jay was so kind to Izzy, gently alleviating Izzy's concerns and shouldering the day-to-day responsibility for the business. I'll never forget the morning Izzy looked at Jay and said, "Once I was busy from daylight until dark, and now look at me. I'm not responsible for so much. It's hard to just sit around all day."

Jay had an answer ready. He had just been waiting for the perfect opportunity to introduce it. Now was the time.

"Daddy," Jay began. "Do you remember I suggested that you leave an oral history of our experiences in Lithuania?"

"Yes. So, what's that got to do with me and going to work?" Izzy asked, a little impatiently.

"I was in Circuit City the other day and I happened to walk by some tape recorders," Jay said, carefully choosing each word. "Maybe you could come into the office, spend a little time helping out and then work on your memoirs. You can do a little each day."

"I don't know, Jay," Izzy replied. "So much has happened since then. It's been too long for me to remember all the details."

"Well, how often have you said you couldn't forget those times, no matter how hard you tried?" Jay asked.

"I'll give it some thought," Izzy finally said.

Izzy asked me about it later when we could talk privately, and I encouraged him to consider it seriously.

"It couldn't hurt," I said. "It would occupy your time, and we aren't getting any younger. It's 1984 already and it seems like every month or so, one of the survivors is dying. Pretty soon there will be no one left to tell the story."

I'm glad Jay didn't ask me to do it. When I dwelt on the past, the nightmares started again. They were never very far from me, and it didn't take much to make them flare up. Izzy was very diligent once he got started. I was really proud of him. I walked by his office one day and heard him speaking about the time when so many of our friends were murdered in Kaunas. I wondered how he could sound so calm but then I understood. I had also pushed the emotion away as a defense; it was the only way any of us could talk about it. After all, none of it was rational, and no one with a conscience could possibly do what had been done to us. Even now, after all these years, I can't understand man's inhumanity to man. Izzy was able to rise above his feelings, though, because he was thinking of the next generation, and he wanted to do his part to leave a record. It took him a very long time to do it, though.

Izzy also started going with Jay to some of the local schools and churches when Jay was giving Holocaust presentations. Izzy even appeared once on Channel 23, our public-television station. Another time he helped organize one of the first Holocaust remembrance programs ever held in the city. Not long after that, he came to me with an idea.

"Edna, I've been thinking. There needs to be a fund to try and keep Holocaust history alive after we're gone. Why don't we start a fund for that?"

"Yes, that's a good idea," I said. "Why don't you call the Jewish Federation and find out what we can do?"

"I'll do it tomorrow," he said, with a look of determination on his face. "It's really up to the remaining survivors to see that the work continues even after we're gone."

Jay was delighted with the idea. In fact, he was relieved. He had been getting more and more calls from history teachers to visit schools. Over time the demand grew and eventually he developed a slide presentation and was traveling to various schools and organizations to present it. Jay's presentation got a boost after he participated in a program that the Valentine Museum organized in Richmond in 1996. The school programs snowballed and actually began to interfere with Jay's work in our business. I overheard a conversation one day that would ultimately prove quite fateful. Al Rosenbaum and Mark Fetter, friends of Jay's, came by the office to talk with him.

Mark started first.

"I've been thinking about something, Jay, especially since you participated in the Valentine Museum Holocaust program. Why don't we start a Holocaust museum of our own, right here in Richmond?"

"There is already a Holocaust museum in Washington. Why do we need another one in Richmond?" Jay asked.

"Well, Washington is quite a ways from here," Mark replied. "There seems to be a lot of local interest here, especially among the schoolchildren."

Jay paused for a minute and then said, "Well, I am getting more and more requests."

Al, a local artist and usually a very reserved man, spoke up rather firmly.

"I agree with Mark," Al started. "You've got a lot of the material already. Mark has contacts that would pay off, and I could help develop the exhibits. I'm sure there are a lot of people who would work as volunteers. It would be tough to do, but it needs to be done."

Mark joined in again.

"There's no question it would be a lot of work, but we could use some of Al's sculptures that were used at the Valentine. It wouldn't be like we'd have to start from scratch."

Jay had been particularly quiet through all of this. He put his head in both hands and thought for a minute.

"I don't know," he finally said, looking up. "That's more than I ever thought of getting involved in. I'm not sure the two of you realize how difficult it is to do these presentations. Every time I do one of them, the memories come back in full force. Some nights I don't sleep at all and then I have to go and do the same thing all over again the very next day. It takes its toll after a while."

"We know it's hard for you," Mark said quietly. "But just think about how much easier it would be if we had the museum in the educational building of Temple Beth-El."

Al chimed in again, "That building is empty now since they built a new school. It's the perfect place. The schools could bus the kids to the synagogue. After you presented your historical lecture, the students could go right next door to tour the museum. You wouldn't be running all over the city then. If you had a central location, you could pay more attention to your business."

"My aunt, Bea Fine, is the president of the temple right now," Mark added. "You know how interested she is in children. I have a feeling she would back us, and we could go from there."

The decision for an exploratory visit to the United States Holocaust Memorial Museum was made. I think Jay and his friends were really surprised at the encouragement they received. The historians there even offered to donate artifacts to help jump-start the Richmond museum. It was ironic, really. The national museum had just finished putting together a yearlong special exhibit on the Kovno Ghetto, the same one we escaped from on that dark night so long ago.

Jay had brought back a collection of ghetto photos from the national museum and had shown them to Izzy one day when they were having lunch at a local restaurant. Izzy was stunned to see some that were taken the day my family was deported to Riga. He recognized Jay, me, and my father waiting just behind the trucks. Jay made the decision not to tell me about having the photos. He was afraid it would upset me.

After a great deal of research, the decision was made to establish the Virginia Holocaust Museum. Izzy was delighted when he learned that the photos he had seen, along with many others taken in the Kovno Ghetto by George Kadish, would become part of the displays in the museum.

Izzy had wanted to tour the museum as it was being constructed, but he had been ill for several months and hospitalized for a time. He kept waiting for his strength to return. It never did. While he had become too weak to even go to the museum a single time, he had acted as an adviser during most of the construction phase, especially for a depiction of our hiding place.

As the work progressed, Jay described each room to Izzy. He took special care to include the details of the sculptures

Al had designed to reflect *Kristallnacht,* the two nights of terror that marked the first pogrom in Europe.

The thing that really caught Izzy's eye was the reproduction of the special menorah Al constructed. The original was about sixteen feet tall and was affixed to the front of the museum. While menorahs usually had more candles, this one had only five tall candles and one half candle. The sculpture, which also had the Star of David dangling among twisted barbed wire, became the defining symbol for the museum. It paid tribute to the estimated six million Jews who died during the Holocaust, the little candle representing the countless number of Jewish children who were annihilated. Al even splashed the menorah with red and blue paint. He explained that the red reflected lost blood, and the blue was a symbol of hope for the future.

When word got out that the museum was being established, a floodgate of memorabilia opened. People came from everywhere to donate artifacts and add to the educational displays. Many of the liberators, soldiers and nurses, came bringing their uniforms and photographs they had taken, as well as flags and other items they brought home from the concentration and slave labor camps. People cleaned out attics and unpacked boxes that had been kept closed for years. The response was nothing short of astounding. Anne Fischer, now almost 100 years old, brought the doll she carried on the ship to America. Inge Horowitz, who lost nearly 200 members of her extended family in the Holocaust, donated table covers her mother had made and some of her family's *kiddish* cups, vessels used to hold the wine that is blessed by a special prayer during a sacred occasion.

Of course, Izzy was also particularly interested in the reconstruction of our hiding place. He had given exact instructions to Jay, carefully describing the dimensions of the place he had dug between the two potato holes on the

Paskauskas farm for us to live in. Jay was rebuilding the hiding place, complete with a doghouse and a replica of Rexxyx. Izzy laughed when he learned that Jay had even recorded the sound of a dog barking and had rigged a sensor to engage the recording when someone walked near the potato hole.

Each time Jay told Izzy that another portion was complete, Izzy recounted his fears to me, especially about the times during the last weeks before we were liberated. He was terribly afraid after Uncle Itzhak and the others came to live with us, because of the boys' rambunctious nature.

One day he said, "Edna, do you remember how scared I was the night Lola and I almost got into a fight? It was foolish of me, I know, but I got so angry when Lola brought up the circumstances of how Nese and Leibel had died again. I couldn't contain myself. I remember picking up the revolver and Lola grabbing the hand grenade, or maybe it was the other way around, but it was a terrible moment. If Raja hadn't intervened and calmed us down, there's no telling what would have happened. Raja was always a wonderful person, but she was worth her weight in gold that time for sure. The amazing thing is that we were liberated just two days later – not a minute too soon. I tell you – I don't know how we managed to survive that long."

Izzy talked about the museum right up until the end of his life. He was especially proud that Lola had contributed $24,000 to help establish it. I think that might have helped a little to ease the sadness Izzy felt about Nese and Leibel. At least this way, their names and pictures would be displayed and museum visitors would know what a hero the Little Lion really was.

Izzy quizzed Jay repeatedly about the work and was delighted when Jay told him he had secured thirteen manne-quins to arrange in the hole, representing all of us who had lived there. I remember Izzy laughed out loud when he learned that his iridescent watch, the one that kept the mice at bay while we were underground, would be displayed, along with the last of my father's rubles, which I had sewn into my sweater. Replicas of the weapons Leibel secured for us would also be on display.

Although Izzy tried valiantly, he didn't live to see the completed museum. He talked to me about it a lot and told me how proud he was of the work Jay and the others were doing. I remember how he smiled one day when I told him that Michael McCauley, our granddaughter's husband, was painting a mural on the walls at night after he got off work. It seemed everybody in our family had a job at the museum, even Joel, Ben, David, and Sarah, our little great-grandchildren. They were all very interested in it, especially the hole where we lived. It gave us an opportunity to tell them a little of our past lives, even though it was so painful.

As the work on the museum progressed, Izzy's health deteriorated. Jay had a hospital bed moved into our apartment, but finally we had to admit Izzy to St. Mary's Hospital. Jay and I had been at the hospital almost constantly for a few days. One evening Izzy seemed to be resting comfortably. Jay and I had continued to speak to him, even though the nurses said he couldn't hear us. Jay told me I should go home and rest. I was worried about Jay, too, so I suggested we both go home for a while. Jay stepped up to Izzy's bed and told him we would return in the morning. Izzy raised his hand, and Jay held it for a few minutes until Izzy's grasp relaxed. We left him resting. In the early morning hours of the next day, February 5, 1997, Izzy's heart stopped beating and my world was changed irrevocably.

You have never seen such a service. Temple Beth-El was packed. I knew that Izzy had lots of friends, but even I was surprised at the number of people who came to pay their respects. I tried so hard to be brave. My beloved Izzy had meant everything to me. He had been my rock, my foundation, and I was lost without him. I tried very hard, for Jay's sake, not to show my emotions, but part of me died along with Izzy, and I knew it would never come back. Now I felt so alone.

Izzy's death had a profound effect on Jay as well, beyond what I had imagined. Although Jay and literally hundreds of volunteers had been working night and day at the museum, Izzy would never be able to see the results of all the hard work.

When Jay told me how good Izzy's memoirs were, I was even prouder of him. Izzy was always good at expressing himself. Sometimes he would ask me if I remembered particular incidents. Sometimes I did, but I'll be honest, sometimes I didn't want to remember or be reminded.

I still missed my mother so much, even after all these years. When I thought about it, though, I realized that we needed to rise above the pain. We had been doing that for most of our lives, but now it had a better purpose somehow. What Izzy had done was very important. Now he was gone, but the record had been made.

Some people still say the Holocaust never happened. It happened. It happened. It has happened every day of my life since it happened. I have never been rid of it. Maybe Izzy's memoirs and the museum will help to wipe away some of the dark cloud I've always carried with me. But what could I do? I had to go on and do the best I could each day. At least now there will be a museum, something that children can look at and learn from.

I was delighted when Jay told me the potato hole was actually going to be constructed just as if it were underground. The visiting children would have to get down on their hands and knees and crawl through one of the tunnels to get inside to the nine feet by twelve feet by four feet hole, just like we used to do. It's impossible to really experience it, though. No one could imagine what it would be like to be almost suffocated in such a small place like that, unable to even see the other people in the room or to stand upright for such a long time. I shudder each time I remember it.

As the dedication for the museum grew near, Jay was spending less time at the office. He and Elly usually rose quite early every day. As usual, Jay hit the ground running, quickly shaved and showered before picking me up and driving to Temple Beth-El, where we said *kaddish*, prayers that Jewish mourners recite for eleven months after the loss of loved ones.

Elly would sometimes join Jay and Frank Seldes for bagels and coffee at Willow Lawn, a nearby shopping center, before going to the office. Frank, Jay's best friend for many years, had been instrumental in helping get the museum on its feet, donating more than 200 gallons of paint to the project. Hundreds of volunteers worked furiously around the clock to get it ready in time for *Yom HaShoah*, the international time of remembrance for the martyrs, survivors and liberators of the Holocaust.

Jay came to get me the night before the museum was scheduled to open. He wanted to give me a private tour. I slowly walked up the steel-covered steps that had been reconstructed to resemble the factory steps where so many Jews were forced to work until they died. Next I walked through a black-hinged door where the words *"Arbeit Macht Frei,"* German for "Work Liberates," had been written in the wrought-iron fixture just like those that greeted inmate workers in the slave labor camps of Europe. I stopped for a moment and marveled at the door, a tragic artistic rendering done by Dr. Kenneth Olshansky, a Richmond plastic surgeon whose family was fortunate enough to escape the Holocaust.

I peered into the first room, which held Al's sculptures of *Kristallnacht*, the beginning of the nightmare, and then steeled myself just before I entered the room that depicted the home where we had lived trapped inside Kovno Ghetto. I was afraid to go in, but I knew I had to do it, especially for Jay.

I looked around for a few minutes, trying to take it all in. I remember turning to him and saying, "Jay, darling, it's so hard to believe that we ever lived through this. Nobody knows what a terrible time that was. How did we make it? So many died. It was a miracle that any of us survived."

When I saw the Ipp and Butrimowitz family portraits hanging there, I couldn't help but cry out loud. Of the thirteen family members pictured there, only three made it out alive.

When I could speak, I finally said, "This is wonderful. I don't know how you did it in such a short period of time." I stopped talking for a minute then, and Jay sensed something was askew.

"What's wrong?" he asked.

"Jay, darling, I hate to find fault, but — " I said without finishing the sentence.

"Well, don't just stand there, Mother. Tell me what it is," Jay insisted.

"The color. It's all wrong," I finally said. "The house is painted the wrong shade of blue."

It was after midnight before they got started, but Frank made sure the color was perfect by morning.

The museum opened the next day, May 1, 1997. Almost overnight, crowds of schoolchildren started pouring in. Since the museum's mission statement was "Tolerance Through Education" and the museum was geared toward middle-school children, it was another surprise when adults started visiting the museum by the thousands. I really don't think it was just the free admission. It was a small, intimate museum where people could quietly reflect on what had happened.

Word about the museum traveled quickly, and visitors started coming from out of state and from foreign countries as well.

Jay became so busy with the museum that he began to phase out the family business. In the mornings he always went straight to the museum after breakfast and joined Elly later at the office to help with invoices and phone calls. Elly usually left our office and went to the post office each morning around 10 a.m. She would then go to the bank and deposit any checks she had received. It was a daily routine that she almost never strayed from.

One day during December, that routine paid off in spades. Elly had gone to the Saunders Post Office on Broad Street as usual and retrieved our company mail from the locked box. She was sorting out the contents when she discovered a brown call slip from John Garger, one of the postal workers. She went to the counter and asked another worker to call John forward.

"Hello, Mrs. Ipson," John began. "I've been waiting for you all morning."

"Why?" Elly asked.

"Well, I have a letter here that's really bugging me. I hope you can help me solve the mystery. It's a registered letter, mailed in Trakai, Lithuania, on November 6. I noticed it the first time it came through because it had really interesting stamps. It was returned to the post office today." John explained, "I got to looking at it again and thought perhaps 'I. Ipoon' was really supposed to be Israel Ipson. I can't explain it. There was just something about it that seemed really important to me. After it came all this way, I just hated to send it back without trying to find the person it was meant for. I thought I'd give you a shot at it before I returned it. Does your family have relatives in Lithuania?"

"No," Elly said, "but my in-laws and my husband were helped by someone who lived there many years ago. And this letter is addressed to our old address on Cary Street, but we moved from there some thirty years ago. I'll take it and ask my husband about it."

Elly told me later that her mind started whirling with questions. She realized the importance of the letter immediately.

"Mother," she began, "you can't imagine how excited I was. Suddenly my whole body got cold and I began to shiver. I knew it could only mean one thing."

At the Virginia Holocaust Museum, Jay Ipson (left) and his cousin, Jacob Kalamitskas, a resident of Israel, examine a replica of their hiding place during the Holocaust (1998).

Courtesy Nancy Wright Beasley

21

Edna's Apprehension

W hen Elly showed Jay the letter, he confirmed that the name on the return address was indeed that of Stasuk, the teenage boy who had helped us. Jay and Elly were so excited that they brought me the letter that same night, thinking I could interpret it. At first, I thought I recognized a few words, but then I finally gave up.

"Jay, I'm so sorry," I said. "Nothing seems to make sense. Who could believe that I would forget my own language, but I have. I don't even know anyone who speaks Lithuanian. Do you?" I asked.

Obviously disappointed, Jay shrugged his shoulders and turned to Elly. She was quiet for a few minutes, and then her face lit up.

"I'll bet we can find an interpreter through the Boys & Girls Club of Richmond," she said. "They're the ones who put on the International Food Festival each year. I've seen a Lithuanian booth there."

"That's a good idea, Elly," Jay said, looking hopeful again. "I'll call them tomorrow. After fifty years, what's one more night?"

I was astonished when Jay called me the next morning.

"We've found an interpreter, Mother," he fairly shouted. "And, you won't believe this. She actually grew up in Kaunas, just like me."

"You're kidding," I said, hardly able to believe what he was saying.

"I'm not kidding. Her name is Rita Ghatak, and she lives in Chesterfield County, just across the James River. She has agreed to come within the hour to read the letter. I'll call you later."

When Jay called, he put Rita on the phone. Slowly she read me the letter:

I'm writing you a letter honored friends. I'm greeting you and wish you health and much luck. Perhaps you won't remember me. When you were with us, my parents hid you from the Germans who had at that time seized Lithuania and were killing your nation. There were 16 people of your nation. If you ever come to Lithuania, please come to visit me. We lived together like brothers and sisters and had the Germans ever found out all of us would have been shot to death. If you come to visit me, I will show you those places where we lived together and I stop writing and say good bye.

My address Lithuania, Traku, Rajonas Traku Pastas, Sejmoniu Koimas Krivicius Stanislovas Telephone 6-82-23

In what seemed to be a whirlwind, more letters were exchanged, and finally phone calls leading to a reunion. Rita was invaluable and our only link to Stasuk, now that we had rediscovered him. Once again, there was a Catholic helping us to bridge the gap. And yet, I still had reservations. It was nearly impossible to believe. Stasuk said he found our address in a bundle of letters in an old cabinet that belonged to his parents. He had written to us without much hope of reconnecting with us again, and now he and his son were due to arrive tomorrow. I went to bed almost dreading the reunion.

Hours later, I sat upright in the dark with my heart pounding at breakneck speed. The smothering feeling in my chest had awakened me several times already, but now it was becoming unbearable. Over the years I had perfected a way to pray and breathe deeply to help ward off the recurring nightmares, but not tonight. A sleeping pill had been useless. Even with my eyes open, the scene kept playing over and over in my mind. As I watched, my father took first my mother's arm and then my sister's, steadying them as they climbed into the back of that death truck.

I remembered that Minnie, always modest, reached to pull her dress down as she climbed in front of our two little brothers. I again envisioned my father looking at Jay and raising his hand a final time to me and mouthing the words, "Don't forget where it is." He couldn't have known that the last of the rubles he was so careful to hide would end up in a museum in another country — a testament to his life and tenacity.

People used to tell me that time heals all wounds, but I don't believe it. It has been more than fifty years, and still I'm often robbed of sleep by that horrific scene. The prospect of reuniting with someone from Lithuania had only fueled the nightmares. Finally overcome with anxiety, I couldn't stay in bed past dawn.

Sitting on the side of the bed, I instinctively curled my toes into the soft tufts of the deep pile carpet and stood to pull on my housecoat. I wiggled my feet into my bedroom shoes and cinched the robe's terrycloth sash as I moved slowly to the bathroom. The light in the bathroom shone off the soft blue walls, a comforting sight.

Three somber faces stared back at me from the tri-fold mirror. Sometimes I wondered if each face belonged to a different woman. My life, after all, has had three very distinct divisions. The first was carefree: my childhood, schooling and my ultimate marriage to Israel Ipp, my precious Izzy, the man of my dreams, followed by motherhood and looking toward a bright future. The second period was so short and had become so unexpectedly terrible: the time when we were persecuted and hiding in fear for our lives during the years of World War II.

The third part, reflected by the face now looking back at me, was my survival of those hellish years and beginning a whole new life in America with Izzy, sustained by faith and family. No doubt about it, I have embraced immeasurable sorrow, but I'm also satisfied with what I have become. Sometimes I think back on it and wonder how any of us survived the madness. It hasn't been easy, but I always remained smiling and acting as if everything is OK. That's why I always say, "I'm doing the best I can," when someone asks how I'm doing. This day, though, would be a special struggle. It was the uncertainty, the not knowing again that made me so anxious.

I wished Izzy were here. He was so stable, so solid. I could always draw strength from him, but now he had been dead just over a year. I still found myself talking to him hoping that I'd feel his presence again.

Izzy, I would say, *I look into the mirror, and I see an old woman staring back at me. I don't look too bad, my grandchildren tell me. Not bad for what? For an 87-year-old woman? What am I supposed to look like, anyway? I tell you what — someone who is a survivor, someone who believes in God, someone who believes in family, that's what.*

The familiar routine of brushing my teeth and washing my face helped anchor the day. I walked down the hall to the kitchen, turning on lights as I went, hoping to push back the dark feeling that still stayed with me. I dropped two slices of bread into the toaster and turned the stove on to heat water for my morning coffee, hoping that food would quell the awful feeling. I knew I didn't have an upset stomach but rather was experiencing the hard knot of apprehension I had often heard Americans call "butterflies."

Apprehension had become a familiar feeling in my life again, especially over the last few months. I could almost sense it standing by the bed waiting for me to take it up each night. It returned with ferocity when the sun went down or when Jay and I talked about the visitor coming from Lithuania. I was having a hard time imagining a face-to-face reunion with the man who helped save us. I feared all the memories I'd been trying to suppress of that terrible time would return with him, too.

I added some extra grape jam to the second slice of toast, still wondering if I was truly awake. I had no trouble imagining the body of a 70-year-old man. But there was a blank spot where the face should be. Stasuk was a teenager when we said goodbye so many years ago. I just couldn't imagine what he looked like now. People sometimes change drastically, even over just a few years, much less a half-century.

I had thought of that good Catholic family so many times as I went about my life. Nothing of the last fifty years of our family history would have been accomplished without their deep faith in God. Other Lithuanians were turning Jews in for rewards and even killing them, but Vaclovas Paskauskas made a decision that his family, although nearly paupers, would stand firm against evil. It was truly a personification of one of their Scriptures, the one where it says you should love your neighbor as yourself.

Although we continued to exchange letters for a while, Izzy and I had finally given up hope of ever seeing the Paskauskas family after moving to America. I often sent packages of clothing and food, which brought a cautious admonition from Mrs. Paskauskas.

"Edna, you are so kind," she once wrote in a letter. "But, please, only send cotton scarves or simple dresses. I know you mean well by sending me such nice linen and silk things, but they are always stolen, and I get only the letter describing them."

The Iron Curtain made communication between our two families eventually impossible. There had been no word from Europe in over thirty years. I was sure that Ona and Vaclovas Paskauskas were long since dead. Izzy and I were in our early thirties when we took refuge in their barn, and I estimated that Vaclovas and Ona had been several years older than we were. We knew it would be a stretch, but Izzy and I had always hoped we might at least reunite with Stasuk.

I remembered Stasuk so well, not just for bringing us food, but because he had taken such a special interest in Jay and had shown such tenderness toward him. Now with Izzy dead and the reunion with Stasuk imminent, I could hardly take it in.

How I longed to put my arms around Izzy and dance with joy. If this worked out the way it was supposed to, it would be a very special day, a little like the one when the Russians liberated us. It had been so long. I really hadn't thought about Stasuk for quite a while. He was so young. I believed he had probably forgotten about us.

Although I had forgotten a lot of other things myself over the years, one thing I remembered clearly was his nickname, "Stasuk," a short version of Stanislovas. He always grinned when I called him that, because it was considered an affectionate term.

I said his name out loud several times, hoping it would help rein in the awful trepidation, but the more I tried to be calm, the more intense the anxiety became. At worst, I thought I would wake from a dream and realize it was yet another re-visitation of the ominous fear I had tried to leave behind in Lithuania.

Izzy, can you believe? Stasuk and his son coming here from Lithuania? We have Stasuk's letters, and Jay bought airline tickets for him and his son months ago. But anything can happen, especially when passing through Customs from Europe. What if they can't leave the country? What if they get sick? Maybe they'll miss the plane. Maybe they won't make all the flight connections. They can't speak English, you know — not a word. Maybe the plane will crash. Oh, listen to me worry. They will come. It's the miracle you always said would happen. I just wish you were here to witness it. How could you be gone just when I need you so much?

I laughed at myself for talking to Izzy, but it was a habit formed when we used to sit opposite each other at our kitchen table looking down over the treetops from our sixth-floor apartment window at 5100 Monument Avenue in Richmond.

It seems I miss Izzy more instead of less as the days go by. We had been a part of each other for so long that sometimes we even finished each other's sentences. So many times we would talk of how we managed to survive the war and come to America. I can see him now and still hear his voice, like watching a rerun of an old-time movie. Izzy always said the same thing. "You know, Edna, despite everything, we have remained a family. God is good to us."

Izzy was right, of course. God had been good to us. How could we not be reminded of our blessings each time we came into our sunny kitchen and sat down in those comfortable chairs with the pretty yellow cushions? Even though I have slowed down considerably, I have always managed to keep the kitchen spotless; everything had its place, right down to the little filigree canister that held the instant coffee we drank early each morning.

Sometimes on the weekends, while Izzy and I waited for our coffee to cool, we would watch young people scurrying to work at the different stores in the shopping center below us. Now that Izzy is gone, I still sit at the table looking at workers dashing in to punch the time clock at the Kroger's below, where I buy groceries every few days. I often wonder if those teenagers could imagine what it would be like to be forced to work as slaves, or to live underground like a mole for months, not daring to speak above a whisper, or to ache as you wished you could brush your teeth, have a bath or see the sun rise again. Ah, but that's impossible. You can't miss what you've always had.

I looked around the apartment and saw such marvelous things. A dishwasher! A stove! I saw all we have attained, but some days, even though I fight it, I have this dark, ominous feeling, like my life is too good to be true, and that once again, as on that sunny day when Jay was just a little boy playing around my kitchen table, it could all turn into a nightmare.

As the day wore on, I couldn't concentrate on any one thing for very long. I tried to clean house but I just wasn't interested. The newspaper even seemed boring. I watched some television but finally cut it off. Nothing helped very much except talking with Izzy.

I finally decided to dress in the early afternoon, just to have something to do. Standing at the closet, trying to decide what to wear, I couldn't help but think of how this day became a reality. I thought again about the strange route that Stasuk's letter took in making its way to us from Lithuania and that there would be a reunion today as the result of it.

I finally decided to wear my navy-blue suit. It was dignified but simple. I settled on a braided gold necklace that looked like a slender rope. I didn't want to wear anything too showy. Stasuk still lived as a farmer not too far from where we had stayed hidden at his home place. He had sent a photograph of himself with his wife standing in front of their house, along with a letter describing their tiny farm, a cow and a few pigs. His wife was wearing what looked like men's galoshes in the picture. It was apparent that their standard of living had changed very little over the years. I thought about the last time that Stasuk saw me, when I still looked half-starved and weighed only 98 pounds, and now how plump I had become and how much I had changed.

I found the earrings that matched the necklace and clipped one in place just as the doorbell rang. I glanced down at Izzy's watch on my left arm and wondered if it was time already. Carrying the second earring in my hand, I went quickly to the door and opened it.

"Jay, darling. I'm so glad you are early," I said. "Suddenly, I'm afraid again. I have forgotten everything. Russian, Lithuanian, German. I still don't even speak English too good. All I really remember is Yiddish. And that's no good for talking to a Catholic."

Jay listened patiently, then hugged and kissed me.

"I'm concerned about the language, too," he said. "But you worry too much. Besides that, Rita will be with us. You remember Rita Ghatak, don't you? She speaks Lithuanian so well. Remember how she interpreted Stasuk's letter for us? It will be all right. Don't you think Stasuk and his son are a little scared, too?"

"Ah, yes, Jay, but not as much as I am. Suddenly I feel old."

"Well, you won't get any younger standing here talking about it, either. Come, put your other earring on and I'll get your coat. Do you have the flowers? I put them in the refrigerator last night."

"They're right here, darling," I answered going into the

kitchen to retrieve the bouquet. "I know exactly why you got them. You knew I would need something to occupy my hands."

I handed the flowers to Jay so I could fasten the belt of my trench coat. I patted the coat pocket to make sure it contained tissues and reached to take the flowers again. I closed my eyes for a moment, took a deep breath, and then walked toward the mirror just inside the apartment foyer, where I inspected myself briefly, squared my shoulders and said, "OK. I'm ready. Let's go."

Jay held open the royal blue door. As I passed through, I instinctively reached above my head with my left hand, exposing Izzy's watch and his wedding ring on my middle finger, reminders of his abiding presence. I lightly stroked the *mezuzah* affixed to the doorway and touched my fingertips to my lips. It's an action I've taken thousands of times when leaving our home, invoking the blessings of the Scriptures. Within minutes we were outside in the April air. After more than half a century, my life had come full circle.

22

The Reunion – 1998

Jay had rented a limousine for the ride to and from the airport. At first, I thought it was a ridiculous extravagance, but the more I thought about it, the more it made sense. Stasuk would be coming to America for the first time, along with his son. While the limousine might have seemed ostentatious to some, why shouldn't we provide the very finest transportation for our savior? After all, had his parents or he wanted to, they could have made money by turning us over to the Nazis or to other Lithuanians. There was a price on every Jew's head at that time. But, here we were, alive and breathing, because of them. On second thought, nothing seemed too expensive or too extravagant.

I had thought of Stasuk and his parents' courage so many times over the years, especially at Jay's bar mitzvah. When I listened to Jay reading from the *Torah*, it was more than music to my ears. It was the sound of our family's future. My heart sang with special joy that day. I remember slipping my hand inside Izzy's and looking at him with such pride.

I think Izzy could read my mind. Later he told me he was thinking the same thing.

"You know, Edna," he said at the reception after the ceremony, "all of this is possible because of some strangers. It's incredible that we were so fortunate. And for them to be Catholics as well. I could have understood it better if other Jews had helped us."

"Yes, Izzy," I said. "I've been thinking of my Uncle Itzhak today as well. He was a savior, too."

Jay was only about nine when we said goodbye to Stasuk for the last time. I wondered that day, as I often did, if we would ever have a chance to show our gratitude to those unselfish people. Because of their insurmountable bravery, our lives had continued, and yes, even prospered when most of our other family members had died. Simply a miracle by anyone's standards.

Those same thoughts returned to me as I was standing on the tarmac at Richmond International Airport beside Jay and Elly. It was a quiet, star-studded night but a little cool with a gentle breeze blowing, not unlike spring nights I remembered when Izzy and I held hands and took long walks when we were dating in Lithuania. Several of our friends had come with us to the airport to greet Stasuk. Jay had arranged special permission for us to meet him on the tarmac, which was most unusual, but so was this event. I was so nervous I could barely stand up. I could see the people around me and the planes coming and going, but I just couldn't grasp the idea that Stasuk would actually be getting off one of them in a few minutes.

"Mother," Jay said as he pointed into the sky. "That's the plane. I just know it is."

Jay was right, of course. He had planned every minute detail of the arrival. I laughed a little to myself thinking that Jay couldn't be any more concerned if he were planning a huge wedding, responsible for the entire affair, from the invitations to the food and florist, along with a thousand other little details like altering bridesmaid dresses. I don't really know how he did it, but Jay managed to get someone to meet Stasuk at all the airports where they had to change planes. He said he didn't want to chance anything going awry. It was quite a feat, but Jay knew Stasuk and his son would need help, especially since they couldn't speak English. Jay had even given them his cell-phone number, but I was nervous because they hadn't called once since their journey began. Jay took it as a good sign, which, of course, it was.

As the plane taxied into place, my heart started pounding hard again, just like it had earlier this morning. I kept thinking again that maybe it really was a dream, and I'd wake up to find myself in bed. I was almost startled when Jay spoke to Rita.

Turning toward our new friend, Jay asked, "Are you ready? It will only be a minute or two. They're pushing the stairs up to the plane now."

"Yes, Jay," Rita answered. "I'm more than a little nervous, but I'm ready. I hope I remember all my Lithuanian."

She turned toward me and asked, "Won't it be wonderful to see him again, Mrs. Ipson?"

"Oh, yes, Rita," I said. "I see the plane, but I won't believe Stasuk is actually on it until I see his face."

"Well, that shouldn't be long, Mother," Jay interjected with a laugh. "They're going to allow Rita to go onboard before they disembark any passengers."

Just then, the airplane's door swung open, and a stewardess stepped out and motioned toward us. Rita took off almost running and went quickly up the stairs. She told me about it later.

"The stewardess asked everyone to keep their seats for a few extra minutes," Rita said. "She explained that a very special reunion was about to take place, and I would need to speak in Lithuanian to two passengers. Then she handed me the microphone.

"When I asked if Stanislovas Krivicius was on board, a portly man got to his feet, lifted his left hand and smiled," Rita continued. "I asked him to stay in his seat until all the other passengers had disembarked."

When I saw Rita come back through the plane's door, I suddenly wondered if I looked all right.

"Elly, look at me," I told my daughter-in-law. "Am I OK?"

"Yes, Mother, you look just fine. Don't worry. They've been traveling for hours, so they won't look their best, either."

"Well, I suppose not," I answered, "but I just want to look nice when I see him. It has been so very long."

"You'll do just fine," Elly reassured me.

Rita was following the other passengers and was halfway down the stairs before Stasuk appeared at the door. He was about average height, with broad shoulders, and was very sturdy looking. He was wearing a dark sport coat with a white shirt and gray pants. Even so, I thought he looked just like a farmer should look. But for some reason it shocked me to see that his hair was completely white. He looked out and saw a group of us moving closer to the plane. He paused and waved before coming the rest of the way down the steps with his son close behind him.

Jay was the first one to greet him, and there was a brief moment of awkwardness because neither man spoke the other's language. Rita had to interpret, of course. When Stasuk realized who Jay and I were, he grabbed us both at the same time. All of us were crying. When I looked around, a lot of other people were crying as well.

Somehow Jay had found a sash that represented Lithuania. He lifted it over Stasuk's head and embraced him again. About then, I remembered the flowers and turned to give them to Stasuk. He took the bouquet in his big weathered hands and gave me one of the tenderest looks I've ever seen. His eyes were as blue as crystal ice. They glittered as he fought back tears.

I suddenly remembered that he used to play the fiddle, and I asked if he still played.

He laughed and said, "No. But tonight I think I could play again. I feel just like dancing."

His son, who is also named Stanislovas, just stood off to the side a little bit. He looked a little dazed, but I could understand that. There were camera lights and flashbulbs going off at the same time. Word had gotten out that the reunion was taking place, and several reporters had come to document the event. They initially held back until the first words between our families were exchanged. Now they were jostling each other for an opportunity to ask Stasuk questions. In order to make the late news at eleven, they'd have to scramble.

Our story had another unusual twist. Holocaust benefactors seldom reunited with the people they had helped. Some of the other survivors who live in Richmond had been amazed at our good fortune. Usually, when someone helped Jews during the war, especially if they were Christians, they gave false names or no names at all to the people they were aiding. That way, if the Jews were ever captured, and that happened a lot, they couldn't reveal the identity of their benefactors, even when tortured.

Once the media interviews were over, we all got into the limousine and went to Jay's house, where Stasuk and his son would be staying for the next two weeks. Alan Zimm, another Holocaust survivor from Poland, was already at Jay's house waiting to greet us and relieve Rita as interpreter. Like most Europeans, Stasuk spoke several languages. It was quite a surprise when Stasuk began to pull out presents for all of us.

"Edna, I wasn't sure what to bring you, but I thought you might like a necklace of amber," Stasuk said, offering me a long strand of amber beads, jewelry which Lithuania is known for.

"Oh, it is so beautiful. It reminds me of when I was a young girl," I said. "Thank you for being so kind."

He brought Elly a necklace as well and some tiny, framed paintings. The artists had used amber crumbs to make a design of a cottage and trees — quite unusual.

Then he turned to Jay.

"And for you," he said, "I have some honey from my bees and the shoes you requested."

Jay accepted the brown bag and quickly reached inside to withdraw a quart of honey and a very small pair of wooden shoes with scant leather straps.

"The honey is nice, but the shoes are perfect," Jay said with such excitement I thought he was going to start dancing.

"I don't know how you managed, Stasuk, but these shoes are exactly like the ones I wore as a boy in the ghetto." With that said, Jay turned and held out the shoes to show Al and Sylvia Rosenbaum, who had accompanied us to the airport.

"Look at these, Al," he said. "My feet hurt just remembering how uncomfortable they were. Even though my grandfather was a cobbler, leather was almost nonexistent inside the ghetto. When he did find a few scraps, my *zeyde* would tack the leather to wooden blocks and make sandals just like these. I've already made a special case for them in the museum. I can't wait to put them on display tomorrow."

Alan, who was quietly interpreting all that Jay said, held up his hand to get Jay's attention. "Stasuk is very anxious to see the museum and wants to know if he can go along," Alan asked.

"Of course, of course," Jay answered as he reached to hug Stasuk again. "I'm anxious for you to see it as well. I want to show you where I have placed your parents' pictures. They are hanging right beside the re-creation of the hiding place. We even have a replica of Rexxyx, your dog."

"No. You don't really," Stasuk said, shaking his head in surprise and delight.

"Well, of course," Jay answered. "Rexxyx is an important part of our family's story, don't you know?"

"Yes! I remember how he barked the night we had to dig your father out of that dirt. It seems impossible that so much time has passed since then."

Then Stasuk held out another small bag whose contents really touched us in a special way. Stasuk had three sap-lings, tiny little cherry trees that he had uprooted from his own garden.

"Here," he said, pulling the almost lifeless twigs from the bag and handing them to Jay. "I wanted to bring something grown in the soil of your homeland. These were growing near my house."

"Wonderful," Jay responded. "You'll have to help me plant them tomorrow, but it's late now and we must go to bed. There is just one thing left to do. We must drink a toast to this day."

As if choreographed for that moment, Elly suddenly appeared with a tray topped with glasses brimming with Benedictine liquor. While she passed out the glasses, she retold the story of how John Garger had been working in the post office sorting the registered letters and again in unclaimed mail, both stations where he ordinarily didn't work, when Stasuk's letter came through the post office.

"Had it not been for John Garger and his belief that the letter had a special meaning," Elly reiterated, "this wouldn't be happening tonight. And they say you can't depend on the post office."

After a hearty laugh, we lifted our glasses in one accord,

saluting the culmination of another miracle before heading for our respective homes and beds.

The following two weeks passed so quickly that it almost took my breath away. After Stasuk told Jay that he couldn't see very well, the first thing Jay did was call an optometrist. Even though it was Sunday, a good friend of ours examined Stasuk and fitted him with glasses almost immediately. You can't imagine Stasuk's surprise when he put the glasses on the first time.

"Everything is so clear," he said, grinning widely. "Now I can really see America. This is wonderful."

Stasuk wasn't the only one looking through new eyes. I had almost forgotten how much we have here in America. When we took him to a grocery store, he just stood in the aisles at first, stunned by the variety of food. He was even more astounded when he visited Virginia State University near Petersburg, where he saw an experimental fish farm. He had told Jay in one of his letters that sometimes he and his son fished as a sideline occupation, so Jay thought he might find the farm interesting. Henry Moss, another survivor from Poland who worked for Izzy for thirty years, went along to interpret that day.

"Edna," Henry said later, "you should have seen the fish. There were ponds as far as you could see. The farm manager took a net and scooped up several. He gave a really fat one to Stasuk to hold in his hands while we took pictures of him."

Henry turned to Stasuk and explained what he was saying to me.

"Yes," Stasuk said laughing, "and be sure you tell her how fat I felt after we went to the steakhouse.

"I tell you, Edna, there was so much food," he said, laughing and patting his stomach.

"You should enjoy," I said. "It is our pleasure to do for you and your son."

"I know," Stasuk replied, "but there is more food in one American meal than we would eat in a whole day in Lithuania."

"Well, you'll be going back too soon as it is," I said. "Enjoy while you're here."

Stasuk also had a chance to eat his native food during his visit. Rita invited all her Lithuanian friends in Richmond to her home for a potluck dinner. Stasuk and his son returned to Jay and Elly's that night so stuffed they could barely walk. It must have been really nice for them to see people who could talk easily with them and eat their native food.

Rita told me that while they were eating, someone asked Stasuk how his parents had decided to take us in. He replied, "What else could we do? There was no other choice. They were human beings, just like us. I still remember seeing how my father cried when he described the little Jewish children he saw leaving the ghetto. He was certain they were going to their death."

When Stasuk and his son weren't eating or visiting, Jay had them busy with different things he thought they would want to see.

One day they visited Paramount's Kings Dominion, where they rode a Ferris wheel for the first time. Another day they went to a dairy farm where an extension agent met them and explained how crops were grown here and demonstrated the milking machines to Stasuk and his son. Carol Shapiro, another survivor from Poland, went along as the interpreter for that day.

The farm machinery especially intrigued Stasuk. Later, at a Southern States store, he could barely pull himself away from looking at all the agricultural supplies and seeds. He examined the hand tools until it was time for the store to close. He couldn't wait to get home and tell me about one of Jay's purchases.

With a wide smile he asked Carol to explain, "Edna, I saw this chain saw. I turned to my son and said, 'Isn't that beautiful, and wouldn't it come in handy when we start to cut wood for this winter?' Jay asked Carol what I had said. The next thing I know, Jay is taking the saw to the counter and paying for it. Can you believe it?"

"Yes, I can," I said. "We have waited for years to repay you for your family's kindness to us. I hope you have much warmth this winter."

"I will," he said. "And when my son and I go out to fell the trees, I'm sure we will tell our friends what a wonderful time we had here in America."

"What will you tell them about not eating bread at Jay's house?" I asked.

"I'll tell them that my Jewish friends were observing Passover and I joined with you by eating matzo."

With another one of his sweet smiles, he added, "For you and your family, we can go without bread for a while."

Stanislovas Krivicius and his son, Stanislovas, stand with Edna and Jay Ipson near the tree planted at the Virginia Holocaust Museum to honor Krivicius and his parents for their part in saving the lives of 13 Jews, including the Ipsons, during the Holocaust (1998).

23

During Yom HaShoah

Because of the fateful timing of Stasuk's letter, his visit coincided with the first anniversary of the Virginia Holocaust Museum as well as *Yom HaShoah*, the international day of recognition for martyrs, survivors and liberators of the Holocaust. A special program had been in the works before we knew Stasuk was coming, but his arrival made it even more meaningful. I shall never forget the feeling I had when Jay was reading the statement we had prepared for Stasuk.

Alan Zimm was on the *bima*, the podium at Temple Beth-El, acting as the interpreter for Stasuk while Jay read the proclamation to the audience in English. We had inscribed a gold medallion with a few words. Jay gave a little history of how we came to be with Stasuk's family and then read the inscription so that all of the people in the temple could share in our joy.

...There is a saying that two mountains will never meet. As

for two humans, that is an entirely different thing. Some things are preordained. Such a thing happened to me in November 1997, when John Garger, a postal worker, handed my wife a letter addressed to my late father. The letter looked like it was addressed to I. Ipoon. John didn't know my father, but he did know that some personal mail was usually delivered to I. Ipson at the American Parts Company post office box. Elly went to pick up the company mail, and John showed her the letter and asked if she recognized the name on the envelope. She came to me with all sorts of excitement waving the letter, which had a return address in Lithuania. It had been mailed to an address on West Cary that we left some 27 years earlier. The letter was going to be returned to Lithuania as undeliverable, when John interceded. Now I can tell you the rest of the story.

It was 1943, and my family had been incarcerated in Kovno Ghetto in Lithuania for almost two years. Our murderous neighbors and the Germans were killing the Jews. The Germans had already started deporting and exterminating the elderly and the children in the Warsaw Ghetto in a program referred to as 'Kinderaktion.' My mother's parents, two brothers and sister were deported to Riga, Latvia, never to be seen again. Miraculously, my mother and I were pulled out of the deportation line by a policeman who was a friend of my father's. My father, of blessed memory, who passed away in February 1997, received word that the children in Kovno Ghetto would be next. A farmer that my father had previously done legal work for offered to help us. Under cover of night, my father cut the wires and we escaped without saying a word, for any word would have meant instant death. We were transported by a horse-drawn cart to a poor Polish Catholic farmer's home, who risked his family's life to save us. They were so poor that their one-room, rented house didn't even have a chimney. Their only furniture was a bench, a table and a wooden frame bed with a straw mattress, which was shared by the farmer, his wife and his stepson, Stanislovas Krivicius. I called him by his nickname, "Stasuk." He was a young man who enjoyed playing the fiddle. One Saturday night, Stasuk was on his way home from a hoedown when he heard his dog, Rexxyx, barking repeatedly. He knew that we were hiding in the barn and we might be in danger. When he went to check on the dog, he discovered a hand sticking out of the ground. My father,who was a lawyer, not an engineer, did not know that it was necessary to shore up the sides of the hole as you tunnel. While he was digging a hole for us to hide in, it caved in on him and he was buried alive. Stasuk and his parents were able to free my father, who completed digging the hiding place where we lived for months without a bath or a change of clothes, or knowing whether we would live or die.

Over time, ten other family members lived underground with us. Because of Stasuk's quick action, thirteen lives were saved. It is my honor and privilege to present Stanislovas Krivicius a gold medallion that was made especially for him. I will now tell you what Alan will tell him in Polish: On behalf of all of us, I present this gold medallion. We give it with love and admiration to a person who, at a very young age, risked his life to save thirteen Jews that were neither friends nor family. You did not receive any pay for this. Your only reward came from God, therefore, it is my pleasure and honor to declare you a 'Righteous Gentile.'

When Jay hung the medallion around Stasuk's neck, I felt an enormous sense of accomplishment. I also felt Izzy's presence right beside me, participating in the day. Finally Jay picked up the *shofar*, the ram's horn blown during special Jewish services. I have heard that mournful sound many, many times and understood its calling to my Hebrew ancestors. But that day it had an even deeper meaning. Here was my little boy, now almost 63, saluting not only *Yom HaShoah* but also one of the people who made our future possible. It was almost too much emotion to bear.

After the service, we gathered again just in front of the museum, behind the temple. Within minutes, we had unveiled a tree that had previously been planted to honor Stasuk and his parents, a living symbol of their sacrifice.

Too soon the visit was over, and once again we were going to the airport. The wait inside seemed interminable. Although I could barely keep from crying, I looked at Stasuk for a long time. He was wearing one of Izzy's suits and a pair of his shoes. I had given him a lot of Izzy's clothes and was so pleased that they were a perfect fit. I think Izzy would have liked that. He always bought the nicest suits, often going to Chicago for them. It seemed right that Stasuk should have them. We stood close to each other without touching. When one of the flight attendants called out the flight number and instructed the first passengers to board, Stasuk and I quickly embraced. I held his face between my hands just for a moment. We didn't say a word. We didn't have to. Those blue eyes spoke to me in silent understanding.

Suddenly it was time for Stasuk and his son to board. Another quick hug all around, and all I could see was a wave of Stasuk's hand as he disappeared down the walkway toward the plane. Jay touched my arm to go, but I was frozen in place. I couldn't turn toward him or even speak.

Sensing my pain, Jay walked away and took photos of the plane through the window of the observation deck. As I watched it disappear from sight, I took the first easy breath I'd drawn for months. Finally I realized the dream that Izzy and I had talked about so many times. Izzy would be proud of what we had been able to accomplish.

Jay touched my arm gently again. This time I could leave. I turned to him and said, "Come, Jay darling, let's go home. The wedding is over."

Stanislovas Krivicius (*left*) receives the Life Saving Cross from Valdas Adamkus, president of the Republic of Lithuania, who honored Krivicius and his parents in recognition of Jewish Genocide Day held in Lithuania each year (1998).

Life Saving Cross
Valdas Adamkus, president of the Republic of Lithuania, presented Stanislovas "Stasuk" Krivicius with a Lithuanian Life Saving Cross during a ceremony held on September 14, 1998. The event was held in the presidential office in conjunction with September 23. That day, known as Jewish Genocide Day, is set aside in Lithuania each year to commemorate the loss of Jewish lives by Nazi genocide during World War II. Krivicius's mother and stepfather, Ona and Vaclovas Paskauskas, were honored posthumously with the same award and praised for offering aid to Jews in spite of danger of death to themselves.

Righteous Among the Nations
A certificate of honor declaring Stanislovas Krivicius as "Righteous Among the Nations" was issued on March 22, 1999. His mother and stepfather, Ona and Vaclovas Paskauskas, received the honor posthumously. The title is bestowed by Righteous Among the Nations, Yad Vashem, The Holocaust Martyrs' and Heroes' Remembrance Authority in Jerusalem.

The authority honors non-Jews who risked their lives to help Jews survive the Holocaust. The criteria, in part, for such a designation is determined when the data on hand clearly demonstrate that a non-Jewish person risked his (or her) life, freedom, and safety without exacting in advance monetary compensation; this qualifies the rescuer for serious consideration to be awarded the "Righteous Among the Nations" title. This applies equally to rescuers who have since passed away.

Epilogue

J ay and Elly Ipson have three children. Edith, the eldest, is married to Michael McCauley. The McCauley's have a son, Joel. Ronny Ipson is married to Teresa Holley. Esther Ipson is married to Terry Minter. She has three children from a former marriage, David, Ben and Sarah Ipson-Minter. The Ipsons and their descendents reside in Richmond, Virginia.

....

Israel (Lola) and Sheina Gillman moved to Germany in 1945, where a daughter, Etty, was born. They moved to Israel in 1949 where Erit, another daughter, was born. The Gillman family moved to Canada in 1953 where Mr. Gillman established a successful hosiery manufacturing plant. He is retired.

Israel and Sheina Gillman have three grandsons and one granddaughter, as well as three great-grandsons and one great-granddaughter. All of the Gillmans and their descendents live in Canada.

In 1982 Mr. Gillman reinterred the bodies of his mother, Nese, and brother, Leibel, in Israel.

Moshe, Sheina and Sara Gillman remained in Lithuania where another daughter, Liuba, and a son, David, were born. Mr. and Mrs. Gillman and several family members moved to Israel in 1971.

Sara Gillman pursued a medical degree in Lithuania and married Joseph Pliamm. They and their son, Lew, moved to Israel in 1972. The family subsequently moved to Canada where a daughter, Naomi, was born. Since 1979, the Gillmans and all their descendents have lived in Canada, where Dr. Pliamm maintains a general practice.

Moshe and Sheina Gillman have four grandsons, two granddaughters and three great-granddaughters. Moshe Gillman died in 1993.

....

Itzhak and Ida Kalamitsky moved to Israel in 1974. Ida died in 1990 at the age of 86. Itzhak died in 1994 at the age of 100.

....

Jacob Kalamitskas   (Lithuanian spelling of Kalamitsky) married Edna Shtukarevitz and had a daughter, Ariela. His family moved to Israel in 1972. Ariela married Moshe Samuel. They had a daughter, Edna, and a son, Hagai.

Edna Kalamitskas died in 1994. Jacob retired as an electrical engineer with Israel Electric Company in 2000.

....

David Kalamitsky and his wife, Lea Mirkin, have three sons: Adir Leshem (a Hebrew family name), Ran and Yaniv, as well as one grandson and one granddaughter. David's family moved to Israel in 1972. He retired as an electronic engineer at Bezeq Telephone Company in 1998.

Sheina Berkman married Meir Shadur, who protected her after she left the Itzhak Kalamitsky group. The Shadurs remained in Kaunas and had two children, then moved to Israel in 1979. Sheina died in 1999. The Shadurs had five grandchildren.

....

Raja and Emmanuel Shlom returned to their hometown of Zosli, then moved to Kovno where she taught school. They entered Poland with forged papers and eventually made it to the American Zone in West Berlin, where they lived in a displaced persons' camp from August 1946 to April 1948. Raja was headmistress in a school there. They later traveled to South Africa where Raja reclaimed her late husband's property. She married David Schiff in 1952. After their retirement, the Schiffs moved to Israel in 1972. David Schiff died in 1983. Raja died in 1986.

Joseph Shlom, who died at six months, was born three years before Emmanuel. Prior to her death, Raja broke a 26-year-long silence with her sister, Ida. Emmanuel says the sisters became quite close in the twilight years of their lives.

....

Emmanuel Shlom moved to Israel in 1963 and married Ilana Braunn in 1970. They had a son, Moshe-Gad, and a daughter, Tali. Ilana Shlom died in 1985.

Emmanuel married Michal Gilad in 1990. She had two children. They resided in Israel with their children. Emmanuel retired as a senior economist from Bezeq (the Israel Telco) in 2000. He died in 2005.

....

Master Sergeant Helmut Rauca fled to Canada after the war. He was extradited to Germany in 1986 when it was determined he lied on his immigration documents, nullifying his Canadian citizenship. Rauca was convicted of the murder of more than 11,500 Jews. He died in a prison hospital in Frankfurt am Main.

....

Research revealed that John E. Garger resigned from the Richmond post office and moved to Florida in 1999. It is believed he has died from complications of cancer.

....

The Virginia Holocaust Museum was established on Roseneath Road in Richmond in a former education building of Temple Beth-El in May 1997. The museum was moved to a new location, provided by the Virginia General Assembly, at 2000 E. Cary Street. The new museum was dedicated during a *Yom HaShoah* memorial service in April 2003. Izzy Ipson's wristwatch and Chananya Butrimowitz's remaining rubles have found a final home in the museum.

....

Valdas Adamkus, president of the Republic of Lithuania honored Stanislovas "Stasuk" Krivicius and his parents on September 14, 1998. Adamkus presented Krivicius with a Lithuanian Life Saving Cross, in conjunction with September 23, the day set aside in Lithuania to commemorate the genocide of the Jews. Ona and Vaclovas Paskauskas were honored posthumously with the same honor.

....

A certificate of honor declaring Vaclovas and Ona Paskauskas and Stanislovas Krivicius as "Righteous Among the Nations" was issued on March 22, 1999, bestowed by Righteous Among the Nations, Yad Vashem, The Holocaust Martyrs' and Heroes' Remembrance Authority in Jerusalem.

The authority honors non-Jews who risked their lives to help Jews survive the Holocaust.

The criteria, in part, for such a designation is determined when the data on hand clearly demonstrates that a non-Jewish person risked his (or her) life, freedom, and safety without exacting in advance monetary compensation; this qualifies the rescuer for serious consideration to be awarded the "Righteous Among the Nations" title. This applies equally to rescuers who have since passed away.

Vaclovas Paskauskas died in 1982 at the age of 92. Ona Paskauskas died in 1992 at the age of 93.

Stanislovas Krivicius died in 2004 at the age of 77.

One of the three cherry trees Stanislovas "Stasuk" Krivicius brought from Lithuania in 1998 has put down roots and continues to grow in Jay and Elly Ipson's backyard.

It is believed that Marchuk, Itzhak Kalamitsky's neighbor and friend who aided the five families in this story, was banished to Siberia after the war.

Jay Ipson and Jacob Kalamitskas still sleep under their comforters every night.

To paraphrase Elie Wiesel, a Holocaust survivor and author who won the Nobel Peace Prize in 1986: More dangerous than anger and hatred is indifference. To be indifferent to suffering is what makes the human being inhuman. Indifference is not a beginning, it is an end — and it is always the friend of the enemy.

Chronology

War and Holocaust

1939

August 23
Molotov-Ribbentrop Non-Aggression Pact, amended September 28, divides Poland between Germany and the Soviet Union and cedes the Baltic States – Lithuania, Estonia, Latvia – to the Soviet sphere of influence.

September 1
German forces invade Poland; World War II begins.

November 23
Nazis introduce Jewish Star of David as identifying badge throughout occupied Poland.

1940

April 30
First major Jewish ghetto, in Polish city of Lodz, is sealed.

June 15
Soviet army occupies indepedent Lithuania.

November 15
Warsaw Ghetto is sealed.

1941

June 22
"Operation Barbarossa" begins: German troops, violating the 1939 Molotov-Ribbentrop Pact, attack Soviet Union, crossing into Lithuania at 3:05 a.m.

June 23
The four Einsatzgruppen units, mobile task forces attached to major German army units, begin their killings in the USSR. SS-Brigadier General Walther Stahlecker leads Einsatzgruppe A in the Baltic States and parts of

Kovno Ghetto

June 23
Soviet armed forces, having occupied Lithuania since June 1940, retreat from Kovno. Lithuanian pro-Nazi partisans begin terrorizing Jews in the city.

Belorussia. In Lithuania, SS-Colonel Karl Jäger commands Einsatzkommando 3, a sub-division of Einsatzgruppe A.

June 24
German armed forces occupy Vilna, Lithuania, 57 miles southeast of Kovno. Jewish population numbers 55,000.

June 26
German armed forces occupy Shavli, Lithuania, 70 miles northwest of Kovno, where 5,300 Jews reside.

July 1
German armed forces occupy Riga, Latvia.

July 4
Jewish council (Judenrat) is formed in Vilna.

June 24
German forces enter Kovno at night.

June 25-26
Encouraged by the SS, ultra-nationalist Lithuanian "partisans" accelerate pogrom against Kovno's Jews, attacking rabbis and their followers in suburb of Vilijampole, known to local Jews as Slobodka. The partisans set fire to several synagogues and burn down some 60 houses. Between 800 and 1,000 Jews are killed.

June 27
While crowds of jeering spectators and many German soldiers look on, Lithuanian "partisans" kill 60 Jews at the Lietukis garage in central Kovno, battering most of them to death, one by one, with iron bars.

June 28
Germans abolish Lithuanian "partisans" and begin forming Lithuanian auxiliary police.

July 4-6
Lithuanian auxiliary police, acting under orders of SS-Colonel Karl Jäger, commander of mobile killing unit Einsatzkommando 3, kill 2,977 Jews in mass shootings at Fort VII, one of several Imperial Russian fortifications surrounding Kovno used as prisons and execution sites during the war.

July 7
Germans inform prominent members of Kovno's Jewish community that a ghetto is to be established for Kovno's Jews in Vilijampole/Slobodka. This neighborhood is characterized by old, wooden, single-story houses without running water. To coordinate the move, a "Committee for the Transfer of the Jews to Vilijampole" is formed from among the Jewish community.

From The Hidden History of the Kovno Ghetto by the U.S. Holocaust Memorial Museum. ©1997 by Walter Reich. By permission of Little, Brown and Company, Inc.

Chronology

War and Holocaust

1941 cont'd

July 31

Nazi leader Hermann Göring authorizes Reinhard Heydrich, head of Reich Security Main Office (RSHA), with organizing a "total solution" to the "Jewish question."

Kovno Ghetto

July 10

Jurgis Bobelis, Lithuanian military commander of Kovno, and Kazys Palciauskas, mayor of Kovno, order Jews moved into Slobodka ghetto by August 15. Lithuanians residing in Slobodka are to be evacuated, and Jews from neighborhoods across the city, the vast majority of Kovno's more than 30,000 Jews, are to join those already living in Slobodka. Jews, regardless of sex and age, are ordered to wear a yellow Star of David sewn to clothing and observe a 6 a.m. to 8 p.m. curfew. Kovno's Jewish leaders appeal to city authorities to cancel measure establishing ghetto, arguing that crowding Kovno's Jews into Slobodka will produce intolerable living conditions and lead to spread of contagious diseases, but the effort fails.

July 24

Kovno municipal authorities order Jews to erect fence around ghetto.

July 28

The German civil administration takes over affairs in Kovno from the German military. Newly appointed Stadtkommissar (city commissioner) of Kovno, SA-Colonel Hans Cramer, issues his first orders, including forbidding Jews to walk on sidewalks, to enter public parks, to sit on public benches, or to use public transportation.

August 2

Einsatzkommandos lead mass shootings by Lithuanian auxiliaries of more than 200 Jewish men and women at Fort IV. Most of the women held at the fort endure rape and other forms of abuse; some are released.

August 4
Acting on German orders, surviving leaders of Kovno's prewar Jewish community form Jewish council (Ältestenrat) for purposes of carrying out German decrees and administering ghetto affairs. Leaders elect as chairman Dr. Elkhanan Elkes, a physician and one of Kovno's most prominent Jewish citizens.

August 7-8
One thousand Jews are arrested and shot at Fort IV.

August 15
Ghetto is closed under police guard, with some 29,700 Jews crammed into a Large Ghetto and a Small Ghetto, the two sections separated by Paneriu Street, a main artery outside ghetto limits. A small bridge will later be built between the two. Jews are prohibited from freely leaving ghetto.

August 17
Ältestenrat announces the creation of Jewish Ghetto Police "to protect public order and to supervise implementation of orders from authorities and Ältestenrat."

August 18
"Intellectuals Action," the first of the German operations to reduce the ghetto population: 534 Jews, including many professionals lured by offer of clerical work in city archives, are removed from ghetto, taken to Fort IV, and killed. (German sources report killing 711 Jews in this "action.")

August 29
Germans forbid transport of food and other items into ghetto.

August 31
Shavli Ghetto is established.

August 31
Vilna Ghetto is formed.

~ 263 ~

Chronology

War and Holocaust

1941 cont'd

September 2
Ten members of the Vilna Jewish Council are executed by the Gestapo.

September 3
First gassing experiments with Zyklon B at Auschwitz; 600 Soviet prisoners of war and 250 ill Polish prisoners are killed.

September 28-29
SS Einsatzgruppe C kills more than 33,000 Jews at Babi Yar, outside Kiev, Ukraine.

Kovno Ghetto

September 3
Germans order ghetto inhabitants to hand over money and valuables, including jewelry, paintings, furs, livestock, and stamp collections.

September 7
Germans prohibit Jews from buying in the city. Illegal purchases nevertheless continue.

September 8
First brigade of workers is marched out of ghetto to Aleksotas military airfield, three-and-a-half miles from ghetto.

September 15
Ältestenrat issues 5,000 craftsmen certificates provided by German specialist on Jewish affairs in Kovno, SA-Captain Fritz Jordan. These Jordan-Scheine, also known as "life certificates," would later protect holders from certain German "actions" by ensuring them work.

September 26
Some 1,000 ghetto inhabitants are taken from the neighborhood of the Slobodka Yeshiva to Fort IV and shot in retaliation for an alleged shooting at Commander Kozlowski of the German Ghetto Guard.

October 4

Germans liquidate the Small Ghetto: After burning the contagious diseases hospital with patients and staff inside, hundreds of Jews, mostly women and children who do not hold "Jordan certificates," are taken to Fort IX. Some 1,800 people are killed.

October 15

Deportations of Austrian and German Jews to Lodz, Poland; Minsk, Belorussia; Riga, Latvia; and Kovno begin.

October 28

The "Great Action": SA-Captain Fritz Jordan and Gestapo Sergeant Helmut Rauca preside over massive, day-long "selection" in ghetto's Demokratu Square, where all ghetto Jews assembled upon penalty of death. By evening, 9,200 men, women, and children, more than 30 percent of the ghetto population, have been sent "to the right" i.e., chosen to be killed. They are shot the next day at Fort IX. Those sent "to the left" return home. The 22-month-long "period of relative calm" begins.

October 29

Vilna's "small ghetto" is liquidated; 33,500 Jews are killed between June and December.

November 24

Theresienstadt Ghetto opens near Prague, in German-controlled Protectorate of Bohemia and Moravia.

November 25

Education Office is established in ghetto under direction of cultural leader Chaim Nachman Shapiro, who begins secret archival project. Shapiro encourages artists such as Esther Lurie and writers to begin documentary efforts. Avraham Tory of the Ältestenrat collects ghetto and German documents for the archives.

November 29

2,000 Jews (including 1,155 women and 152 children) from Vienna and Breslau are shot at Fort IX; 19 Jews from the ghetto are also shot.

December 1

SS-Colonel Karl Jäger reports that "our objective, to solve the Jewish problem for Lithuania, has been achieved." He claims a total of 136,442 Jews killed by Einsatzkommando 3 and Lithuanian auxiliaries. He reports that there remain 15,000 Jews in the Kovno Ghetto, 15,000 in the Vilna Ghetto, and 4,500 in Shavli Ghetto. (A census report prepared by Kovno Ältestenrat in November shows a slightly higher ghetto population of 17,237 men, women, and children.)

December 7

Japanese bomb Pearl Harbor, Hawaii.

December 8

Chelmno killing center, northwest of Lodz, Poland begins gassing operations. United States declares war on Japan.

Chronology

War and Holocaust

Kovno Ghetto

1941 cont'd

December 11
Germany declares war on the United States.

December 12
Acting on German demands for more workers, the Ältestenrat orders individuals previously exempted from work (men ages 16 to 17 and 55 to 60, women ages 45 to 50, and women with children up to age 8) to register with the ghetto Labor Office on December 17. All persons who fail to register are to "be handed over to the ghetto court as shirkers and...severely punished."

December 31
The several Communist resistance groups merge to form the Anti-Fascist Organization under Chaim Yelin.

1942

January 20
At the Wannsee Conference, RSHA head Reinhard Heydrich presides over meeting of key German government leaders to discuss implementation of "Final Solution."

January 5
German ghetto guard chief prohibits demolishing houses or part of houses or fences. Ghetto inmates, desperate for fuel during one of the coldest winters on record in Kovno, defy the prohibition.

January 12
Ghetto workshops, employing prisoners unable to endure forced labor conditions, begin operations, mending uniforms and manufacturing gloves for the German military.

January 14
Germans shoot cats and dogs in small synagogue on Veliuonos Street; the remains are left to rot, desecrating the place of worship.

January 26
Area within three meters of either side of ghetto fence is declared "death zone." Anyone inside this area is to

be shot without warning. This order is meant to deter Jews smuggling food into ghetto or Lithuanians entering ghetto to plunder Jewish homes.

February 6
Gestapo deports 359 Jews, including 137 women, from the ghetto for forced labor in the Riga Ghetto (Latvia), 140 miles north of Kovno.

February 16
Ghetto laundry workshop, employing mostly women, begins work washing clothes of German police and civil administrators.

February 27
Germans order confiscation of all books in the ghetto for recycling into paper. Ghetto inmates hide many books and Torah scrolls brought to the ghetto from city's synagogues.

March 10
A group of 24 Jews from the ghetto are shot for selling goods on black market and not wearing Star of David badges.
Ghetto workshop is set up for manufacture of toys for children.

March 12
Ghetto shoemaking workshop begins repairing military boots and other footwear.

April 26
Ältestenrat issues regulations regarding the planting and protection of vegetable gardens and the operation of a communal soup kitchen.

May 1
Germans again reduce area of ghetto by redrawing boundaries. Crowding worsens.

May 12
Germans arrest four members of Ältestenrat staff, including the head of the administrative Secretariat, for participating in illegal mail service with the Vilna Ghetto. Avraham Tory named head of Secretariat.

March 2
Some 3,000 Jews from Minsk Ghetto (Belorussia) are killed; following this "action," flight of thousands of Minsk Jews to forests begins.

March 17
Belzec killing center in occupied Poland begins operations.

May
Sobibor killing center in occupied Poland begins operations.

Chronology

War and Holocaust

1942 cont'd

July 15
Deportations begin of Jews from Netherlands to Auschwitz and Sobibor.

Kovno Ghetto

June 2
Acting on German orders, Ältestenrat sends 73 people to dig peat in Palemonas, six miles from Kovno. Some escape on way to camp. Forty additional workers are sent two days later. Work conditions and regime at this camp are so harsh that many Jews are killed there or die of hunger or exhaustion.

June 16
Germans order transfer of the ghetto workshops from Ältestenrat to German control.

June 28
The Jewish Ghetto Police orchestra of well-known musicians plays for school-children in former yeshiva. Organizers asked audience to refrain from applauding out of respect for the dead.

July 2
Ältestenrat transmits German order requiring work for all men older than 15 and women aged 17 to 47 with no children under 6.

July 4
Germans order dissolution of ghetto court.

July 7
German ghetto commander issues regulation for fencing off section of Vilija River for bathing.

July 22-September 21
Mass deportations from Warsaw Ghetto; approximately 265,000 Jews are killed at Treblinka.

July 23
Treblinka killing center in occupied Poland begins operation.

July 28-31
At least 10,000 Jews from Minsk Ghetto (Belorussia) are killed by Germans using mobile gas vans and mass shootings.

August 10-23
50,000 Jews from Lvov Ghetto (Poland) are deported to Belzec killing center.

August 15
Births are forbidden in the Shavli Ghetto.

August 16-18
Radom Ghetto (Poland) is liquidated; 20,000 Jews are killed, most of them at Treblinka.

September 12
Battle of Stalingrad begins.

October 19
German army encounters tenacious Soviet defense at Stalingrad.

July 24
Germans issue order prohibiting pregnancies and birth in ghetto: "Pregnancies have to be terminated. Pregnant women will be shot."

August 26
Germans prohibit all religious observances in ghetto and order closing of schools. Prisoners clandestinely continue religious and educational activities and expand curriculum of still-legal vocational school to include regular school subjects.

August 31
Ältestenrat announces German order to end the ghetto's cash economy and the smuggling of food into the ghetto.

September 8
In fulfillment of earlier German orders, the Ältestenrat prohibits births and offers abortions in ghetto hospital.

September 11
Germans order the Ältestenrat to provide 150 workers for the Palemonas peat bogs.

Chronology

War and Holocaust

1942 cont'd

November 7
Allied forces invade North Africa.

November 19
Soviet armed forces begin a counterattack near Stalingrad.

1943

January 5
Lvov Ghetto (Poland) is transformed into labor camp; 10,000 Jews are killed.

February 2
Final surrender of German forces at Stalingrad.

February 5-12
Some 10,000 Jews from Bialystok Ghetto (Poland) are deported to Treblinka; an additional 2,000 are killed on the spot.

Kovno Ghetto

October 23
Germans deport 369 Jews from Kovno to the Riga Ghetto (Latvia). Jewish Ghetto Police help round up those unwilling to leave.

November 15
Ghetto prisoner Nahum Meck allegedly shoots at a German sentry during attempt to escape from ghetto. Germans arrest Meck and hold the Ältestenrat and other Jews as hostages.

November 18
Meck is hanged publicly in the ghetto by Jewish Ghetto Police. The next day, his mother and sister are shot at Fort IX.

February 4
"Stalingrad Action": following surrender by German forces at Stalingrad, Germans shoot 44 ghetto Jews at Fort IX. Pretext is illegal smuggling activities. Shortly thereafter, cultural leader Chaim Nachman Shapiro asks artist Esther Lurie to encourage other artists to speed up documentation efforts.

February 28
Burial of Rabbi Avraham Duber Shapiro, chief rabbi of Kovno and Lithuania, who dies after long illness.

March 15
Deportations begin of Jews from Greece to Auschwitz.

April 19–May 16
Warsaw Ghetto revolt; ends with the destruction of the ghetto.

May 12
Axis forces surrender in North Africa.

June 1–6
Some 10,000 Jews are deported to Auschwitz from Sonsowiec Ghetto (Poland).

June 11
Reichsführer-SS Heinrich Himmler orders liquidation of all ghettos in occupied Poland. This results in mass deportations to Treblinka and other killing centers.

June 21
Himmler orders all ghettos in the Ostland liquidated and reorganized into concentration camps.

July 10
Allies invade Sicily.

August 2
Armed prisoner revolt at the Treblinka killing center.

August 16–20
Liquidation of Bialystok Ghetto (Poland); 25,000 Jews are deported to their deaths.

August 4–September 4
About 7,000 Jews are deported from Vilna Ghetto to Estonia for forced labor.

September 1
Vilna Ghetto fighters clash with German forces.

September 8
Italy signs armistice with Allies.

September 23–24
Final liquidation of Vilna Ghetto: 3,700 Jews are sent to Estonia and Latvian labor camps, and 4,000 are deported to their immediate deaths at killing centers in occupied Poland.

June-July
Zionist and pro-Soviet leftists in ghetto unite to form Jewish General Fighting Organization under the leadership of Chaim Yelin. The two groups agree that "each side will recruit its own men" but will join in a "united program for training and activity until departure to the forests." At its peak, the Jewish General Fighting Organization has close to 600 members.

July 24
Exhibition of ghetto artist Esther Lurie's drawings is held for small circle of friends.

September-December
Seeking to hide crimes in anticipation of forced retreat, Germans use Jewish prisoners and Soviet prisoners of war to exhume and burn corpses from mass graves at Fort IX.

September
Jewish Soviet partisan Gessia Glezer enters ghetto for discussions with activists, including Chaim Yelin, central figure in the Jewish General Fighting Organization. Plans are developed to send armed groups into Augustow Forest, 80 miles south of Kovno.

Chronology

War and Holocaust

1943 cont'd

October 14
Armed prisoner revolt at the Sobibor killing center.

Kovno Ghetto

September 15
SS-Captain Wilhelm Goecke of Gestapo announces takeover of Kovno ghetto administration and workshops by SS from German civilian authorities. Move begins the transformation of the ghetto into a concentration camp and signals end to more than 22 months of relative calm in ghetto.

October 13
Germans order Ältestenrat to collect 3,000 Jewish workers for deportation to labor camps beyond the Kovno area.

October 26
Russian and Ukrainian auxiliaries assist Germans in deportation of at least 2,700 Jews from Kovno. Those of working age are transported to labor camps in Vaivara and Klooga, Estonia, while very young and old are deported to their deaths at Auschwitz. (German documents record a deportation of 2,800 Kovno Jews.)

October 28
At least 43 partisans leave ghetto for Augustow Forest. Only two men succeed in reaching the forest; most are killed or captured, and eleven return safely to the ghetto after imprisonment. This is one of several attempted escapes to forest in October and November involving a total of nearly 100 partisans. Most were arrested and killed.

November 1
SS-Captain Wilhelm Goecke officially reclassifies the Kovno Ghetto as a concentration camp.

November 2
Final liquidation of Riga Ghetto (Latvia); more than 2,000 Jews are sent to Auschwitz.
November 5
Germans murder all Jewish children in the Shavli Ghetto.

November 24
Ten armed partisans leave the ghetto on foot for Rudniki Forest, 94 miles away; six reach their destination. During the following weeks, nine groups of partisans, totaling 180 people, are driven to the forest in trucks; not all arrive safely.
November 30
Some 1,000 ghetto inhabitants are taken to satellite camp in the suburb of Aleksotas. The 7,000 to 8,000 Jews remaining in the ghetto are confined to a small area.
December 2
Chaim Nachman Shapiro, the leader of the ghetto's cultural affairs, his wife, son, and mother (widow of Chief Rabbi Avraham Duber Shapiro) are taken to Fort IX after being led to believe they were to have safe passage to Switzerland.
December 16
Some 900 Jews are taken from Kovno camp to satellite labor camp in the suburb of Sanciai. Later, Jews are taken to Palemonas, Kirdan, and Koshedar.

1944

March 19
German forces occupy Hungary.
March 27
Forty Jewish policemen shot at Riga.

March 27
In an effort to obtain information about the ghetto underground, Gestapo agents arrest and torture some 130 Jewish ghetto policemen at Fort IX. Thirty-six men are killed after refusing to cooperate, including Police Chief Moshe Levin and his assistants Joshua Greenberg and Yehuda Zupowitz.

Chronology

War and Holocaust

1944 cont'd

April 16
The forced ghettoization of the Hungarian Jews begins.

May 15
Mass deportations of Jews from Hungary to Auschwitz begins. By July 9, 437,402 Jews have been deported; most of them are gassed immediately upon arrival at Auschwitz.

June 6
D-Day: Allied invasion of western Europe begins.

Kovno Ghetto

March 27-28
"Children's Action": Gestapo and Ukrainian auxiliaries round up 1,300 Jews, most of whom were children under 12 and adults over 55. Dragged from their homes, the victims are taken to Fort IX and killed. A few women in the ghetto resistance manage to hide 60 children during the "action."

April 3
Final meeting of the Ältestenrat. Chairman Elkhanan Elkes recommends that they flee or go into hiding, although he states he will remain until the end.

April 4
Germans liquidate all remaining ghetto institutions, including the Ältestenrat, whose members are taken to Fort IX but released.

April 6
Ghetto underground leader Chaim Yelin is arrested in central Kovno after an exchange of gunfire with police. He is executed in early May after being tortured.

July 8
As the Soviet army nears, the Germans begin six-day liquidation of Concentration Camp Kauen, evacuating the former ghetto's remaining population by train and by

barge for deportation to the Stutthof and Dachau concentration camps in Germany. The camp is set aflame to smoke out those still hiding in underground bunkers.

August 1
Soviet Army enters Kovno. A few Jews who survived hiding in underground bunkers are liberated.

October 17
Dr. Elkhanan Elkes dies in Dachau.

July 13
Soviet armed forces liberate Vilna.
July 20
German officers' attempt to assassinate Hitler fails.
July 22
Final deportation of Jews from the Shavli Ghetto, mostly to Stutthof in Germany; some 500 survive to see liberation.
July 24
Soviet troops liberate Majdanek concentration camp and killing center in Poland.

August 30
Last transport of Jews from Lodz Ghetto, bringing to 74,000 the number of persons deported to Auschwitz in August.
October 2
After 63 days of fighting, Warsaw uprising organized by Polish underground Home Army is quashed by Germans; acting on Hitler's orders, German army razes the city.
October 7
Prisoners blow up one crematorium in revolt at Auschwitz.
October 13
Soviet forces liberate Riga.

1945

January 25
The evacuation of approximately 50,000 Jews from Stutthof concentration camp and its subcamps in Germany begins; some 26,000 perish by war's end.

Chronology

War and Holocaust	Kovno Ghetto

1945 cont'd

January 27
Soviet troops liberate Auschwitz.

April 11
Prisoners and U.S. troops liberate the Buchenwald concentration camp.

April 29
U.S. troops liberate the Dachau concentration camp.

April 30
Hitler commits suicide.

May 7
Germany surrenders to Allies; war ends in Europe.

May 8
V-E Day: the war in Europe officially concludes.

From The Hidden History of the Kovno Ghetto *by the U.S. Holocaust Memorial Museum. ©1997 by Walter Reich. By permission of Little, Brown and Company, Inc.*

THE ROUTLEDGE ATLAS OF THE HOLOCAUST 3rd Edn by Martin GILBERT ISBN 0415281458 HB & 0415281466 PB Published by Routeledge 2002
Reproduced by permission of Taylor & Francis Books UK

© Martin Gilbert, 2002

AUTHOR'S NOTE

Approximate geographic locations of pertinent areas:

Kaišiadorys - *38 kms east of Kaunas*

Kaunas (Kovno) - *94 km west of Vilna*

Semeliškes - *42 km west of Vilna (not on map)*

Zezmer (Ziezmariai, Zezmar) - *38 km east of Kaunas*

Zosli (Zosle, Zasliai) - *45 km east of Kaunas (not on map)*

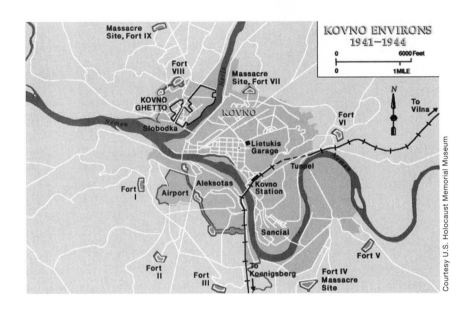

KOVNO ENVIRONS
1941–1944

0   6000 Feet
0   1 MILE

Massacre Site, Fort IX

Fort VIII

Massacre Site, Fort VII

KOVNO GHETTO

KOVNO

Slobodka

Fort VI

To Vilna

Lietukis Garage

Fort I

Aleksotas

Airport

Kovno Station

Tunnel

Sanciai

Fort V

Fort II

Fort III

To Koenigsberg

Fort IV Massacre Site

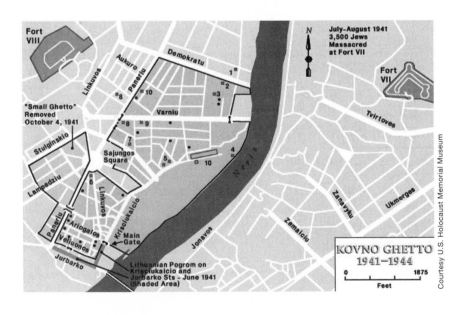

Fort VIII

Demokratu

Aukuro

Linkuvos

Pateriu

Varniu

"Small Ghetto" Removed October 4, 1941

Stulginskio

Sajungos Square

Lampedziu

Linkuvos

Paneriu

Ariogalos

Veliuonos

Kriolukaicio

Jurbarko

Krisciukaicio Main Gate

Jonavos

Lithuanian Pogrom on Krisciukaicio and Jurbarko Sts - June 1941 (Shaded Area)

N

July-August 1941 3,500 Jews Massacred at Fort VII

Fort VII

Tvirtoves

Neris

Zanavyku

Ukmerges

Zemaiciu

KOVNO GHETTO
1941–1944

0   1875
Feet

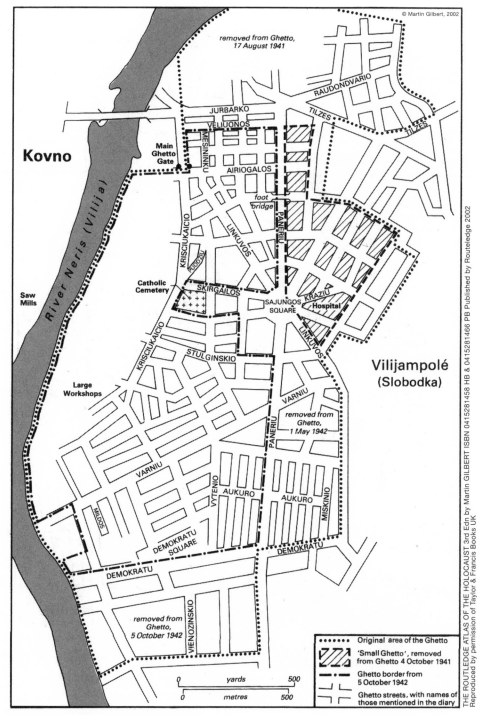

Kovno

River Neris (Vilija)

Saw Mills

Large Workshops

Catholic Cemetery

Main Ghetto Gate

foot bridge

Vilijampolé (Slobodka)

removed from Ghetto, 17 August 1941

removed from Ghetto, 1 May 1942

removed from Ghetto, 5 October 1942

RAUDONDVARIO

TILZES

TILZES

JURBARKO

VELIUONOS

MESININKU

AIRIOGALOS

KRISCIUKAICIO

LINKUVOS

PANERIU

BURZIU

SKIRGAILOS

SAJUNGOS SQUARE

KRAZIU

Hospital

LINKUVOS

KRISCIUKAICIO

STULGINSKIO

VARNIU

PANERIU

VARNIU

MILDOS

VYTENIO

AUKURO

DEMOKRATU SQUARE

DEMOKRATU

DEMOKRATU

AUKURO

MISKINIO

VIENOZINSKIO

© Martin Gilbert, 2002

yards   500

0

metres   500

0

Original area of the Ghetto

'Small Ghetto', removed from Ghetto 4 October 1941

Ghetto border from 5 October 1942

Ghetto streets, with names of those mentioned in the diary

The Kovno Ghetto: streets and boundaries

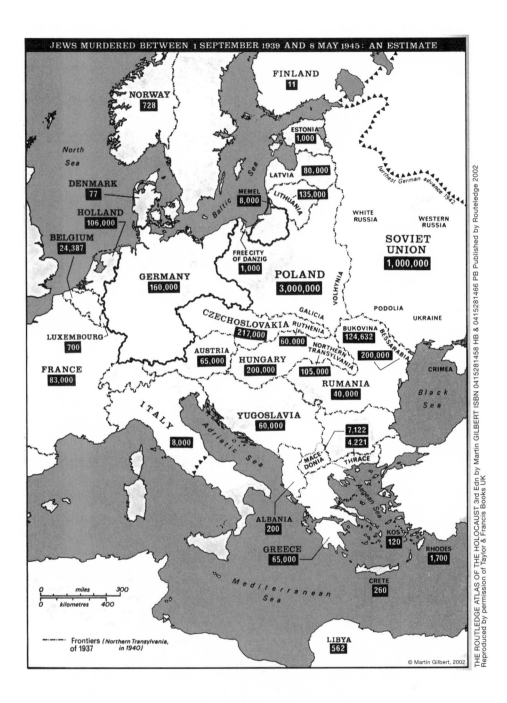

JEWS MURDERED BETWEEN 1 SEPTEMBER 1939 AND 8 MAY 1945: AN ESTIMATE

FINLAND
11

NORWAY
728

ESTONIA
1,000

LATVIA
80,000

MEMEL
8,000

LITHUANIA
135,000

DENMARK
77

HOLLAND
106,000

BELGIUM
24,387

WHITE RUSSIA

WESTERN RUSSIA

furthest German advance 1942

FREE CITY OF DANZIG
1,000

SOVIET UNION
1,000,000

GERMANY
160,000

POLAND
3,000,000

VOLHYNIA

PODOLIA

UKRAINE

GALICIA

CZECHOSLOVAKIA
217,000

RUTHENIA
60,000

BUKOVINA
124,632

BESSARABIA
200,000

LUXEMBOURG
700

AUSTRIA
65,000

HUNGARY
200,000

NORTHERN TRANSYLVANIA
105,000

FRANCE
83,000

RUMANIA
40,000

CRIMEA

Black Sea

ITALY
8,000

YUGOSLAVIA
60,000

Adriatic Sea

7,122
4,221

MACE-DONIA

THRACE

Aegean Sea

ALBANIA
200

KOS
120

GREECE
65,000

RHODES
1,700

CRETE
260

Mediterranean Sea

LIBYA
562

North Sea

Baltic Sea

| 0 | miles | 300 |
| 0 | kilometres | 400 |

‑ ‑ ‑ Frontiers *(Northern Transylvania, in 1940)* of 1937

© Martin Gilbert, 2002

THE ROUTLEDGE ATLAS OF THE HOLOCAUST 3rd Edn by Martin GILBERT ISBN 0415281458 HB & 0415281466 PB Published by Routledge 2002 Reproduced by permission of Taylor & Francis Books UK

Soviet officers preside over the exhumation of bodies in a mass grave at Fort IX following the liberation of Kovno Ghetto. An estimated 40,000 Jews, some of them transported from other areas in central and western Europe, were shot to death at Fort IX between the fall of 1941 and the spring of 1944.

Message calling for revenge written at Fort IX.

The liquidation of Kovno Ghetto (which had become Concentration Camp no. 4, Kovno) began on July 8, 1944, three weeks prior to the Soviet liberation of the city. Approximately 6,100 Jews were transported to concentration camps in less than a week. Believing that several thousand Jews were still hiding, the SS ordered the German troops to raze the site. All houses were blown up and doused with gasoline. Fleeing Jews were shot while many others burned to death. The fire burned for a week. Approximately 100 survived.

Fort VI after liberation.

Masses of Kovno Jews were herded together before their execution at Fort VII.

A chain of nine tsarist fortifications constructed in the nineteenth century surrounds the city of Kaunas. When the Germans occupied the city during World War II, several of these forts, most notably Fort VII and Fort IX, were used as the sites of mass murder against Jews, perpetrated by German *Einsatzkommandos* and their Lithuanian collaborators.

In an attempt to conceal their extermination of Jews, the Germans forced a special unit of sixty-four Jewish workers to exhume and burn thousands of corpses prior to the ghetto's liberation. The concealment effort, which began in September 1943, was later recorded by eleven of the workers who escaped through a tunnel under the fortress on Christmas Eve. Their written description was later used during post-war trials. Mass executions at Fort IX continued through the spring of 1944. The last mass killing action there was perpetrated against a group of French Jews who were routed to Kovno for execution in May 1944, just two months prior to the liberation of the Kovno Ghetto in July.

Glossary

Arbeit Macht Frei – work liberates

bar mitzvah – coming of age for Jewish boys at age thirteen, at which time he becomes fully responsible for performing the commandments

bima – podium in the synagogue where the rabbi delivers his message

bubbe – grandmother

challah – braided bread used especially on Shabbat and holidays

chutzpah – courage, a daring attitude

elderbubbe – great grandmother

Fort VII and Fort IX – most notorious two of nine Russian forts used to massacre Jews in Kaunas, Lithuania

gay – go

gelbe turm – literal translation – yellow tower; also referred to as Yellow Jail

Gestapo – secret, state police (noted for their brutality) that served during the Nazi regime

kaddish prayer – Jewish relatives attend synagogue services and say the kaddish prayer for eleven months following the death of family members

kasher – to cleanse in a ritualistic way in order to make the item kosher; not using leavened bread during Pesach

kiddish cup – a special cup designated for drinking wine at special times

kosher – dietary laws of the Jewish people; separating meat from milk

Kovno Ghetto – established for Jews across the river from Kovno in Slobodka (also known as Vilijampole) by decree of two Lithuanian officials – the mayor, Palciauskas, and the city's military commander, Colonel Bobelis on July 10, 1941. All Jews had to be inside the ghetto by August 15, 1941.

Kristallnacht – usually translated as the Night of Broken Glass - November 9-10, 1938 – when riots were incited against Jews in Germany and Austria, resulting in millions of dollars of damage to Jewish property, the death of 91 Jews and the arrest of approximately 30,000 others. Many were able to buy their freedom; others were sent to concentration camps. Considered the first pogrom in Europe.

lokshn kugel – a dish made of noodles and other ingredients

lit (pl. litas) – unit of Lithuanian currency – (equal to $0.10-0.17) – exchange rate for American dollar - 1930-1940

Maccabi Games – a Jewish athletic competition first started in the 1800s. The European Maccabi Games were outlawed in any territories falling under Soviet rule in the mid-1930s. Following Hitler's rise to power and during World War II, the clubs ceased to exist. Many of the athletes perished in the Holocaust. The games were resumed in 1950 and continue today.

maline – slang for hiding place (literal translation – raspberry) a designated place providing protection, as the thorns of the raspberry bush, for storing valuables

mameh – Mama

matzo balls – small balls made from matzo meal, water and salt and dropped into chicken stock and boiled; especially consumed during Pesach

Min Hashamaim – an order from God (literal translation: from the heavens)

meshuggah – crazy

mezuzah – a parchment containing scripture that is affixed to the doorpost of Jewish homes; usually in a metal or wooden case

Glossary

minyan – a group of Jewish individuals (usually men) required for public prayer services

mikvah – ritual bath generally for women

papeh – Papa

peckel – package of goods usually smuggled inside the ghetto

Pesach – Passover

pogrom – a planned campaign or persecution sanctioned by a government toward a particular ethnic group

Rauca, Master Sergeant Helmut – head of the Jewish affairs desk at Gestapo headquarters in Kaunas. Responsible for the "Great Action" in Kovno Ghetto on October 28, 1941, where he personally selected over 9,200 Jews to be executed the following day at Fort IX.

Righteous Among the Nations – The criteria, in part, for such a designation is determined when the data on hand clearly demonstrate that a non-Jewish person risked his (or her) life, freedom, and safety without exacting in advance monetary compensation. This qualifies the rescuer for serious consideration to be awarded the "Righteous Among the Nations" title. The honor is bestowed by Yad Vashem, The Holocaust Martyrs' and Heroes' Remembrance Authority established in 1953 by an act of the Israeli Knesset.

Schutzstaffel – Nazi police units known as the SS, organized by Hitler's protégé, Heinrich Himmler

Shabbat – Sabbath or Saturday

shofar – ram's horn blown primarily on the holiday of Rosh Hashanah, the Jewish new year celebrated in the fall

strasse – street

Sturm Abteilung – referred to as storm detachment (sometimes referred to as storm troopers or SA), an auxiliary police force used by the Germans

tallis (tallith) – a prayer shawl that Jews use to cover their shoulders and head while praying during services

tzaddik – a righteous man

tzedakah – charity, being careful to share with others who might be less fortunate

Torah – first five books of the Bible; text used for basis of Judaism

Vilna – (Vilnius) was the capital of Lithuania from the fourteenth century through the end of World War I. Vilna became a part of Poland in 1920. For a brief period Kovno became the capital of Lithuania and was continually referred to as the provisional capital of Lithuania, even after Vilna was returned to Lithuania.

yellow star – a badge known as the Star of David that Jews were forced to wear on their left side and also on the back of their coats for identification purposes

Yom HaShoah – a time of remembrance set aside each year to remember those who perished in the Holocaust and to honor the survivors and liberators

zeyde – grandfather

Additional Acknowledgments

To list every individual who supported me in the writing of this work would constitute another book. Besides the ones already acknowledged, so many others have helped, like Rita Ghatak, who provided invaluable translations for several Lithuania interviews.

The research staff at the Bon Air Library; numerous staff members at the U.S. Holocaust Memorial Museum, especially Martin Goldman, Judith Cohen, Maren Read, Robin Harp and Tim Baker; Randi Smith and Dianne Hall of the Chesterfield County Public Schools; as well as Sylvia and Al Rosenbaum, Dianna Gabay and Barbara Hollingsworth of the Virginia Holocaust Museum, have provided untold hours of help. The Kill Devil Hills, N.C., library staff, as well as the staff of Yad Vashem and the Lithuania Central State Archive have offered other assistance. Beth Ahabah Museum and Archives staff, and the Mariner's Museum research staff also assisted.

While Robert Johnston and Faye Toney kept my computer running, Chad Anderson and Andrew Cain, and especially Hew Stith and Leila Beasley, provided the final expertise in editing. Steve Hedberg, who designed the cover and the contents, brought special beauty to the completed product.

Many of my family members, especially my children, Beau and Leila Beasley and Jason Beasley have walked closely beside me. So many individuals have contributed in one way or another that the following list is long and possibly incomplete. Just know that I thank you.

J. Padraig Acheson, American Family Fitness, Southside staff; Martha Anderegg, Father Pat Apuzzo, Liz Archer, Sharon Baldacci and Randy Smith, Les Blackwell, Don Bowling, Betty Jo (BJ) Bridgforth, Sunisa Bridgforth, Sonja and Bud Brodecki, Carlie Collier, Daiúy, Debbie and Pete Daniel, Miriam Davidow, Carla Davis, Lois and Bill Davis,

Additional Acknowledgments

Gail and Don Doyle, Brian Eckert, Harriet Edmunds, Audrey and Brian Hingley, Sundra and Horace Faber, Betty and Ed Fertel, Barb and Randy Fitzgerald, Thomas Gaskins, Jim Gottstein, Julie Grimes and Mark Fagerburg, Johnnie Hamilton, Ellyn Hartzler, Jan Hathcock, Mark Herndon, Dr. Elizabeth Hodges, Harold Horowitz, Suzanne Horsley and Joe Herron, Marcia Horwitz, Sally Stewart Huband, Edna Ipson's extended family, Barbara Irby, Diane and Chris Lawson, Frances Lynch, Liz Pierce, Emyl Jenkins, the Rev. James Johnson, Richard Johnstone, Linda and Sid Jordan, Ed Kelleher, Shirley Kirk, Gertrude Kupfer, Leisha LaRiviere, Sue Landerman, Sandra Langford, Alex Lebenstein, Carol Love, Erin Lumpkin, Betty and Russ Lunsford, Garie Mayer, Eric and Debbie Miller, Henry Moss, Amy Nisenson, Karla Novick, Sandra Ogburn, Paula Otto, Margie and Joe Poole, Rita Peyton, Karen Plummer, Cynthia Price, Liz Puma, Kim Rich, Katie Rosenbaum, Maureen Rosenbaum, Margaret Smith, Dr. Clarence Thomas, William Rothenberg, Pat Russell, Simone Schwartz, Carol Shapiro, Claire Sheppard, Bill Sherrod, Pam Stallsmith and Tom Hohing, Fred and Ruby Thompson, Dr. Linda Tiffany, Art Todras, Sandra Waugaman, Susan Winiecki, and Halina and Alan Zimm.

Bibliography

Izzy Ipson's memoirs, which were dictated and transcribed by several people over a period of years, were the primary source for this book. Numerous interviews, both personal and taped, were conducted with Edna and Jay Ipson between 1997 and July 2004.

A personal interview with Jacob Kalamitskas (whose surname differs from his father's due to Lithuanian spelling) was conducted in March 1998. He also provided written information regarding his parents, Itzhak and Ida Kalamitsky, and his brother, David Kalamitsky, through August 2004.

A personal interview with Stanislovas Krivicius was conducted during April 1998. Several follow-up questions were answered through phone conversations with him and family members, translated by Rita Ghatak, the latest one in July 2004.

A personal interview with Emmanuel Shlom took place in September 1999. He also provided his mother's memoirs, numerous written documents and photos pertaining to his life. Telephone interviews and correspondence continued through August 2004.

Israel (Lola) Gillman answered written questions through his grandson, Neil Bienstock, the last time in August 2004. Mr. Gillman also provided personal photos.

Sheina Gillman, wife of the late Moshe Gillman, answered questions through her daughter, Dr. Sara Pliamm, in 2003 through a tape recording. She also provided photos. Written and verbal information was provided later, the last time in August 2004.

Other sources consulted:

Berenbaum, Michael. *The World Must Know: The History of the Holocaust as Told in the United States Holocaust Memorial Museum.* Boston: Little, Brown and Company, 1993.

Facing History and Ourselves: Holocaust and Human Behavior. Brookline, MA: Facing History and Ourselves National Foundation, 1994.

Gilbert, Martin, *The Routledge Atlas of the Holocaust,* 3rd Edn. United Kingdom: Routeledge, 2002.

Goldhagen, Daniel Jonah. *Hitler's Willing Executioners: Ordinary Germans and the Holocaust.* New York: Alfred A. Knopf, 1996.

Bibliography

Greenbaum, Masha. *The Jews of Lithuania: A History of a Remarkable Community, 1316-1945*. Israel: Gefen Publishing House, 1995.

Hidden History of the Kovno Ghetto, United States Holocaust Memorial Museum. A project of the United States Holocaust Memorial Council. New York: Little, Brown and Company, 1998.

Reitlinger, Gerald. *The Final Solution: The Attempt to Exterminate the Jews of Europe 1939-1945*. Northvale, NJ: Jason Aronson, 1987.

Rosten, Leo. *The New Joys of Yiddish*. New York: Crown Publishers, 2001.

Scheindlin, Raymond P. *The Chronicles of the Jewish People*. New York: Smithmark Publishers, 1996.

The Holocaust Chronicle. Lincolnwood, IL: Publications International, 2000.

Tory, Avraham, *Surviving the Holocaust: The Kovno Ghetto Diary*, ed. Martin Gilbert. Cambridge, MA: Harvard University Press, 1990.

Wheal, Elizabeth-Anne, Stephen Pope, James Taylor. *Encyclopedia of the Second World War*. New York: Castle Books, 1989.

The Virginia Holocaust Museum generously allowed the use of photographs.

The United States Holocaust Memorial Museum generously allowed the use of maps and photographs.

Historical timeline: From *The Hidden History of the Kovno Ghetto* by the United States Holocaust Memorial Museum. © 1997 by Walter Reich. By permission of Little, Brown and Company.

Further information pertaining to this subject was researched at the library and photo archives of the United States Holocaust Memorial Museum as well as through their Web site at http://www.ushmm.org/kovno/ghetto/ghetto.html.

About the Author

Nancy Wright Beasley started her journalistic career as a state correspondent for *The Richmond New Leader* in 1979, while she and her family lived in South Hill, Va. She ultimately settled in Richmond, Va., launching a freelance career and becoming a personal columnist and contributing editor for *Richmond Magazine* in 1998.

In 2000, Beasley earned a master's degree in the School of Mass Communications at Virginia Commonwealth University where she serves as an adjunct professor. The Virginia Press Women named her as their Communicator of Achievement for 2005. The Richmond YWCA chose her as one of Ten Outstanding Women in Central Virginia in 2006.

Izzy's Fire: Finding Humanity in the Holocaust was nominated for a People's Choice Award, a competition sponsored by the James River Writers and the Library of Virginia. It is now being taught in numerous schools and universities in several states.

A second nonfiction book, *Reflections of a Purple Zebra: Essays of a Different Stripe*, a compilation of Beasley's personal columns from *Richmond Magazine* was published in 2007.

The author lives in Richmond and is currently pursuing a master of fine arts in children's literature at Hollins University in Roanoke, Va., made possible through the generosity of Neil November.